THE WINE BOOK

ALSO BY MATTHEW JUKES

The Wine List 2002

The Wine List 2003

The Wine List 2004

The Wine List 2005

The Wine List 2006

The Wine List 2007

THE WINE BOOK

MATTHEW JUKES

TELLS YOU EVERYTHING YOU NEED TO
KNOW ABOUT THE WINE YOU ARE DRINKING

headline

First published in 2005 by
HEADLINE PUBLISHING GROUP

First published in paperback in 2007 by
HEADLINE PUBLISHING GROUP

2

Cataloguing in Publication Data is available from the British Library

ISBN 978 07553 1511 6

Designed by Fiona Pike, Pike Design

Printed and bound in Great Britain by Clays Ltd, St Ives plc

Headline's policy is to use papers that are natural, renewable and recyclable products and
made from wood grown in sustainable forests. The logging and manufacturing processes
are expected to conform to the environmental regulations of the country of origin.

HEADLINE PUBLISHING GROUP
An Hachette Livre UK Company
338 Euston Road
London NW1 3BH

www.headline.co.uk
www.hodderheadline.com

CONTENTS

To Isadora and Elspeth

ACKNOWLEDGEMENTS

This book is a fermentation of sorts. I have been working as a wine buyer and wine writer for nearly two decades, and during this time I have been privileged to meet some incredible people. At every step of my journey, winemakers all over the world have very generously let me know their secrets and taste their finest work; wine merchants and UK agents have kindly let me have first sniff of their precious finds; PRs have kept me bang up-to-date with scoops; wine trade colleagues have generously shared their tips; generic marketing bodies in the UK have helped me access far-flung corners of the wine world; and you have all opened thousands and thousands of bottles with me. Without your phenomenal support I could never have continued in the job that I love. Your energy, enthusiasm and encouragement are very special to me. Thank you all so much – your generosity is overwhelming.

My heartfelt thanks also go to the team behind the scenes – my family, my agent Robert Kirby, and my publishers Headline, in particular Jo Roberts-Miller, an editor in a million.

My aim is to spread the word about wine. This book is my personal blend of all the facts and flavours I have come across over the years, and I do hope you all enjoy it. If it encourages the prospective wine lover to delve further into this joyous subject then I have achieved my goal.

INTRODUCTION

Welcome one and all to *The Wine Book*. You will see when you glance through the following pages that this is not a coffee-table, arty, photo-filled wine book. There are a few maps dotted around to help you visualize the trickier wine regions but, apart from that, it is my intention that you *read* this book – not just flick through it. In fact, I'd like you to read every word, and this is why. Browsing through a cookbook for ideas and perhaps only coming back to cook one of the recipes ten years after buying it may be OK (you can cook a recipe today, next year or in a decade and it should always taste vaguely the same), but the wine world moves at an incredible pace. The information would simply be out of date if you left it that long. This is exciting, of course – nothing stands still when you are growing grapes, making wine and wowing wine lovers. Vintages roll on, the weather is unpredictable, tastes change and vines grow ever older. These challenges and the sheer velocity of change are at the heart of why wine is such an addictive subject.

And in here, all of the information is vital – the fat has been trimmed off. This is a chiselled, honed and toned wine book. Use it to tackle the wild wine world out there. Whether you are already really into wine or just a beginner, this is an essential tome to bring you totally up to speed with what is happening out there *now*. My style of writing has, in the past, been described as 'demystifying', 'for those people who are slightly baffled', 'lacking in snobbery' and other pleasing things (to me, anyway). Translated, this means that if something requires explanation, I do it. If I don't like a region or country, I say it. And, importantly, if I love a style of wine or an estate, I write it down for you. It has always struck me as odd that, in the past, wine writing seemed elitist and inaccessible. What is the point in that? I want loads of people to read this book, get the confidence to tackle wine lists and wine shops, and share their knowledge of this utterly awesome subject.

THE CHAPTERS

I have divided this book into various chapters, focusing on different aspects of wine. I don't get on to the wine regions of the world until halfway through and this is entirely deliberate. In order to understand wine fully, it is important to start at the beginning – at the root of the subject (no pun intended) – with the grapes themselves. This is followed swiftly by how grapes are grown and how different styles of wine are made. A crucial chapter is how to buy wine – giving you tips on what to look for and how to structure your buying habits. Then comes the best bit – how to taste wine! Serving, storing and matching this glorious drink to food finishes off the practical advice. After the comprehensive chapter describing the world's wine regions, I have included a huge glossary that explains terms that might be a little alien. This is divided into sections: viticulture (grape growing), vinification (winemaking), just about every tasting term you can think of (avoiding anything ridiculously florid), some useful French tasting terms and a general section mopping up the leftovers.

THE WINE DIET

No, not another preposterous weight loss programme, but a guide to enjoying an enviable way of life. In the same way that eating a chicken sandwich every day, or wearing the same trousers and T-shirt and listening to non-stop Dire Straits might be construed as being somewhat blinkered (downright worrying, if you ask me), it is important to vary your wine diet. Sadly, most of us are lazy and carry on buying a wine that 'works' for us until it has run out, before switching to a new label. Why is this? If your favourite radio station played the same track over and over again, it would drive you nuts. So why punish your palate with the same wines every day? This book sets out the facts about the wine world and the gems embedded in it. You will learn about the different grape varieties, different methods of production and all the major wine-producing regions. This should enlighten you and arm you with the knowledge to analyse your own vinous likes and dislikes, and, therefore, encourage you to go out and expand your wine boundaries by buying increasingly more interesting and challenging bottles.

If, for example, you know you like the flavour of Sancerre (a white wine made from the Sauvignon Blanc grape, from the Loire in France), varying your wine diet and broadening your tastebud horizons could mean that you find yourself taking the following globe-trotting journey while all the time staying within the safety net of a familiar style. One flavour or region leads to another and if something gets in your way (e.g. you don't like a wine or are not ready for it) sidestep and move on.

Sancerre to **Menetou Salon** (a neighbouring village making similar-styled wines from the same grape)

Menetou Salon to dry white **Graves** from Bordeaux (similar styles and both produce good versions at a sub-tenner price; they share the Sauvignon grape but now Semillon is added to the mix)

White Graves to **Margaret River Semillon/Sauvignon Blanc** (exactly the same style of wine but the flavour has changed a bit because of the different climate in Western Australia)

Margaret River Semillon/Sauvignon Blanc to **Adelaide Hills Sauvignon Blanc** (both regions are cool-climate and Australian, and have similarly tasting, stunning quality, crisp whites)

Adelaide Hills Sauvignon Blanc to **Marlborough Sauvignon Blanc** (from a classic area in Australia to one in New Zealand – arguably the most important region outside Europe for this grape, as well)

Marlborough Sauvignon Blanc to **South African Sauvignon Blanc** (a little more crisp acidity and herbal aromas)

South African Sauvignon Blanc to **Casablanca Sauvignon Blanc** (for when times are tough and you need to save a few quid but not drop your standards – a similar style from Chile but at half the price)

Casablanca Sauvignon Blanc to **Napa Valley Fumé Blanc** (if you've won the lottery and you feel like a similarly flavoured wine but with more oomph and depth, head to California)

Napa Valley Fumé Blanc to **Pouilly-Fumé** (it may sound the same but it's stylistically slightly different; made from the same grape but in the Loire)

Pouilly-Fumé to **Sancerre** (a jump over to the other side of the river and we're back where we started!)

Hoorah – we have travelled the world in the safety of a flavour we like and a style that suits, but along the way we have tasted some remarkable wines. I don't doubt that you could drink Sauvignon Blanc all day, every day for a month and never have to taste exactly the same flavour. As you've seen, one tweak on the 'graphic equalisers' (remember old stereo systems?) – a hop between regions, countries and climates – and the fruit moves up, or the herbal notes move down, and so on. And this is all before you've even switched grapes! So why not do just that? Using the same starting point, Sauvignon Blanc, here's a vinous trail that takes you around the world on different grapes. But don't panic! They are all the same 'shape' palate-wise and flavour-wise.

Sauvignon Blanc to bone-dry Austrian or Clare/Eden Valley (both Australian) **Riesling**; Aussie **Verdelho**; youthful Hunter Valley (also Australian) **Semillon**; crisp Loire or South African **Chenin Blanc**; Alsace **Pinot Blanc**; **Torrontés** from Argentina; **Aligoté** from Burgundy; Galician **Albariño**; English **Bacchus**; **Muscadet** from the Loire; **Pinot Grigio**, **Trebbiano**, **Verdicchio**, **Garganega**, **Greco** and God knows how many other Italian varieties that do the job, too (don't worry they are all in the book!)

Now for the wine diet, treasure hunt finale – this time let's not go globally with one grape or sideways with the same style but massage each tastebud as we experience every wine style from fizz to fortified without leaving one country. Starting at the beginning with a very famous style – Champagne – this is the ultimate dinner party tour.

From fizz to titillate the palate and prick the thirst with interest we head to **Chablis**. Using one of the Champagne grapes – Chardonnay – now we pick up a light, dry, aperitif-style white wine.

Same grape again, but gaining a little more structure for our starters, head south to **Burgundy** proper and uncork a superb Meursault.

Burgundy's other super-famous grape is Pinot Noir. Let's take this new grape and move to the Loire where it is planted in small quantities, and open ourselves a celestial rosé in **Sancerre**. Light enough to go with many starters or fish main courses this does the job well.

But we need a fresh, juicy red for our main course... Where better to find one than **Chinon**? A bit further down the Loire, here we can pick up a crunchy, bright purple Cabernet Franc.

We've got the taste for Cabernet Franc now, but want a little more red impact and weight, so let's open the throttle and wallet a little, and change regions again for a glass of red **Bordeaux** (made from a blend of Cabernet Sauvignon, Cabernet Franc and Merlot).

Now let's downscale the price and find another hearty red to finish off our main course – a juicy Merlot from the **Languedoc**.

The cheese course is coming and earthier reds are required – **Provence**, next door, fills this gap with style.

We'll also need an aromatic, but not too sweet, white for some of the blue cheeses – try another totally underrated French wine region and slip into a Vendange Tardive Riesling or Muscat from **Alsace**.

The Muscat grape makes full on sweeties as well; take a look in the southern **Rhône** at Muscat de Beaumes-de Venise. If budget is an issue, then find the cheaper Muscat de Rivesaltes from **Roussillon**. While you're there, pick up a Maury or a Banyuls (the little-known port-like red) to drink alongside your coffee and choccies.

A banquet fit for Henry VIII!

This is what I mean by a varied and balanced wine diet. Vary the grape, region and style – it just depends on your mood and bravery. If you want to feel safe, stay with a region, variety or producer for a while, and mooch around experimenting within your comfort zone. Once you decide to switch to a new grape variety or find yet more regions that suit or producers that work for you, then go for it! (Friday nights are best, surely, for this sort of treat!) There are no rules, you are the boss – this is one of the major attractions of wine as a hobby. This is also what differentiates wine from almost any other drink.

So, why should you do this? The answer is that the wine world moves at a staggering pace. Tastes change and ever-more exciting wines are being made every day. It is important to be at the forefront of this movement. If you are the sort of person that reads the newspaper every day to keep abreast of current affairs, or someone who feels the need to download the latest music or see the new film releases, then this desire to stay up to date should flow over into your wine intake. Just as foodies rush to buy fresh, seasonal ingredients as soon as they arrive on the shelves, wine should be the same. Each week new wines are shipped into the country and stocked on merchant's wine lists. It is your responsibility to give them your details so they can alert you to new finds. I receive loads of letters each week from people complaining that they have missed the boat on wines that I have written up in my weekly column. More often than not it is because they waited a few weeks before heading out to the shops. As the saying goes, 'If you snooze, you lose.' Every wine is, by definition, a limited release. OK, some bottles are out there in their hundreds of thousands of cases, but others are only made by the hundreds of bottles! Make sure you are at the front of the queue. You will discover new flavours and estates, and constantly push your tastebuds to experience things they have never experienced before. Join with me and my like-minded pals, and get yourself on a palate-thrilling wine diet. You won't regret it.

SMILE – IT IS WINE AFTER ALL

The most important point to remember while reading through this book is that wine is fun! I had immense pleasure putting this book together and I hope that you will have the same fun reading it. Nearly twenty years into what I hope will be a job for life, I love this industry and feel delighted to be working with such a magical, happiness-spreading drink. How many people are lucky enough to wander around the world, opening superb bottles of wine and meeting the inspirational alchemists who are the world's greatest winemakers? Admittedly, it is only 10% glamour (flying around, eating in swish restaurants and tasting awesome bottles) and 90% sitting in front of my computer tapping away, but I wouldn't change it for the world. I hope that you take to this subject with the same fervour that I attack my job.

TASTE – DO YOU HAVE IT?

Finally, before you launch into the heart of the book, it is important to stress that when it comes to matters of taste, *you* are always right. If you don't like a wine, don't buy it again, or at least wait until your palate decides the time is right to have another go. Don't let anyone bully you into believing that you don't have 'good' taste, because your nose and mouth are your own detectors and they decide the parameters in which you operate, so how can they be wrong? I can't tell you what you should like, just why I like what I like and why it tastes the way it does. Listen to what your palate tells you, ignore the snobs and get drinking!

Chapter 1

GRAPE VARIETIES

Grape varieties are the cornerstones of wine knowledge. Understand the concept of grape varieties and you will be well on the way to solving the mysteries behind the taste of wine. Each one has a distinct character and array of smells and tastes. Some are more memorable and impactful on your olfactory system than others. Some work better when they are combined – the team effort. Others prefer to be left to do their thing in peace – the loners. If a wine is made from only one grape variety it is called a 'single varietal' or just plain 'varietal'. If it is made from more than one grape variety, then it is called a 'blend'. The idea behind blending is to create a wine that is better than the sum of the parts. Blends tend to have many flavours, all racing around the mouth at the same time. If you get to know the particular taste characteristics of each grape in this chapter, you will have cracked the code. Combine this with a little knowledge of climate and general winemaking practices and you are there.

Before we start, it is important to explain some of the vocabulary. When referring to grapes, the term 'variety' means 'type'. If I were writing about apples then the varieties would include Cox, Golden Delicious, Russet or Bramley. Over the next few pages there is a whole new directory of names to learn. Some will undoubtedly be very familiar. You may not have realised that these names, in fact, refer to the grapes that a wine is made from, rather than the style of wine made. Chardonnay, for example, is a grape type not a style of wine – which is why not all Chardonnays taste the same. Imagine the difference between two bottles of wine, both made from the Chardonnay grape, but one from France and one from Australia. They will have a certain degree of similarity; after all they are from the same variety of plant. However, as they were grown and made into wine, thousands of miles apart, by different people in different climates using different styles, they will not taste the same.

There are over 5,000 grape varieties in the world. But, don't despair, as the majority of wines available on the shelves in wine merchants and supermarkets use only a fraction of these – the best and tastiest ones, of course. The following list contains two sections within both red and white grapes. The first sections together detail my top twenty grape varieties. These are some of the most commonly available grapes and a few of them are known as 'noble varieties'. I have moved a couple of the lesser-known grapes into this category, as I feel that they are particularly interesting and worthy of note. The second sections contain the more obscure, eclectic varieties. Weird and wonderful they may be, but you are unlikely to come across these grapes every day. (A few other varieties that are not highlighted here pop up in subsequent chapters – these will be accompanied by a short explanation putting each one into context.)

IMPORTANT RED VARIETIES
Cabernet Sauvignon
(Cab-er-nay Soe-veen-yon)
The grape's hallmarks, along with a **blackcurrant** flavour (the

French word *cassis* is used a lot), are a **cigar-box** or **cedarwood** note and sometimes even a **dark chocolate** texture and flavour. A New World Cabernet Sauvignon can often be recognised by a **mint leaf** smell on the nose. Possibly the most famous red grape in the world, Cab Sauv has every right to be proud of itself. It is a classy beast with breeding and universally appealing character traits. Cabernet Sauvignon is the metaphorical chairman of the board of the Multinational Wine Corporation. This grape forms the main part of one of the world's most celebrated styles of wine – Cabernet Sauvignon is the backbone of most red Bordeaux. Its ability to contribute intensity of flavour and masses of ageing potential to a wine has meant that it is a favourite for planting in thousands of vineyards all around the world. Cabernet Sauvignon tends to perform best when it's blended. In red Bordeaux it is joined by two or three other red grape varieties to form a balanced wine. As this style has a proven track record, winemakers all over the world follow this recipe, and so a wine using Cabernet Sauvignon, Cabernet Franc and Merlot is known as a 'Bordeaux blend'. Cab Sauv responds very well to time spent in oak barrels and therefore is often accompanied by a woody flavour. The grape itself is thick skinned. A grape's skin contains colour and tannin elements. Wines using Cabernet Sauvignon grapes tend to be deeply coloured and tannic when young. Tannin is a grape variety's lifeline – generally the more tannin the longer the wine will live. Therefore Cabernet Sauvignon brings longevity to a blend.

There are many famous wines made predominantly from this grape that do not write 'Cabernet Sauvignon' on the label. All 'Left Bank' Bordeaux including Château Latour, Château Montrose, Château Lafite-Rothschild, Château Haut-Brion, Château Palmer, Château Léoville-Barton, Château Ducru-Beaucaillou, Château Cos d'Estournel and many, many more, contain a huge whack of this noble variety in the mix. In California, Cabernet Sauvignon is the lifeblood of the smart wine society. This heroic grape accounts for Opus One made by Robert Mondavi, Beringer's Chabot Vineyard, Joseph Phelps Insignia, Harlan Estate, Ridge Monte Bello, Stag's Leap Cask 23, Shafer Hillside Select, Dominus and countless other frighteningly expensive wines. Elsewhere, the jumbo-priced 'Super-Tuscans', Sassicaia, Ornellaia and Solaia, broke old Italian wine laws by planting a non-indigenous variety and produced mind-blowing wines from Cabernet Sauvignon. Prices went through the roof and the wine's classification went through the floor, all of the way down to Vino da Tavola (table wine)! It just shows how jealous the local authorities were of brave Italian winemakers who put the great grape to the test and won. Nowadays Cab Sauv appears all over Italy.

Australia makes some of the most amazing and affordable Cabernets in the world. Margaret River in Western Australia, Coonawarra, Clare Valley, McLaren Vale and the Barossa Valley – all in South Australia – are home to sensational Cabernets. This part of the world also gave birth to one of the most underrated blends of the modern day – that of Cabernet/Shiraz (or Shiraz/Cabernet). The combination of the elegance of Cabernet and the brazen spice of Shiraz makes for a gripping ride. This is one of my favourite blends and yet there are not enough wineries concentrating on this wondrous coupling – but it will come. New Zealand has come a long way with Cabernet in the last decade. Hawke's Bay, in the North Island, is the main region specialising in this variety, and recent results look very impressive. Chile and Argentina have both managed to make wonderful Cabernet cheapies for years, but they are now moving up the ladder and showing us that they can rival some of the other New World countries with this imposing grape. South Africa is also coming on strong. However, I feel Shiraz (Syrah) will end up being their strong suit. Spain has, for a long time, made some fine Cabernets – Torres' Mas La Plana being my favourite – and you cannot fail to ripen this variety in the Spanish sun. Many other minor league countries make interesting Cab Sauvs, too. The majority of these wines actually declare the grape variety on the label, so thankfully you don't have to try and guess what it is.

All over the world, Cabernet Sauvignon holds a firm grip on wine drinkers' palates and a majority share of most wine lover's cellar space. When it comes to recognising the flavour of this grape just think 'aristocratic'.

Merlot *(Mer-low)*

With **plums**, **fruitcake**, **blackberries** and **red wine gums** on the nose, Merlot tends to have an immediately appealing character, and it is more supple, smooth and velvety than many of its peers. It often has a touch of **oak**, texture and velvety richness on the palate and again, like the big brother Cab Sauv, can be a little **minty**. This grape variety is Cabernet Sauvignon's wingman. If Cabernet is the voice of reason, Merlot is a little bit wayward and often easily led. Rarely does it perform spectacularly on its own, as it needs guidance and direction from a steadying hand. It is the arty, designer-style grape that flatters many blends but cannot really stand alone unless the habitat is exactly suited to its individual requirements. Because it is a juicier style of red grape, it generally needs the structure of Cabernet Sauvignon to bolster its fruity framework. Merlot is in its element on the 'Right Bank' of Bordeaux. Here, it is often the dominant grape in the blend, ably supported by Cabernet Franc and Cabernet Sauvignon. The New World, particularly California, has been guilty of going Merlot crazy in the past. Hyper-expensive, small production Merlot-based wines were all the rage. Thankfully this fashion has calmed down somewhat. Australia and New Zealand plant Merlot and are making some ripe Bordeaux taste-alikes, led by visionaries like Jim Irvine in the Eden Valley, but it is the enormous plantings in Chile that supply the world with most of the Merlot for everyday drinking. Chile and Argentina are also at the forefront of another slightly dubious trend, following on from California's explosion of Merlot-based wines in the mid eighties – the bodybuilder's Merlot. This unnerving style of red wine takes the dashing Merlot variety and transforms it into a pill-popping, fake-tanned freak – over-oaked, over-extracted, high alcohol and, sadly, over here. Merlot is ideally suited to being a medium-weight wine, with balance and harmony. It hates being pumped up and polished.

If you like Merlot's happy-go-lucky, plump, juicy, almost sweet flavours then beware of its flip side – that of the thin, watery, unripe red wines that are made to be drunk young and are found at the bottom end of the price spectrum from Italy,

Eastern Europe and the South of France.

Famous wines made from this grape include most Bordeaux from Pomerol and Saint Emilion – such as Château Pétrus, Château Trotanoy, Château Le Pin and Château Angélus – also an expensive Tuscan blockbuster called Masseto, and a handful of Californian Merlots like Shafer, Newton and Duckhorn. Once again other wines make a point of writing Merlot on the label if it is the dominant variety. It is worth noting that most New World Cabernet Sauvignons have some Merlot lurking inside, sweet-talking the tannic Cabernet into civility..

Cabernet Franc *(Cab-er-nay Fron)*

Grass cuttings, **leafy notes** and **violets** overlay masses of **black fruit** flavours. Cabernet Franc often has good acidity, too. It can smell both green and red, and red at the same time! It is the third most important grape of the Bordeaux 'Three Musketeers' and is the final building block in the making of red Bordeaux. This grape lends a certain aromatic quality to these wines. Apart from some notable exceptions like Château Cheval Blanc in Saint-Emilion, where it forms two-thirds of the final blend with Merlot filling the gap, it generally plays a supporting role. The tannin element of Cabernet Franc is less obvious than that of Cabernet Sauvignon. As well as forming part of the formidable Bordeaux triumvirate, Cab Franc is very comfortable in the Loire. It is as if Bordeaux is its main place of work and at weekends it disappears to the Loire to relax with friends. In the Loire, Cabernet Franc produces the great-value, muscular, scented reds of Bourgueil, Saint Nicolas de Bourgueil, Chinon and Saumur-Champigny. Elsewhere winemakers have cottoned on to the fact that the Bordeaux and the Loire have a good thing going, and so, to some small degree, they have made sure that when a Cabernet Sauvignon is being created, a little Cabernet Franc goes into the mix. Some wineries in California have planted Cabernet Franc extensively, copying the Cheval Blanc pattern, with amazing results. In Australia, Cabernet Franc is a real favourite as it gives another dimension to their Cab-Sauv-dominant wines. New Zealand has also taken Cabernet Franc to its heart, as it is easier to ripen than Cabernet Sauvignon and favours the slightly cooler climate. I love the purity of this variety. It holds its own well in the Loire where the wines are 100 per cent Cabernet Franc. And for this reason I favour this grape over Merlot in world importance.

Pinot Noir *(Pee-no Nw-ar)*

Wild **strawberries**, **redcurrants**, **red plums**, **violets** and **stables** (yes, horses) can pop up on the nose in a Pinot, with a **black cherry** flavour on the palate. Vibrant and juicy in their youth, as these wines age, they can take on a slightly farmyardy feel, and, as the colour fades from dark red to pale brick red, the nose can turn leathery and raspberry-like. The most alluring red grape in the world (to my mind) is also, more often than not, the most disappointing in the wrong hands. Pinot Noir is known as the 'fickle mistress' of the red grape world. So-called because it is a real pain to ripen, and has infuriated winemakers the world over who have fallen head over heels in love with its charms. Pinot Noir's spiritual home is France. You may be surprised to learn that it is one of the three main grape varieties that make Champagne. However, it is best known for producing the great red wines of Burgundy. Names like Gevrey-Chambertin, Chambolle-Musigny, Nuits-Saint-Georges, Richebourg, Volnay and many others, are the wines that owe their fame to Pinot Noir. It is in Burgundy that the celestial elegance and brooding power of this beautiful grape are captured consummately. Fiendishly unpredictable and as often disappointing as not, this grape variety needs you to worship it in order for you to understand what all the fuss is about. When on form, Pinot Noir makes outstanding wines with heroic length and baffling complexity, when off form they taste thin, stewed and unripe. Other French regions that plant Pinot Noir with some success are the Loire Valley (red and rosé Sancerre), some brave people in the South of France and, in a minor way, Alsace. The producer and the vintage are the two crucial factors in the two northerly regions, as a good growing season and a skilful hand are essential for Pinot Noir to do its thing.

Elsewhere, most wines using this tricky variety will have Pinot Noir written on the label. New Zealand's Martinborough, Central Otago and Marlborough regions all make very good examples, while cooler parts of Australia, like Tasmania and Mornington Peninsula, Geelong and the Yarra Valley in Victoria, all make very smart wines indeed. Chile, South Africa and even Italy produce some good Pinots – but choose carefully. In North America Pinot Noir is the new Merlot. California and Oregon's cooler areas are home to the petulant Pinot, and it has been befriended by a small band of infatuated winemakers. Calera, Au Bon Climat, Etude and Kistler make celestial Pinot Noirs, but it seems that, for the time being, the super rich of the West Coast are the only people able to afford to drink the tiny allocations on offer.

Syrah/Shiraz *(Sirrah/Shirraz)*

Ground pepper, **cigar smoke** and **coffee beans** can often form the aromatic elements of what is a totally alluring **blackberry-** and **blackcurrant-**driven palate. In its everyday form Syrah can be a bit of a brute. Often rather clumsy and not especially charming, it needs to be nurtured and encouraged to turn the corner from being a blocky, ungainly red wine into a thoroughbred. In order to experience its purity and explosive blackberry and pepper aromas fully, it is important to head to the top of the Syrah-ladder. The Northern Rhône Valley in France is its true home, although it has been taken to Australia's heart, as its prodigal grape, where it is known as Shiraz. In France, no restaurant wine list is complete without a mention of Côte-Rôtie or Hermitage whose wines are made from this spicy, firm variety. The most famous producer of Côte-Rôtie is Marcel Guigal. His single vineyard wines, La Mouline, La Landonne and La Turque have elevated this grape's fame to unimaginable levels. With this estate leading the way in Côte-Rôtie, and Chave and Jaboulet working their magic in Hermitage, the Northern Rhône has had a new lease of life and Syrah, as it should be, is enjoying the limelight. Syrah is also one of the main constituents in blended Southern Rhône wines, like Châteauneuf-du-Pape. The Languedoc and Roussillon also employ this fine variety to good effect and, these days, they rival some of the Rhône's more serious wines.

In Australia, Shiraz is an institution. Its unlikely and very welcome partnership with Cabernet Sauvignon (in France this would be the unholy blending of Bordeaux with Rhône) works extremely well. The most expensive non-French Syrah in the world is also from Australia, Penfold's Grange. It is no surprise that a grape variety that makes 'Roasted Slope' (Côte-Rôtie) enjoys hot climates. The Barossa Valley in South Australia is almost synonymous with big, inky-black Shiraz. McLaren Vale, Clare Valley and many other areas besides, also make stunning, world-class Shiraz, and if you have never tried one of these top wines, then put your seat belt on because they are simply breathtaking.

Outside France and Australia, Syrah is planted in most winemaking countries and is having particular success in California, South Africa and Chile. The Americans have a fascination with all things Rhône, and the term 'Rhône Ranger' is used to describe a hearty bunch of reprobates whose love of the region is such that they are planting many obscure Rhône varieties in land usually reserved for Cabernet Sauvignon and Merlot. Long may the Rhône Rangers ride. South Africa is the latest country to really turn up the heat with this variety. Paarl, Swartland and Wellington look like ideal sites for this sun-loving grape, and, with a number of good vintages under the bonnet, a few of the top wineries are showing that they have really understood the intricacies of this grape.

Lastly we come to Chile. The Chileans seem to have had a fixation on Cabernet and Merlot for far too long, and they are now realising that Syrah is an important red grape variety with a loyal and thirsty customer base. Some of the super cuvée wines emerging are looking very good indeed.

Grenache/Garnacha *(Gre-nash/Gar-natch-ah)*
With everything from **dark red cherries** to **black fruit**, Grenache often has a **herbal** element to its aroma, not unlike **sweet pipe smoke**. It is the other red Rhône grape that makes it into my top

twenty, and is the swarthy, unshaven cousin of Syrah. Where Syrah likes to go hunting alone – the assassin – Grenache likes to have some company – the shooting party. Grenache forms the bulk of most Southern Rhône blends. It can have as many as twelve other mates on board in a Châteauneuf-du-Pape, but mainly likes to depend on its reliable friends Syrah and Mourvèdre. Sadly, Grenache is a much-abused variety in the South of France bulk market, as it ripens on cue and provides an ocean of wine for 'house' consumption in bars. It plays a similar role in Spain, where it's called Garnacha and is very widely planted. Garnacha reaches its vinous peak in partnership with the deft enforcer Tempranillo (of which more later). This combination makes Spain's most famous red wine, Rioja. In all cases, Grenache is a meaty, earthy variety that only really lets the side down in rosé form when, on account of its unusually high alcohol, it can be thought of as the gangster's moll. The only other style of Grenache-based wine that is worthy of a search party is the rich, Christmas cake, Port-style wines of Banyuls and Maury. These two are fortified, like port, but not to the same degree and are found in the far southwest of France near Perpignan. Presumably, these wines alone account for the ferocity of the rugby players in that corner of France.

Australia shipped in Grenache at the same time as Shiraz and the two old pals are often blended together to form a New World ripeness/Old World dependability wine. Shiraz somehow always takes the credit, but Grenache does a lot of the legwork. You will see GSM, MGS, GMS, but rarely MSG (for some reason!) on bottles of Aussie wine, letting you know that the three old mates Grenache, Shiraz and Mourvèdre (or Mataro as some call it) are doing their magic in the bottle.

California has fun with Grenache in its pink and Porty form, but these two styles are not taken very seriously and Grenache usually plays a supporting role in many grown-up, red Rhône-style blends. The Grenache grape pops up in South America, helping other varieties by boosting structure and presence, and has no trouble fitting in, as it is no stranger to a hot climate. The only other place that uses Grenache successfully is Sardinia.

Here the disguise is known as Cannonau, and this wine can be found in pizzerias the world over, countering the spice of a 'Dragon's breath deep pan' or a 'Spicy Inferno'.

Gamay *(Ga-may)*

The grape has a **bananas** and **bubble-gum** nose on the cheapies, but a **pepper** and **blackberry** aroma on more expensive bottles. Every bottle of Beaujolais is made from 100 per cent Gamay, and for that reason alone you may think that Gamay is the joker in my pack – but no, because I, for one, think that it is a superb variety that makes one of the most underrated and great value red wines of all. Before you get too carried away, though, I do not mean that all bottles of Beaujolais are unmissable and delicious (or offer great value for money) – far from it.

Fine – and by that I mean Domaine-bottled, serious quality – Beaujolais ranges in taste from summer **strawberry juice** lightness to a wintry, robust, **black cherry** and **pepper** concoction. The very best sell for the same price as a middling Bourgogne Rouge, so they are still good value. Unfortunately, bad Beaujolais, generally the Nouveau fiasco and chemistry-set, big brand or French supermarket stuff, is little more than a lipstick-pink, headache-inducing alcopop. The innocent Gamay grape may be responsible for this range of guises, but it is not the grape's fault. The praise or guilt lies at the feet of the winemakers who transform this grape into whichever style suits them best (benchmark quality or fast buck). The one reason to carry on drinking good Beaujolais is that it keeps you smiling. Beaujolais wines require no real concentration, they are 'no-brainers' (I love them), as they are packed with fresh, **red berry** flavours, perky acidity and virtually no tannin whatsoever. The Beaujolais region is wedged into the gap between Burgundy and the northern Rhône and the wines taste like it. They have a juicy character with a hint of earthy spice. They require no extended cellaring; in fact they demand to be drunk the second they hit the shelves. After all, they are rarely expensive and they complement food marvellously (see the Wine and Food chapter). Gamay is also planted in the area of Touraine in the Loire Valley, and there it makes a similarly thirst-quenching red wine. This style is a favourite in Paris brasseries and it's often served as their equivalent of a house wine. The reason for this, and don't argue with Parisian restaurateurs, is that there are precious few wines from France that offer immediate drinking with year in, year out dependable quality at affordable prices. Make a mental note of some of the village names in Beaujolais, and then find the list of reliable producers later on in this book. You will thank me, honestly.

Nebbiolo (Neb-ee-olo)

Coming from Piemonte in the northwest of Italy, and having **leather**, **gamey** overtones, and **spice**, **plums** and **stewed prunes** characteristics, Nebbiolo is an immensely tough variety. It often needs five years minimum in a bottle to be even approachable. It is a regal sort and demands respect – and usually gets it. Even the so-called new wave estates in Piemonte still need years of cellaring to charm this beast into submission. The most famous name that Nebbiolo is responsible for is Barolo. Other lesser-known labels are Barbaresco and Gattinara. Because these wines are in fairly short supply and they invariably require extended cellaring to soften the scary tannins, they tend to be very expensive. A great Nebbiolo can conjure up intense plummy flavours with spicy, gamey overtones. Nebbiolo is a truly memorable variety, if not an everyday requirement for most palates – its size, structure and tannin would undoubtedly be too demanding for our poor taste buds.

Various outposts around the world are planting Nebbiolo with varying degrees of success. I have tasted a few good ones from South Australia, grown in both the Adelaide Hills and McLaren Vale. Intriguing and accurate, granted, but I wouldn't hold your breath for a raft of non-Piemontese Nebs flooding in from all corners of the world because it doesn't like to travel far from home.

Sangiovese (San-geeo-vay-zee)

With **cranberries**, **mulberries**, **fresh herbs** and **red cherries** on the nose, this grape shows bright **red fruit** flavours, overlaid with a whiff of **fresh-cut herbs** and **new leather.** Sangiovese is the second of the Italian grape varieties in my selection of the vinous elite. This time, my star grape variety favours a more Central Italian vista, as Sangiovese is the main ingredient in Chianti. It also makes Brunello di Montalcino, another majestic Tuscan wine. There is no doubt that Sangiovese is a truly sumptuous variety. Extraordinarily charming, this troubadour is warm, ripe and complex in good vintages and troubled, misunderstood, unapologetic but almost forgivable in bad ones. Sangiovese can always be relied upon to reveal an acidic kick on the finish. For this reason Chiantis and Brunellos need some age under their belts to be fully appreciated. Sangiovese occasionally enjoys the company of Cabernet Sauvignon and Merlot in a blend – what a gregarious fellow it is. When blending Sangiovese with Cab Sauv or Merlot the resulting wine is known as a Super-Tuscan. Some of the most expensive and sought-after wines in a collector's cellar are Super-Tuscan. The good news is that Chianti and neighbouring Vino Nobile di Montepulciano are receiving a welcome return to world fame. The trattoria cloak has been cast off and, with help from the US market (they are big Italian fans) and some serious investment from locals, Sangiovese is in better shape than it has ever been. Now, more than ever, is the time to look closely at a region whose wines are synonymous with all aspects Italian. It is worth spending a few pounds more on these Sangioveses, just as you might do on shoes, clothes, cars, motorbikes, prosciutto or olive oil.

Zinfandel *(Zin-fan-dell)*

The taste is like a turbo-charged **blackberry** meeting a **spice** warehouse – a **black fruit** explosion covered in **vanilla** and **mixed spices** – and my top echelon would not be complete without Zinfandel. However, rather than a lifetime membership, I will award it a rolling, one year pass. 'Zin' is rumoured to have ancient Italian roots (Primitivo is a very close cousin). Sadly, its relations are reluctant to admit parentage fully so there will always be an enviable air of mystery about this unruly, yet explosive grape. Some of the most shocking and inspiring red wines in the world are made from this almost exclusively Californian variety. It is a shame, however, because some of the worst wines in the world are made from Zin, too. Over the years Zinfandel has been seen in many unpleasant guises: from 'blush', a ridiculous name for a semi-sweet, bimbo rosé style, via 'jug' wine bought in enormous containers the size of a truck, to a sort of port-like moonshine, with a kick like a mule. Forget all of these, because the correct way to enjoy this exciting variety is in straightforward red wine mode. In the hands of top-flight wineries like Ridge, Cline, Nalle, Ravenswood, Elyse and Turley (all in California), the results are breathtakingly invigorating, palate-bashingly eye-popping and heart-warmingly sofa snoozing.

OTHER RED VARIETIES
(IN ALPHABETICAL ORDER)
Baga (Bagga)
A black, **tarry**, **plum** and **blackcurrant**-flavoured grape, with more than a lick of **spice** and power. This underrated, thick-skinned Portuguese grape variety accounts for the lion's share of the blend in Bairrada and is also used for Dão. You can just about get away with pronouncing it 'bugger', as well!

Barbera (Bah-bear-a)
Nebbiolo's friendly little brother in Piemonte, **black wine gums**, **plums** and fresh **boot polish** can be found here, with a velvety texture and aftertaste. Barbera is a relatively straightforward grape, because it has plenty of fruit and lower acidity and tannin. Although not as famous as Nebbiolo, in the right hands it can produce supreme juiciness and fine structure. Most good Barolo producers have a Barbera in their armoury, and it's always much cheaper, so it's a nice place to start with the wines of Piemonte.

Carignan (Carin-yon)
Spice, **leather** and **earthy black fruit** are Carignan's hallmarks. It is a southern French grape variety that lags behind Syrah and Grenache in terms of style and elegance. It needs the sun, as it

is a late ripener. It's also found further afield in such sunny climes as Spain (Carignano) and South America. Carignan is an awkward, angular fellow that needs support from other varieties to help it along.

Carmenère *(Car-men-air)*

Red fruit, **coffee bean** and **mocha** notes make Carmenère the ideal breakfast red. Only kidding! This grape is championed by the Chileans, who for years mistakenly thought it was a strain of Merlot and bottled it under the Merlot name. In fact, Carmenere is quite different and it is a welcome addition to your wine diet – slotting in somewhere between the aforementioned Merlot and heavier Cabernet Sauvignon. Funnily enough, I am rather partial to this variety, as it tends to be very good value for money; perhaps because it is not that well known...

Cinsault *(San-so)*

Cinsault is similar to Carignan but arguably is a little more rustic and less intensely flavoured. It also performs best in a blend. This unremarkable variety whose home is, once again, the southern Rhône and Languedoc-Roussillon, has one redeeming feature – it is one of the parents of Pinotage (read on). It just about makes good rosé wines in the right hands, too.

Dolcetto *(Doll-chetto)*

Liquorice and **black cherry** are the welcome scents to the grape, and skunky **stink bombs** the not-so-welcome. You have been warned! Like Barbera, Dolcetto is a Piemontese red variety although, this time, it's the funny little brother to Nebbiolo. This grape has low tannin and therefore is the only true glugging red grape from the northwest corner of Italy. Purple in colour and boasting an unusual eggy scent, this variety is worth finding, as it gives another dimension to the wine aroma spectrum.

Freisa *(Fray-za)*

The last of the Piemonte brethren – Freisa is a weird one. Fresh

red fruit with a pick-your-own feel, this is a less muscular grape than many northern Italian reds and can't make up its mind whether it is a Dolcetto-like glugger or a Nebbiolo-like keeper. Both styles are made – I prefer the young, vibrant, cherryade version. You will probably only see this grape on your holidays or in top quality Italian delis, and then only buy it if you are feeling lucky.

Kadarka *(Kuh-darker)*

Swarthy, charmless and brutish, this is a gritty, **blackberry**- and **potting-compost**-scented variety. A Hungarian, Bulgarian (called Gamza) and Romanian grape producing spicy, blunt reds with little charm. Think of a wine whose ideal food partner is poached haunch of yak!

Malbec *(Mal-beck)*

Always deep, dark and brooding, Malbec is sturdy and masculine, with **prune**, **black cherry** and **oaky** flavours. It is an unfashionable, old retainer grown in the Loire Valley, Cahors in central France and South America, where it does its best work in some serious Argentinian blockbusters. This is a heavy-weight red grape, which used to be widely planted in Bordeaux and was used as the tannin/colour provider on account of its thick skin. Also known as Cot and Auxerrois.

Mavrud *(Mav-rood – rhymes with hood)*

This grape makes Kadarka look positively charming. **Black fruit** and **earth** in equal measure. Mavrud is a Bulgarian red grape variety with dark, swarthy appeal. It sounds rustic, even menacing, if you roll your 'r'.

Mourvèdre/Mataro *(More-veh-dr/Mat-are-oh)*

Often with a whiff of **fresh herbs** and sweet **wood smoke**, Mourvèdre is another of the Southern French red grape posse, but, unlike Cinsault and Carignan, this grape has true style. Totally classy and complex **black cherry**, **plum** and **berry** flavours combine with **oaky** nuances usually creeping in, too. In

France, Mourvèdre is an integral part of the finest Châteauneuf-du-Pape blends, loving the company of Syrah, Cinsault and of course Grenache. Other famous wines that owe their flavours to a greater or lesser degree to this variety are Bandol, Cassis, Palette, Tavel and many other Provençal wines. These wines may all be a little esoteric, but are well worth hunting down. If this variety were missing from the blend you would taste the difference. Desperately in need of a suntan, this variety loves the hot weather. It travels extensively abroad to Spain (Monastrell – say what you see), Australia and California where it is known as Mataro.

Petit Verdot *(Pet-ee Ver-dough)*

Having a tougher flavour than most red grapes, Petit Verdot is often a little raw and unpolished with intense **black fruit** flavours but stemmy acidity and heady alcohol. The 'little green one' is sometimes used in small quantities in Bordeaux blends to add acidity to the rich cocktail of Cabernet Sauvignon, Cabernet Franc and Merlot. Keen fans around the world plant this variety in the hope that an ever more complex blend will help them to reach perfection. There are a few plantings in South Australia that work well, bearing in mind that you need a lot of sunshine to turn this little green one into a big red one.

Pinot Meunier *(Pee-no Mur-nee-yay)*

Pinot Meunier is the only grape variety that actively needs a PR agent. Virtually unheard of in everyday parlance, this poor grape is left in the wings while Chardonnay and Pinot Noir take all of the applause. Where is this grape to be found? The answer is in Champagne where it is vinified off its skins (i.e. just using the juice) to produce a white wine that is an integral part of many Champagne blends. It brings up-front fruit and crisp acidity to the party, adds a **floral**, **smooth** and vaguely **raspberry-scented** note, and is generally used in Non Vintage Champagnes, where prolonged cellaring is not a requirement. Pinot Meunier is virtually unheard of outside France, except for some plantings in Australia and some in Germany where it is known as Schwarzriesling.

Pinotage (Pee-no-tahge)

A Pinot Noir/Cinsault cross, developed in 1925, Pinotage produces a rich, rustic wine and is South Africa's most famous red grape. Pinotage is an earthy, spicy, deeply coloured grape with **tobacco** and **plums** on the nose, **crushed berry** fruit on the palate and a hearty finish. It needs food badly, and works well if made by top producers.

Tannat (Tan-at)

Big, heavy, spicy and palate pulverising, Tannat has a no-prisoners flavour of **prunes** and power. Originating in the Basque region this variety did not travel too far to find its home in the two wines, Madiran and Irouléguy. These two quirky offerings tend to be very dense when young and need a few years for the tannin levels to soften. Strangely Tannat also is found in Uruguay where it is transformed into a slightly softer, fruitier version of Madiran. In other words, still a bit of a monster.

Tempranillo (Temp-ra-nee-yo)

This is an immensely important red grape that is the main ingredient in Rioja as well as many other Spanish red wines. **Strawberry**, **raspberry**, **cherry** and **vanilla** appear on lighter wines, which heavy-weights rev these flavours up and add **blackberry** and darker nuances to the mix. It is, confusingly, known as Tinto Fino, Ull de Llebre and Cencibel in different parts of Spain, and Tinta de Toro is a very close clonal brother. It also enjoys a favourite holiday location, this time Argentina, where the style is fruit driven and less oaky than Rioja. Once again, the New World is experimenting with this variety, but none that I have tasted will trouble Spain's vast panoply of sensational offerings.

Touriga Nacional (Too-ree-ga Na-see-on-al)

Of the huge number of grape varieties that go into port, Touriga Nacional is the most aristocratic. Immense power, as you would expect, is the main character trait of this grape. Cram-packed with dense black fruit it is the backbone of the finest and longest-lived vintage ports. This is a mighty red grape with darkest,

pruney, **black fruit** and layers of **spice**. Touriga Nacional is also used to make Douro red wines with some considerable success. They are, not surprisingly, pretty big, spicy, age worthy creatures.

IMPORTANT WHITE VARIETIES
Chardonnay (Shar-dunn-ay)

If Cabernet Sauvignon is the king of the grape world, then Chardonnay is most definitely the queen. World dominance was on the agenda when Chardonnay took the throne, and she achieved it mercilessly. Its hallmarks are **honey**, **fresh butter**, **hazelnuts**, **meadow flowers**, **pear**, **apple**, **fresh-baked bread**, **lime juice**, **butterscotch** and **vanilla** (if oak barrels are used). This remarkably versatile, dry variety has reached fame on the back of a mass-appeal flavour that harmonises nicely with oak barrels and tends to complement food extremely well. Chardonnay is planted in virtually every winemaking country and it can be found in hundreds of different guises on wine shop shelves. If you are bored with seeing the word Chardonnay on bottles of wine then try some Chablis, Meursault, Chassagne-Montrachet, Puligny-Montrachet, Pouilly-Fuissé or St-Véran – come to think of it, any top-notch white Burgundy – for all of these wines are made exclusively from the Chardonnay variety, but do not feel the need to write it on the label. (There are a few exceptions, but we will come to those later.) Chardonnay is also one of the three grape varieties used for making Champagne – ha-ha, fingers in all of the pies! In fact a Blanc de Blancs Champagne is 100 per cent Chardonnay. Chardonnay all over the world aspires to the greatness found in Burgundy's white wines, and in California comes tantalisingly close. However, no one seems to have completely cracked the code. There are plenty of serious Chardonnays made in the South of France, too, particularly in cooler, higher altitude regions like Limoux. Other countries producing excellent Chardonnays are New Zealand and Australia and, in the second tier, Chile, South Africa, Austria, Spain and Italy.

There has been a backlash against Chardonnay, presumably because there is so much ordinary stuff on the shelves these days, but it is a serious variety that is responsible for the most revered and expensive dry white wines in the world. I have never met anyone who would turn his or her nose up at the offer of a glass of Le Montrachet. So don't join the ABC group ('Anything But Chardonnay'). Celebrate this noble grape and keep your standards up.

Riesling *(Rees-ling)*

With **lime**, **rhubarb**, **petrol**, **toast**, **fruit salad** and **honeysuckle** in varying degrees of intensity, Riesling is a grape variety that sends a shiver down a wine lover's spine. Outside the wine cognoscenti, Riesling is mistakenly thought of as a cheap, sweet wine with a comedy German name – Blue Nun, Black Tower and the like. Inside the wine-smart homes around the world, however, Riesling is hailed as the greatest of all white varieties, and that includes Chardonnay. Why? Well, Riesling produces a vast array of stunning styles of wine – everything from bone-dry, nerve-tingling aperitifs, through structured, foody classics, via long-lived, incredibly complex wines and off-dry, sensual afternoon-in-the-garden sippers, ending up at heart-achingly beautiful sweeties. Its trick is that it engenders superb balance. Riesling's acidity and fruit characteristics are stunningly complementary and this can lead to a long and happy existence slumbering in the cellar. This variety is the unspoken, modest, spiritual leader of a wine lover's palate. Riesling has immense confidence in its skills – cool and calculating, but playful and relaxed, never showing the full hand, even when the chips are down. It has spent many years as an outcast in society, but there has always been a hardened band of likeminded disciples keeping the fires burning.

Riesling's home is in Germany, where the Mosel and Rheingau make some of the most beautiful wines I have ever tasted. German Riesling is one of the most captivating and essential world wine styles, and over the border in Alsace more incredible wines are made from this sensational grape. Here,

Riesling Clos Sainte-Hune made from a single vineyard owned by Domaine Trimbach is the finest expression of dry Riesling available. Italy makes some fine, crisp versions and Austria goes one better by crafting the full gamut of styles; unfortunately they tend to be a little on the dear side. Further afield, Australia leads the pack, with the Clare and Eden Valleys making some of the best value, dry Rieslings the world has ever seen. Tasmania, Victoria and southern Western Australia score very well, too. New Zealand Riesling is also having some success at home and abroad. Marlborough and Central Otago are the two best places to send your search party. The rest of the world sticks its oar in a little, but reverentially decides not to dabble too much, since Germany, Austria, France, Australia and New Zealand seemingly have the variety more than sewn up.

The Riesling revolution has been a long time coming, but now it is here, and we are all able to enjoy the stuff at affordable prices. Once bitten, always smitten, so keep your eyes peeled for the producers mentioned in the Wine Regions of the World chapter. Dry Riesling is an uplifting aperitif. Sweet Riesling is a joy to behold. In between there is a cornucopia of flavours and styles. Try one today, you will feel elated.

Sauvignon Blanc *(So-veen-yon Blon)*

Despite **asparagus**, **gooseberries**, **lemons**, **fresh herbs**, **crunchy apples**, **elderflower** and **freshly mown grass** hallmarks, many wine drinkers regard Sauvignon Blanc as the Fool, a court jester, a mere trifle not to be taken seriously at all. This is wrong, categorically wrong. I agree that Sauvignon Blanc does not take to oak barrels as well as Chardonnay, it doesn't age as well as Riesling, it can't cope with sweetness as well as Chenin Blanc or Semillon, and it rarely has the texture or oiliness of Gewürztraminer or Viognier. So why bother? The answer is, it has something all of those other grape varieties don't. You do not need a wine degree to appreciate its appeal. You don't need to have memorised the 1855 classification of Bordeaux Châteaux to understand every element of its charm. Up front, brazen, outgoing and happy-go-lucky, it is a guaranteed crowd-pleaser.

Granted, there is a lot of mediocre Sancerre and Pouilly-Fumé out there, and there are more boring, lacklustre New World Sauvs than you can shake a stick at – but for every crappy example, there is another that sings from the rooftops. At home in the Loire Valley, in northern France, the Sauvignon Blanc grape variety likes cooler climates. These wines are not made to last forever. In fact, the majority of Sauvignon Blancs in the world should be drunk within three years. New Zealand and its vinous charms would never have been discovered by the likes of the English wine drinker were it not for the gooseberry explosions on the nose and tropical fruit on the palate of its Sauvignon Blancs back in the mid eighties. I am always excited to taste great Sauvignons and now the skills of capturing the aromatic nose and zingy palate have made it around the world to cooler parts of Australia, Chile and South Africa. It is also doing great things in northern Italy and southern France. My final reason for you to vote Sauvignon Blanc a winner is that it is a saviour when it comes to oriental food. No other grape copes as well with the sweet and sour, spice and heat of all types of Pacific Rim, Asian fusion or even the real-Eastern-thing quite like this thirst quencher. The jury has decided – Not Guilty of being a Fool. Rather, Sauvignon Blanc is the People's Champion!

Semillon (Sem-ee-yon)

With **honey**, **orange blossom**, **lanolin**, **lemon zest**, **hop sack** and **lime juice**, this workhorse grape variety only really hits full speed in its sweet form. Once again, the birthplace of this grape is in France, more specifically the Left Bank of Bordeaux. Here, often in conjunction with the underrated Sauvignon Blanc, it makes the most celestial sweet wines. Semillon is luckily prone to rot, and this rot is encouraged. Despite the grapes looking unpleasant on the vine, the juice that emerges when they are pressed is incredibly high in sugar. Under the right supervision it can result in a heavenly potion, whose well-known names are Sauternes and Barsac. Sadly these wines are few and far between, not to mention fairly pricey. A dry version of the wine, again often made using a proportion of Sauvignon Blanc in the blend, can be sublime. Unfortunately, there is a large quantity of very dull dry white Bordeaux on the market as well. So, how can such a beauty end up being so drab? Over-cropping and sheer incompetence are presumably the reason, because abroad there are more than enough smart Semillons made.

Like a student on its gap year, Semillon loves to travel. It blends well with Chardonnay and tries to emulate its more talented partner in the taste department. Semillon can handle oak barrels – not as effortlessly as its friend Chardonnay can, but well enough for it to be trusted on its own with these flavours. Flying solo, Semillon has enjoyed considerable success in the Hunter Valley and Barossa Valley in Australia. Over in Western Australia, the Bordeaux model is used to great effect – and loads of high quality Semillon/Sauvignon Blanc blends abound. In New Zealand several estates have pioneered single varietal Semillon and come up with an interesting alternative to Chardonnay. Relying on its CV as a fine producer of sweeties, it comes as no surprise that when asked to perform the pudding wine thing it steps up to the mark in style. In Australia and several other New World countries, Riesling is its only rival in the drop-dead gorgeous stakes.

Chenin Blanc (Shuh-nan Blon)

Chenin Blanc is like your best friend who decides to follow certain music, clothes, food – everything – just as it has fallen out of fashion. Never quite getting the timing right, Chenin Blanc is a dear old thing that tries hard, but only gets invited out when the company can put up with its eccentric behaviour. Retro? Possibly. Fashions always come around again, as you know. Its hallmarks are **beeswax**, **honey**, **apples**, **pears** and **wet woolly jumpers** (!), while sweet versions have the full fruit bowl on the go. So where do we find this grape? The Loire, of course, along with geeky Sauvignon Blanc and awkward, uncommercial Cabernet Franc – what a superb and engaging trio. In South Africa it flourishes, mainly in dry form. One or two estates are treating it like Chardonnay and giving it the full-on oak treatment. I have tasted some amazing versions of this style of wine and they rival the very best in the world. In Australia and New Zealand, Chenin copes admirably with oak barrels, too, and, thanks to the warmer climate, can develop some considerable structure.

Chenin Blanc, like Riesling, has an uncanny balance of acidity and fruit when youthful. Acidity being the vinous equivalent of a healthy supply of monkey glands (or a bloody big aqualung), Chenin always appears to have something in reserve (Loire Chenin Blanc usually tastes a little young). The other fascinating aspect of this variety is that it makes THE full range of styles of white wine. From remarkably efficient, inexpensive sparklers, through lean, zippy, cleansing aperitifs to medium-dry, charcuterie and paté friendly wines, all the way to full-on honey and succulent peach sweeties dripping in unctuous, mouth-filling richness (using the rot that Semillon loves). So despite being a little unusual, to say the least, this grape is a talented individual.

Gewürztraminer *(Guh-vurz-tram-inner)*

Gewürztraminer has the most distinctive smell of any grape variety. Pungent **lychee**, **spice** and **rose petal** nose are accompanied, more often than not, by an **exotic oiliness** on the palate and a long ripe finish. This grape has the unusual knack of always smelling sweet but then sometimes surprising you and, just when you are least expecting it, tasting bone dry. Altogether otherworldly and certainly not immediately vinous, this grape is an acquired taste. Born in Germany but more at home in Alsace, it can produce extremely concentrated, flavoursome wines that range from light, fresh and dry, to unctuous, decadent and wonderfully sweet. Curiously, the nose always gives the variety away, but not until you taste it is it possible to tell whether the wine is dry, medium or sweet. A popular way of making Gewürz is to pick the grapes a little later than the others destined for dry wines. These styles are called 'Vendange Tardive' – literally, harvested later. This suits the grape variety well – they are not usually cloyingly sweet, instead just ripe and smooth. Gewürz is always a treat for your palate, as it exercises the taste buds you never knew you had. Unlike the other well-travelled white grapes in this section, Gewürztraminer doesn't quite make the grade abroad. Seemingly a little jet-lagged or just a bit home-sick, Gewürz lacks the power and concentration of the Alsatian back home. Australia, New Zealand, Chile, South Africa and North America all have a go and make interesting, if not captivating, wines. In Europe, northern Italy loses the Gewürz (German for 'spice') and just plain Traminer is grown to produce the equivalent of a diluted Gewürztraminer nose with a crisp, dry finish. Spain and Eastern Europe do their bit but to little effect. It seems that Gewürztraminer loves its homeland and no matter how nice the tour guide, hotel or weather, it just doesn't enjoy travelling.

Muscat (Muss-cat)

The Muscat grape has a huge family. Whether they are directly related varieties, sub-varieties, clones, or just happen to sound vaguely similar, I am grouping them all together in this sprawling clan. The range of tastes that emanate from this family tree is also extraordinarily diverse. From the lightest, fizzy, soda-siphon grape juice (like fairy dust dancing on your tongue), all the way to the deepest, darkest, headiest liqueur like a rugby player's liniment, Muscat just about covers the full complement of winey flavours. The common factor in all of these wines is that Muscat is the only grape variety that actually tastes of grapes. Think about it for a second, for all of the other varieties in this chapter it is possible to come up with many different descriptors in order to convey their taste but with Muscat it is a struggle to find a more useful word than … **grapey**!

The head of the Muscat family is Muscat Blanc à Petits Grains (no wonder it gets shortened to Muscat). This grape is responsible for the dry wines of Alsace (Muscat d'Alsace – another synonym) and the sweet wines from southern France (Muscat de Beaumes-de-Venise and Muscat de Frontignan). The Italian translation for this Muscat is Moscato Bianco. This variety makes the frothy Asti wines in Piemonte and some fabulous sweet wines in Trentino. It is fairly widely planted in Italy. In

South Africa it is known as Muskadel and in California as the Muscat Canelli or White Muscat.

The inferior Muscat of Alexandria is starting to crowd out the Muscat à Petits Grains and is responsible for Muscat de Rivesaltes, a fortified wine that hits the spot in a clumsy sort of way, and also Moscato di Pantelleria from Sicily, an orange-peel-crossed-with-syrup style of wine. More commonly used as a table grape, Muscat of Alexandria only really feels comfortable in hot climates. It is made in Portugal into the tolerable clodhopper of a sweet wine Moscatel de Setúbal. It is also found in the sensational, fortified Australian icon wines, known as Liqueur Muscats.

The other Muscat worth noting is the Muscat Ottonel, a cooler climate buddy who is trying to shove Muscat à Petits Grains out of Alsace. This grape is happy in Romania, Austria and Hungary – although I'd avoid it if I were you.

The family of Muscat is not a happy one. More dysfunctional than functional, they are continually treading on each other's toes with no one version reigning supreme, as climate compatibility plays a large role in which version is planted where.

Pinot Blanc/Pinot Bianco *(Pee-no Blon/ Pee-no Bee-anko)*

Not the most demanding of grape varieties, it is very easy to condemn Pinot Blanc to the 'B' list but, showing fair play to all comers, I am pleased to welcome PB into our happy band of overachievers. Another grape whose fame is almost exclusively European, Pinot Blanc is found in Alsace, Burgundy (in minuscule quantities), northern Italy (swap Blanc for Bianco), Germany (as Weissburgunder) and, to a lesser degree, in Austria, Chile and California. So, what is Pinot Blanc's appeal? Almost all of the Pinot Blancs made worldwide are unoaked, dry and relatively inexpensive. Find an estate with a good reputation and the chances are that their Pinot Blanc will be on form. It should be a dry, unoaked, white wine that tastes of **appley**, **creamy**, slightly **nutty** flavours with **soft ripe fruit** and some texture on the palate. I am trying to make this sound exciting! The fact is that very few Pinot Blancs will make you rush out into the street screaming with joy. They are, however, not boring; they just seem to like to set the scene for other wines. They are the compères of the wine world – amusing, likeable, dry, multi-skilled crowd-pleasers that shouldn't put anyone off before the real show begins. This makes Pinot Blanc a suitable variety to start off an evening's wining and dining.

Tokay-Pinot Gris/Pinot Gris/Pinot Grigio/ Tokay d'Alsace *(Tock-eye Pee-no Gree/Pee-no Gridge-ee-oh/Tock-eye Dal-sass)*

So called because it has a greyish skin, Tokay-Pinot Gris is another grape variety that loves it in Alsace – it must be the Michelin-starred restaurants. Its flavour is somewhere between Pinot Blanc and Gewürztraminer – though admittedly, there is a world of flavours in that gap! The distinctive nose of this grape is one of **spice** and **honey**. It does not have the rose-petal-perfume that Gewürztraminer has and tends to be drier like Pinot Blanc. There are some notable exceptions to this, however. Late, judicious picking can lead to extremely sweet wines, but on the whole it is a savoury taste collision between a fruit bowl and a spice rack. This grape is the definitive split personality. While the Alsatian version of this grape is not that commonly available, the Italian style, Pinot Grigio, is everywhere. And what a different can of beans this wine is. The richest, most exuberant Pinot Grigio is still a virtual light-weight next to the oleaginous Alsatian. Pinot Grigios from Trentino, Alto Adige and Friuli are spicy on the nose and then spritzy, almost buzzing with electricity, on the palate. This freshness comes from the Italians' eagerness to harvest a little early and capture all of the mouth-watering acidity that this grape has to offer.

In Germany, Pinot Gris is called Ruländer and it enjoys a fair degree of success in the relatively warm Baden region. Here it puts on some of the weight in which it revels in Alsace, and for that reason is appreciated as an enjoyable, food-friendly wine. Never quite reaching the aromatic zip of Pinot Grigio or the weight and spice of Tokay d'Alsace, this grape also manifests itself in Austria and Eastern Europe.

There are precious few Pinot Gris in the New World, although a few terrific versions pop up in the Adelaide Hills, Tasmania, King Valley and Mornington Peninsula in Australia, and New Zealand is tackling this variety by making everything from light-weight Grigio to full on sexy styles, but only a few have really hit the balance mark to date. Argentina, South Africa and Chile all have a go at the lower price points and some are showing promise.

Viognier (Vee-yon-yay)

Divine, sensual, provocative temptress, or fashion victim's folly? Your guess is as good as mine. With a haunting perfume of **peach kernels** and **apricot blossom**, **honey** and **nutmeg**, followed by an ample body with plenty of charm and a lingering aftertaste, Viognier seems hard to resist. But resist it you must, as there are so many new Viogniers out there, hitching a ride on the bandwagon, that rarely capture the full allure of this captivating grape. Viognier is the enchanter who found initial fame in the fiendishly expensive Northern Rhône white wines of Condrieu and Château Grillet. And, to give credit where it is due, these grapes from the steep slopes around Côte-Rôtie have spawned some magical wines. However, it was only a matter of time before somebody had the courage to plant Viognier elsewhere. Suddenly there were not one but thousands of estates clamouring for attention, and it is now widely planted in the Languedoc-Roussillon and Southern Rhône, and abroad in Australia (Yalumba leads the way, but many more are following closely), Uruguay, Chile and California (never one to miss a trick). Viognier blends well with Rhône stable mates Roussanne and Marsanne and it also forms a fine partnership with Chardonnay where the Viognier is all forward fruit on the nose and the Chardonnay fills in the palate and the finish. Where Viognier lacks acidity, and therefore longevity, Chardonnay gives it the ability to age a little longer than normal – and who could turn that offer down?

The main thing to remember is – be careful. In Viognier's case, all that glisters is not gold and beauty could only be label-deep.

OTHER WHITE VARIETIES
(IN ALPHABETICAL ORDER)
Aligoté *(Alee-got-ay)*

Most of the white grapes planted in Burgundy are Chardonnay. Pinot Blanc appears in minuscule quantities but barely rates a mention. The other grape that is seen around is Aligoté. Having a neutral flavour with occasional **apple** and **pear** notes, it produces a dry, refreshing, lean style of white wine that is designed to be drunk young. Traditionally this variety was mixed with a dribble of *cassis* (blackcurrant liqueur) to make a Kir. The dry flavour of the wine balances nicely with the rich blackcurrant taste for a delicious aperitif. As most of France's Aligoté is planted in Burgundy, it is no surprise that vineyard plantings have shrunk in favour of the nobler Chardonnay, so Aligoté is often relegated to the worst vineyard sites, such as next to the motorway. Only in the village of Bouzeron is Aligoté upgraded to be a relatively serious commodity. Here it has its own appellation, 'Bourgogne Aligoté-Bouzeron', and yields are closely monitored to ensure high quality. Further north in the Chablis district, Aligoté is again viewed with a touch of respect and makes simple and refreshing summery wine.

Albariño/Alvarinho *(Al-ba-reen-yo/ Al-va-reen-yo)*

I once described this grape variety as having a Viognier nose with a Riesling palate and a Sauvignon Blanc finish. High praise indeed, for it was a particularly good example of a Galician Albariño. This really can have a **peachy** aroma like Viognier, a **flowery**, **spicy** palate like Riesling and a **citrus tang** on the finish like Sauvignon. I'll also stick my neck out and claim that it is certainly the best indigenous Spanish white grape variety. Sadly, however, that is not saying very much. In the far northwest corner of Spain, the province of Galicia churns out fine Albariño for wealthy Spanish wine drinkers to enjoy. The Rias Baixas zone in Galicia produces Albariño that has a cult following, and several examples have made their way out of Spain to test the international waters. The reception has been surprisingly warm and a love affair with Albariño has followed. The Alvarinho spelling refers to the superior grape used for a version of Vinho Verde, from across the border in Portugal.

Bacchus *(Back-us)*

With a **floral**, fresh aroma, usually followed by a **fruity**, **lemony** palate and a dry aftertaste, Bacchus is a Riesling/Sylvaner cross, crossed with a Müller/Thurgau (or is that a 'criss-cross'?) with some redeeming characteristics. It ripens in cold climates and is responsible for some of the wine made in England and, to a greater degree, in Germany. Oh, and it is named after the god of wine. Not to be sniffed at, if you see what I mean.

Colombard *(Column-bard)*

Often boring and insipid, a good version can have fruit-salady notes. Colombard is one of the grape varieties whose primary job is making the dull, acidic base wine that, once distilled, is transformed into Armagnac and Cognac. It has very high natural acidity and so enjoys work abroad as a blending partner, mainly in Australia and California, but work is hard to come by these days.

Furmint *(Fur-mint)*

A native of Hungary, this distinctively spicy grape helps to produce the legendary sweet wine Tokaji (not to be confused with the grape variety Tokay, which is pronounced in the same way). In dry form it is **spicy** with **pear**, **lemon** and **apple fruit**, when sweet it is crammed with **honey**, **orange marmalade**, **roasted almonds** and **caramel**. Several dry wines have emerged using this variety, and have shown the grape to be a fairly talented, if quirky individual.

Macabeo/Viura *(Mack-a-bayo/Vee-your-ah)*

Macabeo is a dreary grape variety found in the South of France

– dull, unremarkable and hard to put a reliable descriptor to! Known as Viura in Spain, it found success enlivening white Rioja and now represents more than 90 per cent of the white vines planted in the region. Viura is better suited to producing light wines, which might account for the recent change in styles of white Rioja from the old fashioned, oaky breed to a more fruity, fresh and forward wine. In Penedès, Viura teams up with local grapes Parellada and Xarello to make the Spanish sparkler, Cava.

Manseng, Gros and Petit (Man-seng, Grow and Pet-ee)

Gros and Petit Manseng are found in southwest France where they produce, among others, the superb wines of Jurançon and Pacherenc du Vic-Bilh. These two wines, particularly Jurançon, have become very fashionable indeed. The complex nose and **citrusy**, **floral** palate accompanied by a very crisp finish have made them highly sought-after restaurant wines. Thankfully, prices have stayed down and they are certainly worth looking out for if you are struggling to stay within some sort of affordable budget while eating in an expensive French restaurant. Petit Manseng is the finer of the two grapes. It has an enviable ability to hang on to its vine well into autumn when the grape shrivels and the sugar content is concentrated, thus resulting in a delicious sweet wine. Some wines are named after the month of harvest, almost as if the vine has won an endurance award, like Jurançon Symphonie de Novembre, by Domaine Cauhapé.

Marsanne (Marce-ann)

Marsanne is a plump, rich, oily white grape that makes Hermitage, Crozes-Hermitage, St-Péray and St-Joseph in the northern Rhône. It can fly solo, where **waxy honey** and mildly **tropical** nuances can be found on good examples but likes to have a co-pilot to achieve perfect balance. The experienced Roussanne (see below), or trendy Viognier (see above) are usually first past the post. In California, 'Rhône Rangers' feel the need to plant Marsanne to complement other French varieties in residence.

In Australia, a few fans, mainly in Victoria, plant Marsanne (with other Rhône whites) and make MVRs (you figure this one out) and the like. Marsanne loves the warmer climate and behaves like a slightly giddy Chardonnay.

Melon de Bourgogne *(Melon duh Bor-gone-yuh)*

Neutral and refreshing, with the best ones offering **apple** and **pear** notes, this is the variety responsible for the super-famous and much maligned white wine Muscadet. Found at the mouth of the Loire River in northern France, this hardy grape manages to achieve a good degree of ripeness in most years, rewarding the wine drinker with a fabulously dull wine that somehow still catches the eye. Show me a restaurant without Muscadet on its wine list! The gulf between fine Muscadet and bad may be less like a gulf and more like an ocean, but there is no better wine with which to enjoy a dozen oysters or a *plateau de fruits de mer*.

Müller-Thurgau *(Mooller Tur-gow)*

With mild **tropical notes** and a whisper of **honey**, Müller-Thurgau is widely planted in England and fast disappearing from New Zealand (where it inexplicably used to occupy the number one spot!), but this cold climate grape is most prolific in Germany. Müller-Thurgau, a Riesling/Sylvaner cross, is a pretender to the Riesling throne but lacks its character in just about every department. It does ripen early, so it is not as prone to disease and downpour as its noble parent, and it also produces a huge crop – in some cases, double that of Riesling's yields – but these two points do not make up for a loose-knit structure, weird green smell and short life span. I am sure that you have guessed what is coming next. Yes, Müller-Thurgau is responsible for the more hideous examples of Liebfraumilch and various other brand names worth avoiding. If you are a Liebfraumilch lover, then please do not be offended, as there are some proper ones out there. My advice is to taste a Riesling from the Mosel region and discover the definition and complexity of the true star of Germany.

Muscadelle *(Musk-a-dell)*

Confusingly, this grape has nothing to do with the huge Muscat family despite the fact that it is another grape whose best tasting note is grapey. Muscadelle is found in Bordeaux where it plays a supporting role to Sauvignon Blanc and Semillon. Third best by a long way, the majority of Muscadelle is used for the lesser-known sweet wines of Sauternes' neighbouring areas, Ste-Croix-du-Mont, Loupiac, Cadillac and further afield in Monbazillac. In fact, out of fashion Muscadelle is being pulled up as opposed to planted. It does, however, have a following 'down under' where it is responsible for a blunderbuss of an Australian liqueur called Tokay – nothing to do with Hungarian Tokaji. The plot thickens – so does this wine.

Palomino *(Pal-uh-meeno)*

Palomino deserves a very brief mention in this section, as it is the grape that is grown around Jerez in southern Spain and makes – you guessed it – sherry.

Pedro Ximénez *(Ped-roe Hee-men-eth)*

This grape produces the sherry-like wines of Montilla in Andalucía in southern Spain. More interestingly, Pedro Ximénez is used to make a fortified wine that is rich, dark brown, sweet, tastes of **espresso coffeebeans**, **dark chocolate**, **sweet raisins** and **homemade toffees**, and goes under the name of PX. It is like a top-secret potion. It can keep, after uncorking, for weeks and is not only delicious poured over ice cream but actually could replace pudding altogether. (It is also an awful lot easier to pronounce than Pedro what-d'you-call-it.)

Roussanne *(Roo-sann)*

Edging towards Viognier in aroma and flavour, this is a wonderfully restrained **peach-scented** grape, with more **lemony** acidity and a sleeker chassis. Roussanne is the more delicate, talented half of the Northern Rhône white grape double act. It is leaner and more aromatic than its fat friend Marsanne, and it also holds the distinction of being one of the four grapes allowed into white Châteauneuf-du-Pape (an exclusive vinous fitness club, with a tough membership policy).

Scheurebe *(Shoy-ray-buh)*

A Sylvaner/Riesling cross that works well in Germany and Austria. When dry, it makes delicious ripe, zesty wines. When sweet, Scheurebe gives succulent, **fruit cocktail** aromas on the nose with balanced, not cloying, fruit on the palate. There is always a zip of acidity running through the centre of the wines. This grape is also grown, with good results, in England.

Sylvaner *(Sil-vah-nur)*

This is the most boring of the Alsace wine-growing fraternity – or is it just misunderstood? Frankly, this widely planted grape rarely gets into second gear and is often left at the lights by Pinot Blanc – and that is saying something. A good Sylvaner generally has some texture and good acidity, but its marked lack of classic descriptive adjectives leaves the palate unexcited and the brain soon switches off. If Sylvaner had to be in a mixed case of Alsatian wine it would be the cardboard packaging ensuring the other bottles didn't break.

Ugni Blanc/Trebbiano *(Oo-nee Blon/ Treb-ee-ah-no)*

Ugni Blanc (French) and Trebbiano (Italian) are names for the same white grape, but, whatever the name, this little grape tends to produce low-end, dry, one-dimensional wines. It is possible to find bucketloads of cheap wines made from this grape in your local wine shop, like Vin de Pays des Côtes de Gascogne. Occasionally, these wines exhibit a fresh, lively **lemon zest** character with a nice, tidy finish, but, more often than not, the flavour disappears the second it touches the tongue. It is widely planted in France and Italy and makes some good wines – Frascati and Soave are some of the better-known names. Surprisingly this plain grape also makes a simple base wine for Cognac and Armagnac (as does Colombard).

With one or all of these raw materials at their disposal, it is then down to the winemakers to perform their wizardry and transform the harvested grapes into wine. That is the subject of the next chapter.

Chapter 2

GROWING GRAPES AND MAKING WINE

Well, it's pretty simple really. Find a vineyard, grow and pick some grapes, crush them, ferment them – sugar turns to alcohol – bottle it, *et voilà*, wine. It sounds easy, so why all the fuss? Making wine should be a relatively straightforward process. The truth of the matter is that each one of those stages is a little more complicated than you might expect. Since no two vineyards are alike and thousands of grape varieties are available, it is crucial to decide upon both site and variety first. When you are up and running – this could take three or four years – then more decisions have to be made as to how to make the wine of your dreams.

In this chapter, I will take you through the process of vineyard site selection, viticulture (the farming of grapes) and vinification (the alchemic transformation of grapes into wine). This chapter alone should slow your eager corkscrew down a touch as you consider where the content of your bottle has come from and what went into creating it.

WHERE IN THE WORLD

Most of the world's wine regions are found between 30° and 50° latitude in both the Northern and Southern hemispheres. This is because outside these two zones, it is either too hot or too cold for vines to grow grapes that are suitable for winemaking. Within these boundaries there are huge chunks of the Earth that could, in theory, be used for vineyards, but there are other factors that have to be considered.

As a vine is a plant, in theory it can be planted anywhere, but imagine popping down to the local garden centre and buying a rose bush. There are many different sites in your garden where you could plant it – you could even give it to a friend for their garden – but one thing is certain: roses grow best in particular spots and green-fingered gardeners will do a better job of deciding on that site than a novice would. Like roses, vines are very picky about where they are planted. Also like roses, there are many different types, each with its own specific likes and dislikes – which soil is best, how much sunlight is needed, what sort of drainage is required and what style of trellising is essential for a good bloom. Enough of that analogy because vines are far trickier to grow than roses and the resulting crop is a damn sight tastier, too.

The most important factors affecting the growing of vines are the location, the climate, and the conditions below ground.

The **location** means the country, region, sub-region, area and exact plot of land on which the vineyard is situated. In the Old World, where most of the region's vineyard areas were mapped out hundreds of years ago, it is possible to see where the best sites for vine growing are. In most New World areas, where there tend to be fewer rules governing where and what you plant, new vineyard sites are springing up every day: some successful, some not quite so.

Above ground at the location several factors come into play. The aspect or topography of the vineyard refers to the angle of its slope. A vineyard planted on a hillside will absorb more sunlight than a vineyard planted on flat land. Generally, sloping vineyards not only have a better view of the sun but also have better drainage than flat ones. However, not all slopes in wine regions are cultivated. In the Northern Hemisphere south-facing slopes are chosen as they maximise the length of sunshine hours on the vines. In the Southern Hemisphere north-facing slopes are often favoured, unless your grapes prefer it a little cooler. The direction of the rows also plays an important part, whether it is to concentrate the sun's rays down on to the vines for the longest period of time possible or, in hotter countries, to avoid some of the rays during the day. It is also important to determine where the prevailing winds come from (to protect from wind damage and to ensure the vines dry out after a downpour – like laundry on a washing line), where the sun rises and sets, and to take into account whether the vineyard is flat, on undulating hills or on a steep hillside. All these aspects will be considered when deciding the orientation of the vine rows.

The altitude of the vineyard can have an effect on the grapes. The higher the altitude, the cooler the temperatures overall, but particularly at night, and the longer the growing season for the grapes. High altitude vineyards are fine in hot climates as they take the edge off the searing heat, but they are not so good in cool climates. For this reason, many vineyards in Northern Europe tend to have trees on their hilltops, the best portion of the vineyard being the middle of the slope. Valley floors tend not only to lack the full direct power of the sun but also are more prone to flooding and frost. They also tend to be too fertile, giving rise to inferior crops. Many vineyards are planted on the slopes of river valleys. The Rhône, Mosel and Loire are but a few. These spots are ideal provided the slope is angled in the right direction, as they receive the added benefit of reflected sunlight from the water, too.

We cannot affect the **climate** and therefore must try to pick a kindly one before choosing a vineyard site. Depending on your specific chosen grape varieties, as some require more sun than others do, the ideal climate should be a long warm summer, allowing the grapes to ripen slowly and evenly, with a dry, sunny lead-up to picking time in the autumn. The winter can be pretty cold as vines can withstand −20°C, though this would be regarded as extreme. Vines, like most fruit-bearing plants, spend the winter months lying dormant waiting for the spring sunshine.

Unfortunately, it doesn't always work like that. Just think of the last time you went abroad skiing when there was no snow, sailing when there was no wind or sunbathing where it bucketed down for a fortnight. The weather is very much in control of this stage of winemaking and you just have to make the most of it (as I'm sure you've said to yourself while huddled, freezing, under a beach umbrella).

At particularly vulnerable times such as flowering or ripening, hail, frost and strong winds can damage the crop and even strip it of flowers or grapes. Uneven flowering due to a particularly cold or rainy spell can result in partially developed grapes that are not suitable for wine. One of the worst problems is rain at harvest time. The vines can, if given the chance, drink their fill in a short space of time and the resulting grapes will be dilute and lacking in varietal flavour and power. Rainy weather can also lead to rot on the vines and, unless there is a breeze to dry the vines out, this will lead to an imperfect harvest.

Vines need heat – an average throughout the year of about 15°C (60°F).

They need sunshine for photosynthesis – 1,500 hours over the growing season is perfect.

They also need water – whether it's falling from the sky or brought by irrigation, a vine needs approximately 80cm of water per year.

So, above ground we have our shopping list of ideal conditions. The amount of land suitable for planting vines is narrowing by the minute.

We must now take into account the soil's profile **below ground** – the type and depth of the strata. The profile indicates the soil's ability to hold or drain water and retain heat. Vines live through their root systems: too dry or too wet, and you have problems. They like relatively thin topsoil for good drainage, and subsoil with some water retention characteristics. The best for heat retention are gravel, loamy soils or sandy soils. Chalk comes next with clay bringing up the rear. Good heat retention is essential for an even ripening of grapes and can make up for very cool evenings by keeping the vine's toes warm.

Many of the great vineyards of the world have particular soil types. The chalk soils of Champagne have a huge influence on the famous wine itself, not least having given rise to the most fabulous cellars in which to age the bottles. It follows that chalky soils promote grapes with high acidity, but also allow good drainage (essential in a rainy northern European climate). The gravelly soils of the 'Left Bank' in Bordeaux have good heat retention, superb drainage and relatively low fertility, thus forcing a vine's roots deep to search for nutrients. Cabernet Sauvignon thrives in this 'stressful' medium. The Bordeaux commune 'Graves' (gravel) is named after its soils. The Gimblett Gravels area in Hawke's Bay, in New Zealand, also benefits from this type of soil. The extra-large gravel pebbles ('galets') in the vineyards of Châteauneuf-du-Pape are famous for their heat retention qualities, capturing the sun's rays during the day and acting as hot-water bottles at night, keeping the vines warm. Slate soils also warm up quickly and then retain their heat which helps the grapes for the great wines of the Mosel-Saar-Ruwer, in Germany, to ripen fully in a fairly cold climate.

VITICULTURE

The next stage is viticulture – the growing and tending of the vines. These days it is not unknown for wineries to employ viticultural consultants whose sole job is to look after the vineyards. They are in charge until the crop is handed over to the winemaker at harvest time. These people are expert geologists, biologists, botanists, meteorologists and, no doubt, a few other ologists as well. Battling against the weather for the whole year is a thankless task and, as great wine is 'made' in the vineyard, everybody expects viticulturalists to do a good job. Sadly, rather like goalkeepers in football, they are rarely awarded the top honours for superb wines, as the winemakers (the centre forwards) tend to get the plaudits. The Holy Grail of making wine is to find both skills in the same person and employ a winemaking viticulturalist or a specialist viticultural winemaker! Over the years I have met people responsible for some of the greatest wines on the planet – without exception they all have both skills in abundance.

The old adage that wine is 'made' in the vineyard is absolutely true. The best winemakers can make something out of nothing, but truly great wines can only come from epic quality fruit. The neatest, tidiest, best-planned and, of course, best-situated vineyards often yield the finest fruit. Before planting a vineyard the method of vine training must be decided upon. It is necessary to make the most of your naturally occurring conditions, such as aspect, soil and climate. There are loads of training techniques used in vine growing. The main aim is to maximise the sun's effect on the vine and to try to allow air movement around the bunches to prevent any excessive humidity that would lead to rot or mildew. The buzzwords in vine training are 'canopy management'. For years, it was thought that a low yield concentrated a vine's efforts into the smaller crop and this would directly lead to a higher quality harvest. This is, to a certain extent, true. However, with the advent of enormous research by some key players in the business, notably the Aussies and Kiwis, the science of vine training was born. Nowadays the methods of spreading the canopy of leaves out, designing the trellising systems and measuring the distance between each vine and each row of vines to match the microclimate exactly are being implemented by keen viticulturalists the world over.

With the 'training plan' sorted, the next hurdle is planting. It is now time to introduce you to the demon of the wine world, a little bug (or more correctly a louse) whose name is Phylloxera vastatrix. Sounding more like a comedy mate of Asterix and Obelix, this little beast has ravaged the wine world for ages. It first appeared in a starring role in Europe, hailing from America, in the nineteenth century, and proceeded to munch its way through the roots of over 6 million acres' worth of vineyards in France alone. At the time, this was viewed as one of the greatest agricultural and economic disasters of the century. In hindsight, however, and after finding a way to prevent it, Phylloxera was seemingly the single most important cause of a newfound replanting programme that raised quality and concentrated the minds of winemakers. In effect, the huge clear out resulted in the best vineyard sites and wines remaining. From this major upheaval, the French *Appellation d'Origine Contrôllée* system was born.

How did they get rid of the Phylloxera? Resistant rootstocks were the answer and the louse quickly lost its appetite. In vineyards around the world, American resistant rootstocks have been planted with a vine variety grafted on to them. In effect two vines are joined together, one which works well below ground, and the other which works well above. Without trying to overcomplicate matters, there are many different resistant rootstocks available, and yet again it is a matter of matching them to soil, climate and the actual vine variety destined to be joined at the hip to them. Curiously, Phylloxera has not infected some parts of the world. Sandy soils are not the natural habitat for this bug and, as yet, Argentina, Chile, some parts of Australia and a handful of other regions have not been forced to graft over. Recently, however, the so-called 'billion dollar bug' charged through the vineyards of California. The University of Davis in California, specialists in wine education, had recommended a rootstock called AXR1 However, a strain of the Phylloxera bug called 'biotype B' enjoyed the taste of this rootstock, and the rest is history. Anybody that used AXR1 succumbed to the louse and has had to replant. Anyone who disregarded Davis's advice has continued to make wine without a hitch.

We now have the vineyard, training system and correct rootstocks. There is one last detail to contend with. Believe it or not, once the vine variety has been decided upon there is the little matter of clones. Without wanting to sound too *Star Wars*-y or big brotherish, clones are pure versions of grape varieties. Taken from the best vineyard sites, they have been reproduced over and over again, thus eliminating any offspring that are inferior. This concentrates the characteristics of the individual clone and ensures (cross fingers) a good result, as long as the chosen vineyard site for the young nursery plant is compatible with that of its original host. The only problem with relying too much on individual clones is that even if the crop is fabulous, it may lack complexity of flavour in the end wine. In this case, several different clones with slightly varying taste characters can be planted alongside each other in the same vineyard, giving a far more varied base from which to make the end wine.

The annual life cycle of a vine is much the same as any other fruit-bearing plant. There are crucial periods during the cycle when long-range weather forecasts (and even prayer mats I'm sure) are employed to try to calm the nerves of anxious winemakers. The following section explains the changes that occur in the vineyard over the eight-month period leading up to and including the harvest.

As the harvest in the Southern Hemisphere (March-ish) takes place six months ahead of that in the Northern Hemisphere (September-ish), I have used seasonal periods as opposed to actual months to describe what is going on.

Late Winter – The dormant vine, having survived the cold winter, wakes up gradually. This can be seen when the cane ends start to weep sap (presumably for joy), which shows the vine is warming up and the roots are starting to absorb water in the soil. At this point frantic pruning takes place in preparation for the subsequent spurt of growth. Frost alert – early pruned vines are at risk.

Spring – A month or so after the weeping has started and then stopped, the budbreak (or budburst) takes place. Vines planted in warmer soils or with warmer weather, and certain grape varieties like Chardonnay, break first. These are more likely to be prone to frost. During this period the vines are fastened to their various training systems. By late spring, leaves and shoots begin to appear and tiny green circular clumps are visible on the vine. These little 'bunches' are the flowers that eventually blossom two months or so after budbreak. Spraying will prevent any unwanted diseases (Coulure and Hen and chicken – see Glossary). At this time of year it is important that the weather stays fair until after the flowers have been pollinated. Once again, frost here would be a killer. Fertilisation occurs and the flower turns into a berry. At this point they are tiny, round, hard and green. This stage is called 'fruit set'. It is now possible to check the success of the fruit set and estimate the maximum size of the potential harvest.

Summer – The weather should be sunny and warm throughout this period in order to ripen the grapes. Summer pruning is the cutting off of excess leaves to focus the vine's energy into the grapes. This will only be done if necessary. The grapes grow in size and become more recognisable as true bunches when 'veraison' happens. This is the moment when the skin on the bright green grapes either turns yellow/green for a white grape or purple/blue for a red one. The sugar content in the grapes is now increasing gradually. Pruning excess bunches of grapes at this time will focus all of the vine's efforts into a smaller but higher quality harvest. Once again, leaves can be plucked off the vine to create more space for airflow around the bunches – thus avoiding rot.

Autumn – This is the most important period in the wine year and human intervention plays as big a part as the weather. The harvest takes place as soon as the grapes reach target ripeness – sugar ripeness (which corresponds to the potential alcohol level in the wine) and physiological ripeness (taste-wise – balance and varietal complexity). Measurements are taken of the sugar content in the grapes to see when they are at their peak, and winery staff munch hundreds of grapes, checking for fruit purity and astringency in the crop. Usually white grapes are picked first. With this head start, they can sometimes whizz through the winery before the arrival of the red grapes. Each winemaker generally knows the order in which the different grapes will arrive at the cellar door. If the estate has only one grape variety growing in the vineyards, such as Sauvignon Blanc in the case of a Sancerre producer, then specific vineyard sites will tend to ripen quicker than others, because of differences in soil, microclimate or aspect. Practice makes perfect in this department. The only spanner in the works is the all-important weather. If there is any sign of rain, the winemaker's gambling instinct will emerge. You have two choices: pick right away to avoid the grapes getting bloated and thus diluted or even rotten; or hold on and hope for a sunny patch just around the corner, straight after the rain. This could dry out the grapes, and then the ripening could continue even further after their little impromptu drink.

Early Winter – The only grapes left on the vine in late autumn/early winter are destined for the production of sweet wine. These grapes start to shrivel as their supplies from the vine are cut off and their water content begins to evaporate. Late-harvested grapes are not particularly pleasant to look at, but this concentration in sugar and acid is what's needed. One stage further than this would be when the rot, Botrytis cinerea, attacks the grapes. This occurs naturally in some vineyards thanks to favourable weather conditions, but can also be introduced (inoculated) by the winemaker. This 'noble rot' further concentrates the sugar within the grapes and the result is the production of tiny amounts of unctuous, rich, sweet wine. If the climate is suitable then Eiswein (literally, ice wine) can be made. This can only occur when the temperature in the vineyard drops below zero and the grapes actually freeze on the vine. They are picked as late as three months after the normal harvest, and pressed lightly so that only the intense sugary juice is collected while the water content is still frozen in the press.

VINIFICATION

Given the finest quality grapes, there is no doubt that it is possible to make an incredible wine – but it would be far easier and less stressful to make a mediocre wine. The greatest winemakers have to seek to retain all of the goodness and taste of the vineyard in their wines, and attempting to lose none of the natural power and aroma of the grapes at harvest is an art. After all, it is not very easy to add flavour, but it is all too easy to take it away. Great winemakers also have an ability to turn a poor harvest into something special.

As some winemakers actually control the vineyard management as well as that of the winery, their knowledge is understandably broad. If a vineyard manager is employed, then the importance of the relationship between him and the winemaker should not be underestimated. There is a right hand/left hand aspect to these two positions. In the weeks leading up to the harvest, the winemaker will work closely with the viticulturalist, spending time in the vineyards tasting grapes and checking their sugar and acid levels. The winemaker is the person who decides exactly which day to start the harvesting. The viticulturalist will then instruct the pickers, or the mechanical harvesters, to go into the vineyards and remove the crop as quickly and efficiently as possible. Any delay after harvesting will endanger the grapes, as once picked they are susceptible to oxidation and heat spoilage. For this reason the grapes are taken straight to the winery where the cellar-hands will have cleaned and tested the winery apparatus, ready for the off. Adrenaline will be at an all-time high and sleep will be very low on the agenda.

I have set out in the next pages the classic ways in which white, rosé, red, sparkling, sweet and fortified wines are made. This could be done in a very scientific fashion that would not only baffle me but also bore you. I have therefore decided to explain these techniques with reference to the way that they affect the taste of the end wine.

First, there is a brief explanation of some of the key stages and practices that occur during winemaking. If you can understand these principles, the rest will be a doddle. Remember that the elements of winemaking are universal. Like making a cake, casserole or cocktail, the basic method is the same; only the ingredients differ.

Alcoholic Fermentation

This is the chemical process that turns sugar and yeast into alcohol and carbon dioxide – in other words, when grape juice turns into wine. Yeast occurs naturally on a grape's skin as the so-called 'bloom', seen as a dusty coating. If crushed grapes are left in a tank, then fermentation will eventually occur naturally. These yeasts are called 'wild yeasts' and this method is the time-honoured, old-fashioned way of making wine. However, with the advent of chemical engineering, cultured yeast can be added to the grape juice by the winemaker. This process is called inoculation and these yeasts have proven characteristics that control the fermentation with favourable results. Certain yeast strains work well with specific grape varieties, enhancing the aroma of the final wine or enabling the wine to be pushed to higher alcohol levels.

Fermentation halts when all the sugar is exhausted or when the level of alcohol reaches a point where it is actually poisonous to the yeast. This is the natural end to fermentation, but it can also be stopped in a number of other ways:

Racking

The process of draining the wine off its lees (the cloudy sediment at the bottom of a fermentation vessel), thus removing it from its yeasts.

Pasteurisation or Chilling

This is heating up or cooling down of the wine. It is effective because yeast cells are unable to work at extremes of temperature, approximately below freezing and above boiling point.

Fortification

This is the addition of alcohol, in the form of grape spirit, to a level that is toxic to the yeast.

Filtration

Simply filtering out the large yeast cells from the wine.

Centrifugation

This spinning process separates the wine from the denser yeast cells. It is a rather expensive, time-consuming method.

Malolactic Fermentation

Malolactic fermentation (often shortened to 'malo') follows the alcoholic fermentation. Although it is called a fermentation, it is really a degradation of the malic acid in the wine into lactic acid. Malic acid is a hard, bitter-tasting acid found in grapes (and in unripe apples – leading to cheek sucking and facial contortion). Lactic acid is much softer. The riper a grape is at harvest, the lower the acid. In cooler climates, where the natural acidity in the harvested grapes is fairly high, 'malo' is almost always encouraged. Only in hot climates, where acidity is hard to hang on to, and where the grapes ripen at a very fast pace, might it be necessary to inhibit the malolactic fermentation. Conversion of malic acid to lactic acid tempers the raw taste of a wine and softens the palate out, often adding another flavour dimension. Malo usually occurs naturally straight after the alcoholic fermentation as the enzymes needed to start this stage are again found on the grape skins. Just to make sure, the winery is usually warmed a little to help start the malo process. Some grapes are more susceptible to malo than others. Chardonnay is a natural candidate, whereas Riesling and Chenin Blanc often avoid it.

Stainless Steel

Stainless steel is the perfect material for tanks as it is:

Inert

Does not affect the taste of the wine inside.

Stainless

Easy to clean.

Long-lasting

Much better than a barrel, in that respect.

Perfect for temperature control

Cold water is pumped around pipes surrounding the tank to chill it, thus allowing the wine to retain all of its aromatic qualities and freshness. Conversely, hot water can be pumped around the pipes to encourage malo.

At one time it was rare to see stainless steel tanks in Old World wineries. Nowadays proud French winemakers show you their gleaming tanks, as if to say, 'Check this out, I'm bang up to date.' Don't tell them the rest of the world got rid of glass-lined cement tanks and dirty old barrels decades ago. Stainless steel is so popular that any wineries with more than a few stainless steel tanks are called 'tank farms'.

Oak

Oak barrels have been used for winemaking since the times of Herodotus. In the past they were almost exclusively used for storage and transportation. These days oak barrels are used for two purposes – fermentation and maturation. While stainless steel imparts no taste whatsoever to a wine during fermentation or maturation, oak barrels do. When wine is either fermented or matured (or both) in oak its flavour greatly alters the taste of the wine. This is the primary use for barrels – to enhance the flavour of a wine by adding another dimension of taste, namely that of oakiness and other associated nuances.

Before talking about the different types of oak barrels available it is important to explain the pros and cons of oak. The one massive pro is that, if oak is handled correctly, the flavour of the wine should be augmented considerably. Now for the cons: barrels are very expensive; they are labour intensive – cleaning, repairing, leaking and manhandling; they are awkwardly shaped;

they are porous which means that the wine inside will gradually evaporate, needing to be topped up occasionally (costing money) and, of course, allowing oxidation of the wine – accelerated ageing if you like; and they have a shelf life – new barrels have tons of flavour, one-year-old barrels, a lot of flavour, two-year-old barrels, some, three-year-old barrels, a little, and four-year-old barrels, not much at all. A little bit like reusing a teabag!

The bigger an oak barrel the less is the surface area to volume of wine ratio. The smaller the barrel the more wood touches the wine. The classic dimension of an oak barrel is the Bordeaux 'barrique'. These barrels hold 225 litres of wine, which equates to about 25 cases of twelve bottles. The other piece of important barrel trivia is that during the barrel assembling process, the staves are heated in order to bend them into a curved shape. This is often done over a fire. If so, the finished barrel will have a slightly charred inside. Winemakers can order barrels with various levels of 'toast' from low to high. The charring of the barrel can complement the flavours of the wine and this accounts for the 'toasty nose' of many bottles of oaked wine.

There are three main sources of oak barrels in the world of wine: France, America and Eastern Europe. French oak barrels are largely considered to be superior to American oak barrels in that they impart subtler, more complex oaky flavours to the wine. They also tend to have more tannin content – the natural preservative of wine. This means that wines using French oak tend to need a little longer ageing than those using American oak. These qualities are also reflected in the price of French oak barrels. A single French oak barrel can cost £500. This cost in turn impacts on the final cost of the wine. Oaked wines tend to be that bit pricier than their stainless steel cousins. The broader, 'sweeter', dry-roasted flavours that American oak gives to a wine are considered less elegant and more 'in your face' – or should I say up your nose. Eastern European oak is starting to become fairly fashionable – less expensive than French but imparting intriguing nuances. A lot of forward-thinking companies are trialling this oak. It is not as simple as just using French oak if you are loaded, or American or Eastern European oak if you are a bit strapped for cash.

French, American and Eastern European oak bring different taste profiles to the wine. Where would we be without the soft vanilla flavour that has become the accepted hallmark of Rioja? It may be a surprise that this stunning taste is picked up by the red wine spending a considerable amount of its life slumbering inside American oak barrels. The peak of Chardonnay excellence found in the Burgundy cellars of France would never occur using American oak as a taste enhancer, because the bold flavour would overshadow the tight-knit, compact, young fruit, thus pulverising the final wine. The massive boom in South American wines could not have had such a huge impact on the world market were it not for their immediate drinkability. Many of the juicy red wines are oaked, but had French oak been used, then the wines would be more expensive and require a few years cellaring before drinking, thus blowing any chance of a fast sale. So there is an argument to support each case.

Most red grape varieties can handle a sojourn in an oak barrel. The richer the wine the longer the time spent in the barrel, or the newer the barrels used. Either way, barrels should be used to complement the wine, not overpower it. A popular analogy is the use of salt and pepper on a plate of food. Just the right amount brings the flavour to a peak – too much can ruin it.

Very few white grape varieties can handle the strong flavour of oak. Occasionally Sauvignon Blanc has a go – but easy does it. Semillon can handle it on a good day. There are unsuspecting varieties that get forced, kicking and screaming, into a barrel by brave winemakers, but one grape variety with more than enough muscle to cope is Chardonnay. 'Oak Aged' or 'Barrel Fermented' can be seen on the labels of many a bottle of Chardonnay.

Fining

This winemaking process clarifies and stabilises a wine. Minute particles held in suspension in the wine can, in time, cause haziness or greater problems, such as bacterial spoilage. Fining is a speedy way of clarifying a wine, thus preventing faulty bottles. Clarification would naturally happen if a wine was left to stand for several months; however, most wines are ready to bottle shortly after the end of vinification and fining quickly stabilises the finished product.

A clarifying agent is added to the wine and then sticks to the invisible, unwanted particles and falls to the bottom of the tank or barrel, forming sediment. The fining agents themselves are an unlikely bunch: egg whites, Isinglass (fish bladders), milk, bentonite (clay), charcoal and a few others can all be used. It is important to stress that none of these substances are left in the wine that is bottled. They form the sediment at the bottom of the barrel or tank, and once the wine has been racked off it is clean and clear.

Cold Stabilisation

This is a method to stop crystals forming in the bottom of a bottle of wine. With cold stabilisation the wine is chilled to a very low temperature, little crystals form and fall to the bottom of the tank, and the wine is then racked off and bottled. These crystals are tartrate deposits that are completely harmless but can cause a fair degree of panic for an unprepared drinker because they look like little pieces of glass. Cold stabilisation is practised by almost all commercial winemakers. However, many expensive wines are not cold stabilised, as the process can remove some of the original, valuable taste elements. Fine winemakers prefer to print a little disclaimer on the label – *vin non filtré* or some such – warning the drinker that should the wine have crystals, pour carefully and enjoy. I, for one, actively enjoy seeing tartrates at the bottom of a bottle of fine white wine, as it is an extra hallmark of quality.

Lees Contact

Lees are the dregs or sediment that settle at the bottom of a barrel or fermentation tank. They are made up of dead yeast cells, grape-skin fragments, grape seeds and tartrates. Usually the lees are discarded as soon as fermentation is finished. However, some wines are deliberately left 'on' their lees in order to extract more flavour from these heavy particles. This is called 'lees contact', and it is incredibly trendy. It not only encourages malolactic fermentation, but also adds complexity to the finished wine. Lees stirring affects the taste of wine, particularly if it is in oak barrels. These wines will have much subtler, softer, more integrated oak flavours than those that are left undisturbed. Most Chardonnay producers are very keen on lees stirring, as it gives their wines depth and texture. You stir the lees with a big oar or a chain on a stick. In France this process is called *bâtonnage* (i.e. done with a baton). Another famous wine that traditionally utilises its lees to good effect is Muscadet. Muscadet is rarely made in oak barrels, but the lees contact does make a big difference to its taste. Watch out for *sur lie* (on the lees) on labels of Muscadet. The difference that it makes to red wines is less obvious as they are generally more structured than white wines. However, lees contact also helps to start malolactic fermentation in reds and has a discernible impact on structure and texture.

DRY WHITE WINEMAKING

The first few stages of white winemaking are performed at speed, with the main aim being to retain all the flavour and freshness of the harvested grapes. Any delay can result in air and heat causing unwanted oxidation in the bunches. So, after the grapes have been picked they are taken straight to the winery. A quick check through the bunches will be carried out either in the vineyard or winery to remove any rotten or unripe grapes. Then, depending on the style of wine, one of two techniques will be used. For lighter wines, the grapes will be lightly crushed and destemmed, and then pumped into a press. (The stems are removed because they contain bitter flavours.) For heavier or aromatic styles, the grapes will be crushed and destemmed and then left to 'macerate' in a temperature-controlled stainless steel tank for twelve to thirty-six hours. Cold maceration extracts more flavour compounds from the skins into the juice. This practice is sexily entitled 'skin contact'.

At all times, the winemaker will ensure that the temperature of the white grapes, juice and wine is cool. This is crucial in order to retain freshness and aroma in the wine. For that reason, if the climate is particularly hot, the grapes will be picked at night, when it is cooler. The harvest can be refrigerated on its way to the winery if necessary. The grapes can also be refrigerated at the winery before crushing, in large, walk-in cold rooms. The maceration will be temperature controlled and the next stage, the pressing, will also be fairly quick in order to get the juice into a tank to settle at a cool temperature again. It may seem fairly paranoid but, of all the modern skills learned over the last few decades in the winery, temperature control is the most important.

The grapes are pressed gently and the juice, known as 'must' is collected. The reason for a gentle pressing is that the juice that naturally falls out of the grapes first is of the highest quality. Even before the press is started juice will have been released from the grapes as a result of the crushing process; this is known as 'free-run juice'. Rarely will the second or third pressings be used in the best wines, as the harder the press squeezes the grapes, the more bitter the flavours in the must.

The must is pumped into a stainless steel tank for settling (*débourbage* in French). At the very least a basic settling of the must is carried out, usually at a cool temperature. In some cases two separate settling stages are done to brighten the must further (to make it even cleaner). The must can now be manipulated before fermentation. Loads of tricks can be used like filtration, fining, centrifugation and cold stabilisation, all of which clean up the must and remove any solid particles and unwanted impurities. At this stage sulphur dioxide (SO_2) is usually added to kill any bacteria and prevent oxidation.

The juice is now pumped into a fermentation vessel. This could be a tank or a barrel, depending on the grape variety and style of wine. The winemaker can now add cultured yeasts or just let the naturally occurring yeasts in the cellar start the fermentation. A cool cellar, or temperature-controlled stainless steel tanks, will ensure that the fermentation takes place in a relatively cool atmosphere, between 10° and 17°C. This will enable the wine to have good aromatic qualities and crispness on the palate. Any warmer than that and the wine might lack zippy freshness but gain complexity. Very few white wines are fermented at any warmer than 25°C. In cool climates, where the grapes have failed to reach optimum ripeness, a process called 'chaptalisation' is practised, where allowed. This is the addition of sugar or concentrated grape juice to the must, before or during fermentation, to raise its total sugar content. This can increase the final alcoholic strength of the wine by one or two degrees. In hot regions, the harvested grapes can have a lot of sugar but too little acidity. To correct the overall balance of the wine, tartaric or citric acid can be added.

Malolactic fermentation (see above) follows alcoholic fermentation either naturally or, once again, inoculated by the winemaker. Some producers will not allow their wines to go through malo as they wish to retain the extra acidity. This only happens in wines where high acidity is required for the style (like for fresh, dry whites) or where the fruit was especially ripe in the first place with low acidity at harvest.

We now have wine! However, there are a few last details to take care of before it is bottled and labelled. The final few decisions are purely 'recipe' procedures, and they will be wine-style or grape-variety specific. After malo, tank fermented wine can be transferred into barrels for a period of maturation. These wines pick up an oaky taste, and often 'oak aged', or words to that effect, will be used on the wine label to denote this style of wine. Oak-aged wines are a little different to barrel-fermented wines, which usually ferment *and* age in oak barrels, thus resulting in a more pronounced oaky flavour. A little *bâtonnage* (see above) may be used if it will enhance the style of the wine. Depending on the type and age of the oak barrels, the wine could hibernate here for anything from a few months to well over a year.

Finally, after fermentation and maturation, when the must is well and truly converted into wine, the racking, fining, stabilising and filtering options can be brought in prior to blending (see Red Winemaking), bottling, labelling and at last – hurrah! – drinking.

RED WINEMAKING

Red winemaking is always regarded as being a little trickier than white winemaking. There is one small but desperately important difference between the two techniques – the skins! Red wine can only be made from red grapes, as the skins contain the red colour pigments. Take a peek inside a grape and you will see that the pulp is clear, regardless of the colour of the grape's skin. So you can make a white wine from red grapes if you crush the grapes quickly and get rid of the skins. The best example of this is Champagne, which is usually made from two-thirds red grapes.

As with white winemaking the first step is to crush and destem the bunches in a cleverly entitled crusher/destemmer (*égrappoir* in French). The stems contain very harsh tannin flavours and they tend to unbalance the wine and rarely soften, even with age. It is sometimes advisable to put a small percentage of stems into the fermentation if the vintage conditions are warm/hot and the fruit is particularly juicy, as this will give the wine a touch more grip and balance. There is not the same urgency with red winemaking as there is with white winemaking. In fact, the process is often deliberately slow. This is because, during the first few stages, the grape juice has to macerate with the skins in order to extract colour, flavour and other qualities, and this takes time. In some wineries, a 'pre-fermentation maceration' takes place at cold temperatures, just to try to extract even more of the potential goodness out of the skins. If it were not done at a cold temperature then the natural yeasts on the grapes' skins would kick off fermentation.

Every red winemaker wants rich, dark, juicy red wines. However, not every vintage produces these hallmarks. In wet years, when the crop is dilute, some technological wizardry can be employed. This is the science bit. Some estates' winemakers remove water from swollen grapes via some very expensive machinery. This hardware can extract water using reverse osmosis or evaporation under a vacuum – baffling stuff! This can concentrate the sugars in a wine that would otherwise have ended up pretty weedy and watery.

Once the crushed grapes have been pumped into a tank, vat

or large open fermenter, the alcoholic fermentation will start either naturally or with cultured yeasts and a warm winery. Late autumn is one of the best times to visit a winery, as the cellar is usually warm (a rare event) and the smell is heavenly.

Fermentation can take anything from a few days to more than a month. The temperature is allowed to rise to much hotter levels than in white winemaking, around 30°C (no more than 35°C, otherwise the yeasts could die and the fermentation will become 'stuck'). The warmer the temperature, the more flavour is extracted from the skins and the deeper the colour of the wine. During fermentation a mass of grape skins and pips (and stems if some are included) form a 'cap' (*chapeau*), which rises to the top of the tank on account of the carbon dioxide released from the fermentation. This accumulation of skins will sit on top of the must (juice) at the top of the tank, reducing the amount of colour extraction unless it is either plunged down into it (*pigéage*) or the must is pumped or sprayed over the cap. 'Pumping over' is a widely practised technique. The French term for this is *remontage*. Chaptalisation can be employed at this time if the grapes lack sufficient sugar to reach an acceptable level of alcohol (see White Winemaking). At all times the temperature police keep an eye on the thermometers, making sure it stays within a safe range. If the temperature rises too high then cold water will be pumped through the cooling jackets surrounding or placed inside the tanks. Some wineries these days have control panels similar to a space shuttle.

After fermentation has finished, the skins can be left in contact with the wine for a further period, extracting yet more flavour and richness. Lighter reds will be separated from the skins immediately. The total time that a wine spends in contact with its skins is called *cuvaison*. The wine that runs out of the tank of its own accord, leaving its skins behind, is called 'free-run juice'. Left behind is the sodden cap (or *pomace*) which, once pressed, releases 'press wine' which, as you would expect, is much darker, heavier and more tannic. These two liquids are kept apart, as the press wine is coarse and often inferior to the free-run wine, and it will only be added in small quantities if the harvest was poor and the wine needs beefing-up. Very occasionally, if the harvest is a blockbuster, the press wines can be exceptional and a larger percentage than normal will be added back into the blend because the flavour is too good to miss.

Over the next few months all of the different batches and barrels of wine will be tasted over and over again by the winemakers. They will know which tanks or barrels come from which grape varieties and also from which vineyards. As all vineyards differ, not just in aspect and the like but often in vine age and reliability, the winemaker will watch and taste, making a mental note of all the different lots. Usually the best vineyard sites produce the best wine, so experience and local knowledge count for a lot in the art of blending. The best tanks or barrels will be selected as the premium label and the rest will be sold as lesser labels or even in bulk if it doesn't come up to scratch. If the estate makes blended wines (red or white) then test blends will be made up. Once the best blend has been assembled, the other separate lots will be blended (*assemblage*) in bulk in a large tank, and from now on they will be earmarked as the estate or 'Château' label, second label or *Prestige Cuvée*, or whatever. Lesser blends will spend their time following a different regime from the top wine, as they tend to require a separate 'oak programme'. Some winemakers, usually of single varietal wines, leave the final *assemblage* until just prior to bottling. Dealing with only one grape variety means that the two variables are the quality level, and either oak or stainless steel handling. Having said that, it is still pretty difficult.

The wine is then pumped into clean tanks or barrels for malolactic fermentation – the softening of the acidity. Following this, after a short wash and brush-up, simple, forward-drinking wines can be bottled. More complex wines will be put into oak barrels for a period of maturation. Fine reds will spend a considerable amount of time in oak barrels picking up the flavours and mellowing out. Decisions will be made as to what percentage of the wine will go into new barrels and what into one year, two year or older barrels. This choice will be based partly on the strength of the harvest – good years can handle more pungent new oak – and partly on the style of the wine – heavier grapes need more oak than light ones, and local tradition will play a role as well.

During oak ageing the wine will be racked to clarify it. The lees will be left behind in the barrel. Fining (see above) may also take place in the cellar, once again, to clean up the wine prior to bottling. Many winemakers will use a filtration system to further remove any solids from the wine, as it provides them with the safety of a perfectly clean and stable wine. Filtration is rarely used for top reds, as it can strip out too much flavour and leave the wine a little hollow. It is widely believed that judicious racking and fining will make red wine stable and clean enough without removing any of the character of the wine.

The freshly bottled wine will now be rushed out of the winery on to the shelves for sale, into merchants' cellars for ageing or kept back by the winery for ageing. 'Bottle ageing' as opposed to oak ageing is crucial for many fine wines, both red and white. Occasionally wineries take the noble, if costly, decision to hold bottles back, delaying their release in the hope that the wine will benefit from this period of rest and development. If not, then we, the consumers, are expected to do that on behalf of the wine. Hence the need for wine cellars.

Carbonic Maceration

Before we move on to rosés, sparkling wines and sweeties, there is one other method of red winemaking that is worth noting – *maceration carbonique* or, in English, carbonic maceration (usually shortened to MC). This process makes forward, juicy, low acidity, low tannin but highly coloured wines, ideal for immediate consumption. Think of the fruitiest, most forward style of red wine – Beaujolais. This wine and many others besides employ this practice. It involves whole berry fermentation in sealed tanks. Carbon dioxide forces uncrushed grapes to ferment quickly under pressure inside their own skins. Some producers use a 'semi-carbonic' process in which only some of the grapes are crushed beforehand. This is all very chemistry-orientated and awfully difficult to explain in detail, but it works and thank goodness we can drink some red wines while they are young and fruity.

ROSÉ WINEMAKING

Making rosé wines is dead easy. OK, there are a few twists, but the basic principle is straightforward. The crucial word is skins. As red wines get their colour from the skins then rosés do also – but just not quite as much colour and therefore not quite as much skin contact. Several rosé-making methods are detailed below.

Bled rosés (*saignée*) are made from the free-run juice that 'bleeds' from just-crushed red grapes. This is very high quality, very aromatic juice that makes the finest, palest and most succulent of rosés. As a result of bleeding the red grapes of some of their juice, the remaining just-bled grapes will have a greater proportion of skin to juice and will go on to make a red wine of improved concentration and structure.

Limited maceration rosé is the easiest style to understand. This is red winemaking stopping short of making red wine. Set your stopwatch and remove the skins when the colour suits. Eight to twelve hours usually works. Then, ignoring the colour, just proceed as normal for a white wine.

Blending red and white wine – horror of horrors – a terrible suggestion that has, in the past, given rise to some hideous wines. They are generally and understandably out of balance, as they are neither red nor white but some Frankenstein blend. The only serious wine that is made with this method is the thoroughly delicious rosé Champagne.

SPARKLING WINEMAKING

Remember that carbon dioxide is a natural by-product of fermentation, Sugar + yeast = alcohol + CO_2. Normally this gas is allowed to escape from the wine into the atmosphere. If, however, this gas is prevented from leaving, either by putting a lid on a tank or a cork in a bottle, then the gas dissolves into the wine. The resulting wine, when uncorked, will release the CO_2 in the form of bubbles. Eureka – fizzy wine. Dom Pérignon and his keen winemaking monk pals discovered that some of the bottles of wine in his cellar were fizzy when opened (some bottles even exploded). In this case, the fermentation had not completely finished when he had bottled the wines, so some carbon dioxide was still in the bottles. This was the precursor to modern day sparkling wine production. Sparkling wines are now made from one of the following methods.

Champagne Method (méthode champenoise, méthode traditionnelle, méthode classique)

Due to European Union law no one outside Champagne is allowed to use the term *méthode champenoise*, although you are allowed to say the other two above. This is the finest way to make sparklers, and many estates, not just in Champagne, use this labour intensive, costly method to produce their wines. The main difference between this style of winemaking and the others is that the second fermentation is carried out in the bottle in which the wine is sold. I will fully explain this method later in the Champagne section starting on page 187.

Transfer Method

A touch down-market, this style copies the Champagne method until the crucial last moment. The second fermentation is in bottle, but not the bottle in which the wine is sold, as the wine is transferred under pressure into a tank for filtration and re-bottling.

Tank Method (Cuve close, Charmat)

The entire process takes place in a large temperature-controlled tank (including the second fermentation). This process is used for bulk sparkling wines, but does not always result in low quality. Asti is the most famous wine made in this style, and while it is not everybody's cup of tea, there is no doubt that it can be absolutely delicious.

Pompe à Bicyclette (bicycle pump method – a comedy expression for Carbonation)

This is simply pumping carbon dioxide gas into a wine in a similar way to making fizzy soft drinks. Cheap and effective, but not a good way to make long-lived or elegant wines.

SWEET AND FORTIFIED WINEMAKING

The normal way to make sweet wines is to aim to harvest fully ripe fruit, in most cases leaving the grapes on the vine as long as possible and picking them late. The riper the fruit on the vine, the more concentrated the sugar in the grapes and therefore the higher potential of sweetness ('residual sugar') and alcohol. Some grape varieties are more suited to making sweet wines than others. My favourite three are Semillon, Riesling and Chenin Blanc, although a few other varieties do the job well. The trick is to pick late. With luck the grapes may be affected by 'noble rot' (Botrytis cinerea). This rot lives on the skins and dehydrates the grape by sucking out its water. Despite sounding rather dangerous and looking very unattractive, it actually does the job of concentrating the sugar within the grape to levels that would be impossible to achieve naturally. The great winemakers of Sauternes, Loire, Alsace and Germany all cross their fingers at harvest time, willing their vineyards to attract this rot if the weather conditions are favourable. It is possible to cheat slightly and spray the vines with a potion that introduces Botrytis to the vineyard. This trick is used in California, Australia and elsewhere where the weather conditions would not always give rise to the rot naturally.

The winemaking process for sweet wines is the same as that for dry white wine except that the grapes are naturally much higher in sugar before they start. Then, before the fermentation is totally finished, while there is still unfermented sugar in the must, the fermentation is stopped. This can be done by the addition of sulphur, which kills off the yeast. Of course, if the sugar levels were naturally very high in the first place, once the level of alcohol reaches 16 per cent, the yeast will be killed anyway, leaving a high alcohol sweet wine.

There are other ways to make sweet wines, the crudest of which is straightforward chaptalisation – the addition of sugar. However, there are some other interesting techniques employed. If Botrytis does not occur, then grapes can be left on the vine until they dry and shrivel, like raisins. This, once again, concentrates the sugars in the grape. The French term for this is *passerillé*, and wines such as the tangy, tropical Jurançon Moelleux are made with this method. Drying the grapes after the harvest, either on mats or hung up in barns, can also be a way of raisining the grapes and raising the sugar levels for making sweet wines. *Recioto* is the Italian term for wine made in this style, such as the delicious, honeyed Recioto di Soave. 'Cordon cut' wines are made by cutting the vine's umbilical cord (the cordon) and starving it of water and nutrients. This results in the grapes shrivelling and the sugar levels becoming markedly more concentrated. Practised in Australia, among other countries, this technique can result in very high-quality wine.

The final way to make sweet wines is by freezing the grapes, either naturally on the vine – *Eiswein* (German for ice wine) – or in the winery, cryogenically. 'Cryoextraction' is a process designed to freeze the water content of the grape then crush out the sugar only. Wines from this process can be made any year, unlike the ice wine process that needs particular weather conditions. These wines are excruciatingly sweet and consequently rarely found in any size bigger than a half-bottle.

Fortified wines come in many shapes and sizes, from light, refreshing Muscat de Rivesaltes to the huge, monstrous Aussie Liqueur Muscats. The one common theme is the addition of alcohol, usually grape spirit, to the wine. This addition of spirit immediately stops fermentation. The earlier the spirit is added the sweeter the resulting wine. Fortified wines generally have an alcohol level of between 16 and 20 per cent. Curiously, despite the huge range of flavours of fortified wines, they are all made by a very similar method. It is just the raw materials and the amount of alcohol that vary. *Vin Doux Naturels* such as Muscat de Rivesaltes, Muscat de Beaumes-de-Venise and Banyuls, as well as Madeira, Marsala, Port and Australian Muscats, are all made where alcohol is added to the fermenting grape juice. Sherry is the only fortified wine where the alcohol is added to sweeten the wine after it has already fermented to dryness.

That covers all of the winemaking bases. Interestingly, keen winemakers love to dabble in various different styles of winemaking even if their regions or grapes are not particularly suitable. It is fun to make sherry or port if you have a few barrels of wine left over. Aussie sparkling reds, for example, came about because in the old days there was not enough dry, lean whites to make traditional sparkling wines, so they just made do with red. This is now a very important and massively enjoyable category of wines. The wine world is a very diverse place and the continual quest for improvement is riveting. Over the years I have tasted hundreds of funky wines that were made in very small batches and did not find their way to the retail shelves, but which represented an attempt by winemakers and grape growers to push the boundaries and experiment. You can bet your bottom dollar that if one of the micro-parcels works, more vines will be planted and the wine will be made in larger quantities. And, to be honest, it is great fun. Winemakers need avenues to express themselves in the same way that bands often splinter for a while to pursue solo projects and chefs cook outside their restaurants for special events or friends.

Chapter 3

BUYING WINE

Buying wine can be more than a little bewildering at times. There are so many different independent wine merchants out there, let alone the huge choice of supermarkets and off-licences. Where do you start? Well, if it were clothes that you were after, then you may have a favourite designer, local high street standard or at least a good department store in which to hunt around. You would probably buy your socks from one store, your shoes from another and jeans from the next. It would not be too difficult to know which shops sold the sort of clothes that suited your taste. While buying, you would then choose a few items and try them on in the fitting room and imagine which of your own clothes might go with these new items.

That seems to work well for clothes and probably many other items of shopping, but we seem to forget this tactic when buying wine. The question we must ask ourselves is 'Which wine shop is best for which style of wine?' There are no wine merchants in the world that have comprehensive coverage of all the world's wine – that would be impossible, as the choice would be infinite. Every wine seller stocks a specific style of wine, whether it is dependent on the customer profile, the palate of the owner/buyer or the proximity to the market. Wines for sale in supermarkets invariably endeavour to be as commercial as possible – not downmarket necessarily, just 'commercial' as in 'universally appealing'. These wines, on the whole, don't need laying down, as they are all meant to be bought for immediate consumption. Once again, that does not mean that they do not have the ability to age, just that they are all chosen for drinking now.

It is also very convenient to buy wine in supermarkets when you are getting the rest of your groceries, and that is the main reason why wine departments in the large supermarket chains have expanded enormously of late. The last point in favour of supermarkets is that their buying power is enormous, compared to a small independent shop, so the prices that they charge will probably be the cheapest around for the bottles they sell. They are able to put a huge amount of pressure on their suppliers, which drives prices down, and most supermarkets offer discounts seasonally, or 'wines of the month' etc., so, if you find a wine that you particularly like subjected to an unmissable discount, that is the time to weigh in heavily with a purchase. All in all, this makes supermarkets a force to be reckoned with in the world of wine buying. Points against supermarkets are that the selections rarely contain unusual or eclectic wines, preferring to favour safe bets and big world brands. This, inevitably, makes the choice in supermarkets a little boring for the adventurous wine drinker. Also, the wineries that supermarkets buy from tend to be huge, as they have to be able to keep up with the demand from several hundred outlets. This again means that smaller wineries lose out – most of the finest estates in the world tend to be on the smaller side. Lastly, supermarkets only rarely offer wine tastings in store (logistics would be tricky for a start), so you don't get the chance to try a wine for size. They do have grading systems to help you find the dryness to sweetness of whites and the lightness to heaviness of reds, but that clearly does not always tell the whole story.

My advice is to use supermarkets for everyday wines or party gluggers that are designed to be simple quaffers. You will find they do the job well and don't cost a packet.

That leaves the other side of the spectrum – the wine specific retailers: both national chain stores and independent wine merchants. Chain stores usually provide good ranges of wines that tend to be more exciting than those from supermarkets. They also, on the whole, offer discounts for buying in bulk (this can mean deals on as little as two bottles, not just case purchases). Also, they often conduct in-store wine tastings, giving you an opportunity to decide for yourself whether the wine is for you. Still large in terms of buying power, chain stores deal with the same big boys the supermarkets do, but also have the ability to pick up smaller parcels of wine and drop them into stores where the local clientele would best appreciate them. This is where the action is!

Independent wine merchants, as the name suggests, rarely have the buying clout of a big chain, so they have to rely on clever buying, good contacts and a good palate to woo the customer. They can also move much faster on a deal than the bigger companies, so they snipe around the edges of the industry, kidnapping parcels here, there and everywhere, in the knowledge that they have a thirsty customer base back at the shop, waiting in anticipation for the wine. They will perhaps spend half of their life searching high and low for unique wines and exclusive agencies and the other half trying to spread the word. The personal touch is crucial in independent wine merchants, so it is important to let the shop assistant know your precise likes and dislikes. They will always be able to find exactly the wine for your palate. Always offering discounts, the 'indies' are battling against the big boys for market share, and a good shop assistant will often open bottles for you to taste if there is the sniff of a worthwhile sale. Not wanting to compete directly with the chain stores, independents rarely list any of the same wines found in the multiples, so the selection will not only be different but usually more challenging and exciting. Wine knowledge in independent wine merchants is also generally very good, as most of the staff will have tasted the wines and often had some say in selecting them. These shops stock wines that can be laid down as well, and will usually have a far larger choice of older wines. Independents also tend to stock a selection of more expensive wines, which tend to be out of the average spending range for a supermarket customer. These guys are the lifeblood of the vinous society.

Remember that, just because a wine merchant is not on your doorstep, it doesn't stop you buying their wines. Get together with some friends and order a case over the phone. Virtually every merchant in the UK delivers nationwide and the charge should only work out to fifty or so pence a bottle, which is a small price to pay for a hand-selected bottle of wine.

In conclusion, there are horses for courses. I recommend a blend of all three styles of wine buying, to suit your wine diet and life style. That way you can get the best of all worlds.

Here are a few tips to look out for when buying wine.

1   If you find a good quality, cheap wine (red or white), then buy as much as you can afford. This will not only save time and money in the future, but will also save any disappointment when shopping around.

2   Don't buy Port in December, as prices will always be high in anticipation of Christmas. Buy a few bottles in the summer instead when the prices are low. This technique applies to all seasonal styles of wine.

3   Southern Hemisphere wines usually arrive in the shops in autumn, so watch out for old vintages, that will still taste great, but will be rushed along to make way for the new ones and are likely to be discounted. The same goes for Northern Hemisphere wines in the spring.

4 Look for wine at sale time. Summer sales and New Year sales can be a good way of finding uncommercial oddities that will broaden your wine knowledge.

5 Always ask for a case discount or find out if any offers are available in the shop. Quite often there are 'seven for six' deals or BOGOFs (buy one get one free), and if you don't ask you won't get.

6 Ask wine merchants about the wines you are buying, as they will know how long they need to breathe, if they need decanting, what temperature to serve them at and so on.

7 Make a note of wines that you like, and then try to follow your taste buds when buying. Let a merchant know your thoughts on wines that you have bought, because they will try to understand your likes and dislikes as well. After a time they will be able to accurately recommend wines for you to enjoy.

8 Wine shops usually have glasses that they rent out for parties. As long as you buy your wine there, there will be no charge for the glasses.

9 Don't buy any wines that are in window displays or near bright shop lights as they will not be in top condition – go for the wine behind, in the shade.

10 Avoid wines that are too ullaged. The ullage is the space between the top of the wine and the bottom of the cork. In wines of less than ten years old there should be no more than a 2cm gap. If it is greater than that, then there may be a leak or the wine could possibly be oxidised.

WINE LABELS

A wine label is its birth certificate. It is the only piece of information that can help you figure out what is going on inside the bottle. After studying all of the writing on a label you should be in no doubt as to what the wine will taste like. Sometimes bottles have back labels with additional background information about the wine. Here is what to look out for:

A geographical reference

This could be a country name, region, specific appellation or even the exact vineyard. Within Europe, all of the wine must come from the region stated. However, in the United States or Australia, there is an 85 per cent rule, allowing up to 15 per cent of the wine to come from another region.

The vintage

In Europe the vintage does not need to be stated for table wines – they are usually drunk young so it is pretty safe to assume that a non-vintage French *Vin de Table* is only a year or two old. If a wine does declare a vintage (most do), then the 85 per cent rule comes into play again.

The quality level

Wines made in the European Union must carry a quality level description on the label – for example, in ascending order of importance, *Vin de Table*, *Vin de Pays*, VDQS or *Appellation Contrôlée*, all terms used for French wines. Spain, Italy, Germany and other countries have their own classification systems. If the wine is made outside Europe, then the word 'wine' must be written on the label in order to be allowed to enter the EU.

Volume of the bottle

This must state the amount of wine in the bottle. The most common sizes are: 75cl a full bottle; 37.5cl a half bottle; and 150cl a magnum.

The alcoholic strength

Usually stated as a percentage of volume.

Name and address of the producer

Straightforward enough.

Bottling information

Château bottled, Domaine bottled, Estate bottled. The main French term used is *mise en bouteille* followed by where it was put into the bottle. In Italian the word is *imbottigliato* and in Spanish *embotellado*.

Grape variety information

It is not compulsory to include this information but a lot of winemakers choose to let the buyers know what grape(s) the wine is made from. You may have thought that if only one grape is written on the label, then the wine is 100% that variety, but this is not the case. In Europe and Australia, a 'single varietal' need only be made from 85% of the stated grape, with the remainder being made up of any others. In the USA it is even less – only 75%. I think this is taking it a bit far – 25% of another grape can radically change the overall flavour of a wine!

In addition to this information some governments require health warnings, heavy machinery warnings and pregnant mother alerts ('do not drink wine if you are pregnant', not 'this wine may lead to pregnancy'!). Wine made in Europe does not need to list any additives used in the winemaking process. The USA warns that wine 'contains sulfites' [sic] and Australians have to declare any additives, like sulphur dioxide which has its own code number, 220. This does take away from the romance of the product, but as most wine is made using some degree of sulphur dioxide (or sulfites) then I suppose it is inevitable that this warning will appear, despite its seemingly ominous tone.

Those are the main, and in most cases, legally binding details that have to be included on a wine label, but bottles can have a lot more information listed. Labels have become increasingly more 'designer-styled' in order to stand out from the crowd on a retail shelf, but beware of skin-deep beauty. Many of the wines available in shops today have a back label that will tell you how irresistible the nectar is within and no doubt regale you with a cute story as to why the wine is called 'Koala Ridge' etc. These back labels can have useful details. Sometimes a little map, or a breakdown of the grapes if it is a blend. Occasionally the method of vinification is outlined. All of these pieces of information can be put together to form a mental picture and help you decide whether it is the wine for you. Bottle shapes and glass colour can also make for an attractive and eye-catching twist to the art of selling wine. The Italians (who else) came up with neat designer bottles, which are bicep-achingly heavy or fridge-defyingly awkward. These now seem to be the norm for any expensive, top-of-the-range wine. 'Art labels' are an interesting proposal kicked off by Château Mouton-Rothschild in Bordeaux, who invited top artists to design a different piece of art to put on each vintage of their wine. So far they have notched up Dali, Henry Moore, Picasso, Chagall, Miró and Andy Warhol to name but a few. Not surprisingly with this roll call, they are the leaders in this style of design. Their wines are not only eminently collectable, but the labels are too. There have been many attempts to copy this attractive style of labelling, but only one other estate has really succeeded and that is Leeuwin Estate in Western Australia, which focuses purely on Australian artists.

Ultimately, however, I am only interested in what is in the bottle and you should be too. Label design plays a non-existent role in the taste of a wine. I can't tell you how many wine salesmen have told me how beautiful a wine label is on a bottle that they want me to buy for a restaurant. Don't they realise that most people choose wine from a list? Many classic wines have unusually simple labels that just let the Domaine, winemaker or winery name alone do the talking.

There are a number of extra titbits that some producers write on a label. There is a full list of these in the Glossary, but here are some of the most common.

French Wine Labels

Blanc de Blancs

Literally 'white wine from white grapes'. On a bottle of Champagne this would mean it was 100 per cent Chardonnay.

Blanc de Noirs

Literally 'white wine from black grapes'. Sometimes seen on Champagne, this means it has been made from Pinot Noir and Pinot Meunier (and not Chardonnay).

Brut

Dry.

Château

'Castle', although they rarely are – some are no more than a potting shed!

Clos

A term for a walled vineyard.

Côtes

A slope or hillside, followed by which specific slope or hillside, for instance, Côtes du Rhône (Hills of Rhône).

Crémant

Fizzy, but not as much as normal Champagne.

Cru

A term for a specific vineyard's quality status, as in Burgundy's *1er Cru* and *Grand Cru* and Alsace's *Grand Cru*. In these cases the individual name of the vineyard would be attached to the *1er* or *Grand Cru* prefix, unless the wine was a blend of several *1er Crus* in which case it would not list each vineyard involved, just state *1er Cru*. The other meaning is 'growth' as in *1er Cru*, *2ème Cru*, down to *5ème Cru*, translating as 1st growth, 2nd growth etc. This is a classification of Bordeaux's top-ranking Left Bank Châteaux.

Cru Bourgeois
A Bordeaux classification for wines one level under *Cru Classé*.

Cru Classé
Literally, a 'classed growth', referring to a classification system covering the finest Left Bank Bordeaux Châteaux.

Cuvée
The blend or a style of wine. A pretty uninformative term that only really differentiates the normal version of a wine from a slightly better one, as in *Cuvée Spéciale*, *Grande Cuvée* or *Tête de Cuvée*. Sometimes winemakers write this on every wine that they make, thus rendering the term meaningless.

Demi-Sec
Literally 'half dry' – therefore medium dry or 'off-dry'.

Domaine
A winery that owns its own vineyards and makes its own wine.

Fût de Chêne
Matured in oak barrels.

Moelleux
Pudding wines use this term if they are rich and ripe rather than cloyingly sweet. Seen on Loire whites and Jurançon.

Mousseaux
Sparkling.

Négociant
A producer who buys in grapes or wine for vinification, bottling, labelling and selling.

Réserve
A meaningless term that implies a superior bottling, but in practice is used as often as *Cuvée Spéciale* (see above).

Sélection des Grains Nobles

The ultimate in sweet wine levels from Alsace or the Loire. Literally meaning 'a careful selection of noble rot affected grapes'.

Sur Lie

Meaning 'on the lees', used for higher quality Muscadet and other whites that are made in contact with their lees.

Vendange Tardive

Meaning 'late picked or late harvested'. Used for sweet wines.

Vieilles Vignes

Meaning 'old vines'. This should signify a superior wine, with a more concentrated flavour, although there is no recognised age at which vines become 'old'.

Vin Doux Naturel

Written on some fortified wines, so watch out. Sweet wines and after-dinner drinks such as Muscat de Rivesaltes, Muscat de Beaumes-de-Venise, Banyuls and Maury.

Italian Wine Labels

Abboccato

Medium-sweet.

Amabile

Sweet.

Amarone

Dried-grape red wines.

Azienda Agricola

The equivalent of *Domaine*, where the grapes are grown and made into wine on the estate.

Bianco
White.

Casa Vinicola
The equivalent of a French *négociant*.

Castello
Castle, like the French term *Château*.

Frizzante
Sparkling.

Passito
A term for a white wine made from dried grapes.

Recioto
A Venetian term for a strong sweet wine made from dried grapes.

Riserva
Indicates the pick of the crop that usually spends longer in oak barrels and has higher alcoholic strength than the *normale* wine.

Rosso
Red.

Tenuta
Estate.

Vendemmia
The 'vintage'.

Vigna
Vineyard.

Spanish Wine Labels

Abocado
Medium-sweet.

Blanco
White.

Bodega
Winery.

Castillo
Castle, like the French term *Château*.

Crianza
A term for a wine that has been aged for two years before release, one of which has to be spent in a barrel.

Generoso
A term for a wine that is fortified.

Gran Reserva
A term for a wine that has been aged for five years, of which a minimum of two years is spent in a barrel.

Reserva
A term for a wine that has been aged for three years, of which a minimum of one year is spent in a barrel.

Tinto
Red.

Viña
Vineyard.

German Wine Labels

Auslese

A 'selected harvest', meaning that the wine will be more ripe than normal and often sweet.

Beerenauslese

A sweet style of wine made from individually selected overripe berries.

Eiswein

Made only in vintages where the grapes freeze on the vine. These are so concentrated in sugar they result in tooth-achingly sweet wines.

Feinherb

A more intense wine than a straight *Trocken* (see below), often with slightly more residual sugar.

Halbtrocken

This means 'half-dry', so one up from *Trocken*, and one down from *Auslese*.

Spätlese

A style that is 'late-harvested' but not always sweet. More often less sweet than *Auslese*, and usually fermented dry to result in a higher-alcohol, more foody wine.

Trocken

Dry.

Trockenbeerenauslese

A mouthful in all senses of the word. A mega-sweet style of wine, made from individually selected, 'noble rot' affected grapes, usually shortened to TBA, and bloody expensive.

Other Labels
Barrel-fermented
Any white wine that has been fermented in oak barrels resulting in a stronger oaky flavour than those wines just aged in oak barrels.

Botrytised
Or 'botrytis affected', is a term for an unctuous, rot-affected, sweet wine.

Importer's details
A blatant advertisement, serving no purpose to the consumer whatsoever. I suppose it is good for the ego.

Late harvest
Vines that are picked later than normal in the quest for extra ripe grapes with which to make sweet wines. (Also called 'late picked'.)

Miscellaneous terms
Either viticultural or vinification terms to help to add weight to the style of wine. For instance, 'Bush Vine' Grenache; 'Vat 65'; 'Bin 7' or 'Old Vine Selection'.

Unfiltered
Just that – a wine that is not filtered, probably with a more intense flavour. More likely to throw a sediment and may, in time, require decanting. (*Vin non filtré* in French.)

Specific numbered bottles
Used to indicate the exclusivity of the wine, a bit like a personal numberplate. Only found on wines from relatively smart estates – there would be no point in Gallo using numbered bottles, as there would be no space on the label for any other writing.

Next time you are out and about in a wine shop, take a second or two to study all of the information on a wine label. By combining all of these separate details, you will undoubtedly pick up more pointers to the taste of the wine than you would expect.

Chapter 4
HOW TO TASTE WINE

I taste between eighty and one hundred wines every day of the year, and no matter how many new bottles I open, the anticipation leading up to the first sniff and slurp is electric. It is a wonderful moment when the first drops of precious liquid are poured. Next time you open a bottle, just before you take a sip, wait for a second. I don't want to spoil this magical moment, but there is something I would like you to think about. That bottle, no matter where it is from, or what it cost, has taken a minimum of a year to be created. The winemaker has inevitably sweated blood and tears to make it and get it to you. The wine has been slave to the weather, human error in the vineyard, human error in the winery, the bottling line, the economic climate and countless other variables that might have prevented it from ever making it this far. You have already seen its birth certificate (its label) and it has a story to tell. So please, take a little time to get to know it and acknowledge it for what it is – much more than just a drink. In that split second before taking a sip, realise that in order ever to understand and totally enjoy wine, it is crucial to remember that it is a living breathing thing, made with love and skill, and it requires love and a little bit of skill to enjoy.

Why taste wine, though? After all, tasting is little more than slow drinking with the brain switched on. But tasting is also the process by which all of a wine's secrets can be unlocked, revealed and enjoyed. Tasting is like reading a book rather than guessing the story from a glance at the cover. With previous knowledge of an author's work and a racy title, coupled with the blurb on the back cover, one can guess at a book's story. The same is true of wine – a reputable Domaine, good vintage and back label can serve the same purpose. But reading the book or tasting the wine is the true test.

Can you taste? Do you have what is required to be a wine taster? The answers are yes and yes. You taste things every day. Wine might not occupy your daily regime as much as it does mine, but toothpaste, coffee, toast, lunch, dinner and choccies in front of the telly can all form part of the daily tasting schedule. Within each mouthful you can, for instance, easily identify between the roast potato, broccoli and chicken. Eyes and nose help, but if you were blindfolded it would still not be too difficult. It is honestly very similar with wine. Everybody has the apparatus in their own head and you usually use it without thinking. Wine tasting just involves a bit of memory and application – and it is wine, so it's fun, too!

Before embarking on your wine tasting, remember that the wine you have in front of you has been tasted many times before to assess its quality, readiness to drink and potential. The winemaker will have tasted it countless times during the winemaking process, to ensure that it is representative of the style of wine that they are trying to make. An agent or buyer will have tasted the wine to decide whether or not to buy it to sell on. Then a wine merchant, restaurant or other outlet will have sent a taster to the agent to assess the quality of the wine, perhaps comparing it to other similar wines, in order to determine which one fits the slot in their shop or wine list and whether or not it might appeal to their clientele. Only then do you get a chance to see for yourself what the end result is.

Wine tasting is an organoleptic assessment, or sensory examination. Sounds painful? Well it isn't. Tasting involves using all of your senses to analyse a wine's elements. The natural order in which to taste a wine is luckily the same as the one used when drinking. So here comes the skilful bit…

Sight

Hold a half-full glass of wine by the stem (this will prevent sticky fingerprints and warming the glass inadvertently) and tilt the glass over – but not too far! Look through the glass on to a pale background – a white tablecloth, plate or piece of paper. It is helpful to be in a room with natural light because artificial light can affect the colour and tone of the wine. Before concentrating on the colour, just check that there is nothing floating in the wine. This may sound a little absurd, but there have been occasions where pieces of cork, flies, dust, sediment (I encountered a large earwig once) and many other unmentionables have found their way into the wine or the glass. Check that the wine is clear and not hazy (this could indicate a problem). It should just appear 'bright'. Are there any bubbles? If there are, the wine will probably be a full-blown sparkling wine. But there may be just a few tiny bubbles on the surface of the wine, known as a 'spritz'. These indicate that the wine is young and perky, a good pointer to a zippy, refreshing style of white.

Now assess the colour and its intensity. Try to get beyond just white and red. White wines can be described as: colourless, pale yellow, yellow-green, yellow, yellow-gold, gold, and deep gold. You do not need to stick to these, as there are many other words that can be used. For reds: opaque, black-red, deep purple, red-purple, ruby, red, garnet, brick-red, orange-brown – again, make up your own if it helps you.

Colour can tell you a number of important things. For white wines, the paler the colour, the lighter, dryer and – if there are green tinges to the wine – the younger the wine. The deeper the colour, the heavier, richer, older or sweeter the wine. Oak-aged whites will be a little deeper in colour than a similar wine made in stainless steel tanks. For red wines, the lighter the intensity, the lighter the weight of the wine. If the colour is 'bright' and has a blue or purple rim, then the wine will be younger than that of a wine with a brown or brick-red rim. Climate can make a huge difference to a wine's colour. Hot climate wines will be riper and so tend to have stronger, more intense colours.

Remember, colour is only useful when combined with the smell and the taste. As you progress through the discipline of tasting a particular wine, you will build up an identity for it.

Just a quick note about 'legs' – the patterns that wine makes down the side of a glass after having been swirled around. Ignore this phenomenon – it is merely a demonstration of the viscosity of the wine. It doesn't tell you anything about where the wine is from, what it is made from or how good its quality is.

Hearing

Not really worthy of a listing – the only time a bottle of wine really makes a noise is the glorious moment when the cork is popped. This will always raise a smile and, you hope, herald the arrival of a glass. Other wine noises are of course the pouring of a glass of wine and the fizz of a Champagne or sparkling wine.

Smell

This is the big one. In order to release the maximum amount of smell from the wine, gently swirl the wine around in the glass, again holding the glass by the stem. A little practice at this movement will enable you to swirl in mid-air. To start with, however, this may introduce a wine spillage problem, so place the glass on a table or flat surface and, holding the stem like a pencil, 'draw tiny circles'. This should get the wine swirling slowly around the glass. You will soon graduate to fully fledged aerial swirling. If you think that this is all a little too pretentious, then take a non-swirled glass and have a sniff. It will not smell nearly as intense as the swirled one, so there is a point to it, beyond that of looking like a pro.

And now for the first sniff. This is your first formal introduction to the wine, so take a steady, long, gentle inhalation, resisting the temptation to snort the wine as this can be particularly painful. When sniffing, try to bend over the glass rather than tilting the glass to you. Don't be afraid of sticking your nose into the glass, as the smell will be strongest close to the wine. This part of tasting is known as 'the nose'. The fun part is breaking this whoosh of winey smells into parts and trying to give them names. We are very privileged to have an awesome olfactory system that possesses a busy department that I call 'smell memories'. Whenever a smell whizzes up your nose the smell memories get working. You can be stopped dead in your tracks by a smell and then spend the next five minutes trying to remember where and when you last encountered it. It could be a familiar pipe tobacco, an alluring perfume, honeysuckle blossom, old leather car seats, a freshly mown lawn, home baking, freshly ground coffee, warm summer rain or a beautifully balanced salad dressing – all engage the brain for a fleeting moment. Many of my friends have the enviable talent of being able to detect a kebab shop, after pub closing time, several streets away.

The purpose of trying to identify wine smells is to look for links between one wine and another, to try to attach a regional or grape variety 'smell memory' to it. Practice makes perfect and although a bit of effort is required to remember these smells, it is remarkable how quickly specific triggers in the brain begin to identify characteristics in the glass, so stick with it. An important rule to remember when tasting is that *you are always right*. Which is brilliant because, if you detect a specific smell on a wine, nobody can tell you that you are wrong. After all, it is your nose that has sensed the aroma and your 'smell memories' that have unearthed the name for the smell. It is then a matter of applying that knowledge to the wine in question, and unravelling its story. In 'blind tasting', where the objective is to guess at the origin of a glass of wine without looking at the label, many triumphs have occurred just through smell recognition alone.

Overall the wine should smell clean; by that I mean not 'out of condition'. 'Corked' wines occur with alarming regularity, and should be weeded out instantly by the nose. The smell will be pungent, musty and mouldy, not unlike a particularly ripe pair of soggy, five-year-old jogging shoes. Some corked wines are very pronounced, others less so. If you are in doubt, taste the wine and you will find that the musty, unpleasant flavour is there as well. This flattens out the flavour and makes the wine taste dull and lifeless.

Once the wine has been given a full bill of health, the challenge begins to give names to the smells in the glass. It is like photo-fit. First, check out if there is oak present or not, as your nose is the best judge of this. Then search for fruit smells. Are there any spicy or earthy overtones, and then any other aromas that come to mind – honey, nuts or flowers on whites; beetroot, boot polish or cough syrup on reds? Also decide how much fruit intensity there is behind the nose, as this could be a guide to quality and/or climate. This may all sound a little bizarre, but you will be surprised what you find.

Taste

OK, you have waited long enough for this moment, so go ahead and take a medium-sized mouthful. This part of the operation is called the 'palate'. Roll the wine around your mouth. A weird expression for this is 'chewing' the wine – it may sound strange, but if you literally try this manoeuvre it will become clear what this term really means. If you are feeling brave you can attempt to unlock yet more flavour from the mouthful by drawing in a small stream of air through your lips. This may also sound a little strange, but it is all in a good cause – you are, in effect, aerating the wine steadily in your mouth. Make sure that you don't choke, though! It is worth practising with a glass of water in order to perfect the action. Then swallow the wine or, if you are intending to taste a range of bottles, you can spit it out to keep your head clear. Finally, concentrate on the 'finish'. As you would expect, this is the flavour left after swallowing and it is measured in the length of time that it lingers on the palate. Repeat this process – in reality it only takes a few seconds from start to finish – if necessary, and then head straight to drinking as soon as you are happy with the information that your brain has amassed.

That is all you have to do to taste wine.

But what can the palate tell you about a wine? It will not really reveal many more elements or key flavours, as your nose will have done much of that work already. It will however, determine the texture, weight and other characteristics of the wine. When the wine is swirling around your mouth, your nose will continue its good deeds, collecting flavours and nuances while your palate detects other elements.

Firstly, the **dryness or sweetness** of a wine is only revealed on the palate. Some white wines smell 'sweet' but taste dry – like Gewürztraminer. These wines are not therefore 'sweet', just 'ripe'. Again, a New World Chardonnay may have more body and structure than a Chablis but it is no sweeter (in sugar terms), just riper, as they both have good levels of 'acidity' and are dry on the finish.

Talking of **acidity**, the palate is also the determining tool of this vital element of a wine's make-up. Acidity is a crucial component in the balance of all wine, giving it lift, bite and freshness on the finish. If you feel it is difficult to separate the sensation of acidity from the rest of the flavours in a wine in your head, then just taste a young Sauvignon Blanc. As white wines do not have tannin, the 'perky', 'zippy', 'zingy' refreshing quality that lends tartness and crispness to the taste is the acidity. White wines without balanced acidity are often referred to as being 'flabby'. In red wines, as they may have discernible tannins, it is sometimes tricky deciding which part of the flavour is tannin and which acidity. They both give rise to a drying sensation in the mouth, and varying levels of cheek sucking, but the acidity is the refreshing element whereas the tannin is the more bitter part.

With red wines, **tannin** (the natural preservative in a red, and the 'battery pack' for a wine's lifetime) can be a major slice of the overall flavour. This happens when a wine is too 'young'. If the tannins are not in balance with the fruit, oak (if oak-aged) and acidity, then this will indicate that a wine has yet to reach its peak of drinkability. Tannins do soften with age, but a young red in perfect balance is still drinkable. If the tannins are hard, the fruit flavours huge, and the acidity firm, there is no reason why the wine cannot be enjoyed immediately (probably with some hefty food). Only wines with prohibitively strong tannins should be sent back to the cellar for rest, recuperation and further hibernation. Every wine – fizz, white, red, sweet and fortified – has its own 'drinking curve' (the period in its lifetime when it tastes at its peak). Most unoaked white wines start their lives ready for action and live for a year or two happily. Bigger reds seem grumpy and uncommunicative in their youth, but mellow and improve with age. Some styles last longer than others (I have tasted eighty-year-old reds that were still in great nick), but more serious reds always take a while to get into their stride. With practice, you will be able to guess at a wine's drinkability from its style and age. This will mean you will be able to avoid wines that are 'too young' or 'too old'.

Your palate can also detect **body/structure**, within a wine. The best way to explain this sensation is to use a great American expression – 'mouth feel'. The richness of a wine, its texture and weight on the palate are all self-explanatory. Wines can range from 'thin', via 'creamy', through 'smooth' and ending up at 'velvety' – not to mention 'light-weight', 'medium-weight', 'heavy-weight' and 'blockbuster'. This is a guide to the alcohol levels, vinification techniques and grape variety (or varieties) that the wine is made from. Taking the point even further, along with **colour**, the **body** of a wine should also point you to a style, climate-type and even a good guess at the country of origin. Body and colour are generally connected as a result of the intensity of sunshine that a vine has been subjected to during the year. So a luscious, golden white wine or a deep, dark red wine will probably be from a hot area or country. Conversely, pale, thin whites and light, weak reds usually come from cooler climates. Sometimes you may get a really tricky wine that has a deep, dark colour but is from a cooler region. If this is the case, then either a brilliant winemaker has had a hand in making it or it was a particularly brilliant vintage.

Oak flavours on the palate should always complement the fruit flavours in the wine. Over-oaked wines either need more time in the cellar to 'knit' together or else the winemaker has been a little over zealous with the barrels and not concentrated hard enough on the wine's balance. The trick is to achieve harmony between the oak flavours and the grape flavours, and, as a result, add an extra dimension to the taste. If you detect oak on the nose, cross your fingers that the palate is balanced. Also, remember that oaked wines are generally more expensive than un-oaked wines (smart barrels cost a bomb), and this may help with your deduction process when playing the Price Point Game (see Glossary).

Flavour, like the nose on a wine, is very much a personal thing. Once again, you cannot be wrong, as your palate tells you what it recognises. Don't worry if everyone else tastes passion fruit and you get kiwi fruit. This is not important – they are both tropical fruit tasting notes, so you are clearly in the same ballpark. I find that more general wine tasting terms are worth voicing out loud, but the more personal ones are better kept to yourself, as they are just that – personal.

The **finish** is an all-important quality marker. Fine wines tend to hang around on the taste buds for minutes, whereas cheaper styles can be gone in a matter of seconds. Make a mental note of which flavours remain on the palate. If the fruit is last to go then the wine will probably be at its peak or about to slip downhill. If the tannin or acidity, or both, are last to leave, then the wine will probably be better off being kept for a few months or even years depending on the style, as it will need to soften further. The units of measurement for 'finish' are short, medium, long and heroic (I threw the last one in).

I am a **balance** freak and, as I have already mentioned, balance is a fundamental element in truly great wines – and by 'great wines' I do not necessarily mean expensive bottles. The one element that unites all of the world's best wines is that they have in-built, impeccable balance. If the concept of balance is a touch baffling then I have a good, simple analogy to throw in. Imagine two seesaws, one for reds and one for whites. The red seesaw has four arms, and on each arm sits a different element in a red wine's make-up: fruit, acidity, oak and tannin. For whites, there are only three arms to the seesaw: fruit, acidity and oak (if present; if not then only two arms). If any of these elements is too dominant on the palate then the seesaw will be weighed down on one side. If they are all present in equal and complementary proportions, then the wine will have perfect balance.

The final part to consider is the **complexity** of the wine. I often refer to simple wines as one-dimensional and others as being multi-dimensional. A simpler wine could be like hearing a solo instrument playing (albeit beautifully), and a complex wine like hearing the whole philharmonic orchestra going for it with gusto. There are occasions, perhaps when sitting over a meal and relaxing, that call for a wine that can awaken the taste buds and challenge the mind. Other times a glass of wine isn't called to do anything other than be partner to a quick salad at lunchtime, so complexity is unlikely to be an issue. The complexity of a wine is another hallmark of quality, and, more often than not, has an impact on the price of a wine. However, usually genuine, regional wines made by skilled winemakers have in-built complexity and integrity coming from the soil and microclimate that transcend price.

Social drinking can, and should, involve tasting – done at high speed for your own benefit or privately in your own personal space. Pour, observe, swirl, sniff, sip, swallow, think, and return to the conversation. Now, that didn't hurt and it only took two seconds and it will also have heightened your enjoyment of the glass of wine enormously. Finally, remember, with wine in mind, practice makes better, never perfect. The most important aspect to tasting wine is the very simple question that many of us fail to ask ourselves – do I like it?

SETTING UP YOUR OWN TASTING

This can be good fun and a novel way to storm through copious bottles of good wine in the name of furthering your powers of deduction. Here is a short checklist of what you will need:

An invitation
Obviously, it is good to know when and where the tasting is, and it is important to emphasise the start time – it is hard to catch up in a wine tasting if you are late.

A theme

It is best to concentrate on a single grape variety, region or vintage. There are so many wines in the world, so narrow it down for the purposes of a tasting.

The order

Dry to sweet for whites, and light to heavy for reds, grouping similar grape varieties along the way.

Lighting

Natural daylight is best; artificial light tends to make wine look dull.

Glasses

ISO (International Organisation for Standardisation) glasses are the world standard wine-tasting glasses. They are relatively inexpensive, useful for all styles of wine and widely available from wine shops or glassware manufacturers. If you do not have any of these, then tulip-shaped glasses will do. This shape should prevent wine whizzing out when swirling! Avoid cut, engraved or coloured glass, as these all interfere with the colour of the wine. Make sure that the glasses are clean with no detergent smell.

No smoking

Smoke will mess with your taste buds and other people's noses.

No strong perfume

Perfume will also mess with your taste buds and other people's noses.

Tasting sheets

A numbered sheet on which to record your thoughts, tasting notes and perhaps marks (out of ten or twenty) for each wine. This will serve as an *aide-mémoire* at a later date.

Spittoons

If necessary (but a must if you are tackling more than eight wines).

Food

Again, if necessary, but crackers or water biscuits are a bare minimum. It is good to try to match wine to food, and it does fend off alcohol's undesirable effects, at least for a time.

Wine

The most important ingredient! Ensure that each wine is served at the correct temperature (of which more later), and poured in no more than half-glass quantities. After all, there may be some left at the end for avid fans of particular wines. Always keep the receipts for the wine in order to play the 'Price Point Game' (see Glossary).

Remember that when tasting in groups, the 'sheep phenomenon' sometimes takes over. One person might say, 'This tastes like strawberries', and everyone else will lazily nod and agree. It is always important to give everybody a fair crack at analysing a wine, as this will throw up loads of adjectives and nuances that will benefit the entire crowd.

The Wine Taster's Language

I am sure that you are aware of the extraordinary language used for describing the taste of wine by professional wine tasters. While many of the words and phrases used are common and recognisable, there are some bizarre expressions that can appear totally alien when referring to wine. Please turn to my extensive Tasting Terms section of the Glossary for details of some key phrases. I promise you that these are all genuine.

WINE FAULTS

How do you know when a wine is genuinely faulty, as opposed to just not very good? There are a few ways to find out. After all, if you are served a faulty wine in a restaurant or you go to a shop and buy a wine that turns out to be faulty, you are entitled in both instances to a refund or to swap the bottle for another of the same. The one point to remember is that you must speak up. It is always easy in a restaurant to catch someone's eye and rustle up another bottle; however, people are generally lazy about bringing a bottle back to a wine shop and so miss out on the opportunity to claim a refund. Do not feel guilty about complaining, as the merchant or restaurant will themselves get reimbursed in turn from the winemakers or importers. It is important that this information gets back to the winemaker, so they can monitor any faulty wines and try to eliminate the problem. Always record the date that you opened the wine on the label, as the shop will taste the wine to try to determine the fault as well. It is helpful for them to know how long the wine has been exposed to air, in order to discount any mild oxidation from its list of possible ailments.

Points to Look Out for (or Smell Out for) in Faulty Wines

Apart from sediment in red wines and tartrate crystals in whites there shouldn't be any visible problems. These two naturally occurring substances are, if anything, indicators of confident winemaking – a lack of filtration before bottling. Filtration can take flavour and body from a wine, so you could argue that these two elements are, in fact, positively attractive. Anything other than true sediment or tartrates is questionable, however. If a wine shows a permanent **haze** or cloudiness, then there could be a bacterial problem with the wine, usually yeast still present. This is a genuine fault and the wine should be returned as soon as possible. Wines with haze will not necessarily harm you; it is just that they are biologically unstable. They may be unpalatable but, more importantly, they are clearly not what the winemaker intended, so it is best not to drink them.

Occasionally, you may spot **bubbles** in a still wine. Some whites are given a little squirt of carbon dioxide when they are bottled, to give them a lift in order to retain the freshness of the style. This is not a problem, as this spritz will disappear shortly after pouring a glass of wine. A difficulty arises when a wine is actually and actively fizzy. 'Still' reds and whites can be unintentionally bottled with yeast still active in the wine. This is a huge error because, whereas in Champagne this trick is used for the positive development of bubbles, in non-sparkling wines it gives rise to unwanted fermentation.

Nosing is the best way of detecting faults. A browning in the colour of a wine could be an indication of **oxidation**, but the best check for an oxidised wine is to take a sniff. The smell will be sherry-like. Any **vinegary** or strong **sulphur** smells can also be off-putting and point to bacteriological or winemaking cock-ups. Mouldy smells could indicate dirty wooden barrels, bacterial spoilage or just plain unhygienic winemaking. Wine should always smell 'clean'. **Bottle stink** is a term used to describe slightly musty wines that need air to freshen up. If you have a wine that is not obviously faulty but just a little stale smelling, then allow it to breathe or, better still, decant it. This could give the musty wine a much needed kiss of life.

The biggest problem of all is **corked** wines. Until all wines are sealed with screwcaps or synthetic corks, this problem will continue to plague drinkers. A corked wine is the result of a contaminated cork affecting the taste of the wine (not a few pieces of cork floating in a glass). This problem is irreversible, and as many as one in twelve bottles that I taste during the course of my job are affected. This fault is not just associated with cheaper wine, although the chance of a corked bottle of fine wine is, thankfully, reduced because top estates spend up on their corks and tend to carry out more stringent tests. Corkiness arises from a problem encountered during the cork production process. Chlorine is used to bleach corks prior to washing and drying. This chlorine reacts with phenol in the cork and is converted, by mould found on them, to a chemical compound called trichloroanisole (commonly referred to as TCA). It is thought that changing the bleaching process could make a difference; however, mould growing on corks can still generate these corked smells, and corks can be contaminated at any time during the production process. All manner of bleaching techniques are being researched – washing cork granules in super-critical carbon dioxide and then reassembling them into cork shapes seems to be the most successful answer at the moment, but the results are not aesthetically very beautiful. If I were a winemaker, I would head to **screwcaps** for guaranteed safety; even if people don't think they are quite as romantic, they do the job perfectly! The Clare Valley in South Australia and Marlborough in New Zealand both pioneered screwcap closures at the turn of the century, and thank goodness they did. This perfect seal is now gathering considerable momentum and you will see wines all over the shelves with these terrific closures. Despite an initial backlash from stick-in-the-mud old farts, the message is getting through that this closure guarantees a wine against corkiness. You do not need to test the wine – it will be exactly as the winemaker intended it to be.

Screwcaps are not a cheap alternative. There is little or no saving to be had in converting your production to screwcaps as the bottles and caps themselves, added to the bottling equipment, are very expensive. A friend of mine in France estimates that it costs 25 per cent more for the bottle and cap, than it did for his old bottle and cork (and capsule). The additional cost to him is significant, but it is worth it if all of his bottles are pristine. As the years roll by we will see a seismic expansion in the number of wines bottled this way. Perhaps a better idea will come along? If it does, so be it. Until then I am a fully paid-up member of the screwcap adoration club.

And this is why – corked wines have a distinctive mouldy, stale, pungent aroma. They are usually easy to spot, as the smell is not remotely winey, more like a strong musty, woody smell. If you are eating in a restaurant and are in any doubt, ask a wine waiter to check the wine. If you are at home, do not pour it out but re-cork it and return it to the shop that you bought it from. If it is corked, they will replace it; if not then there should be an explanation as to why the wine smelled so peculiar and you will probably be given a replacement anyway, to try again. The palate is not really required to detect faults, merely to confirm them. Corked wine generally tastes pretty awful, as does vinegary wine and so on. I would avoid tasting anything that smells unpleasant anyway. If you have a problem with a bottle of wine and a second shows the same problem too, it is definitely a sign to move to a different wine. It is rare for two or more bottles of the same wine to be corked or oxidised, but if bad winemaking is the reason for your concern then you are unlikely to enjoy the same wine again.

One word of warning that should send a shiver down your spine – I have described the smell and taste of 'corked' wines above, but there are a large percentage of wines that are what I call **cork affected**, which creep through the system, often unnoticed. These bottles are a menace. Not smelling too awful, and just tasting a little flat and dull, cork-affected wines are not remotely enjoyable. They are the vinous equivalent of sticking a thick towel over a hi-fi speaker. You can still hear the song, but it is muffled and you miss the depth and richness of the instruments and the detail in the melody. The problem is that, more often than not, drinkers are unaware of what the wine should taste like in the first place, and so drink it, thinking that it is just dull and they wouldn't want to buy it again. This is desperately sad. I see hundreds of bottles like this every year. If you could taste a good one next to the dull one, and compare the two, you'd see just how flat and soulless the affected one was. But we are not always able to do this, and in the absence of a 'real' discernible fault it is hard to muster up the courage to complain – perhaps you even blame yourself (a cold, a bad mood, a rough day at work etc.). Screwcaps eliminate this infuriating issue, too. I despair at the number of wines out there that are dull, flat and boring because rogue corks have unwittingly stolen their character. Screwcaps have the effect of heightening the lift and fruit in a wine, so this is another good reason to support these terrific closures.

I hope these last few paragraphs have put one of the biggest issues of recent years to rest in your minds.

HOW TO SERVE WINE

There is an amazing amount of pomposity associated with the rituals surrounding wine drinking. Crusty old buffers would blanch at the youth of today drinking Zinfandel with chocolate, chilling down red Crozes-Hermitage or decanting a Meursault. Some of the old practices are necessary in order to get the maximum flavour possible from the wine. Others, sadly, just perpetuate the myth that wine is a snobby drink, enjoyed by those privileged enough to be 'in the know'. In this chapter I will strip away all the unnecessary wine etiquette and leave for you the bare dos and don'ts of wine drinking. After all, how difficult is it to drink a glass of wine? In my experience, not very tricky at all. Here are a number of logical steps and some useful information to ensure that you enjoy your wine to the full.

Corkscrews

There are thousands of corkscrews on the market these days. I am sure that they can all manage to extract a cork from a bottle of wine. However, I do favour certain styles over others. First consider the objective. Corks can vary greatly in length and composition. Old corks can be very crumbly, and new corks very hard. So the screw needs to be sharp and long (5.5cm minimum). The helix, or the spiral shaft, needs to be straight, so look down the helix from the pointed end to see a clearly defined inner and outer circle of metal. It also needs to be smooth in order to facilitate the manoeuvre. I am not keen on corkscrews with a central shaft that resemble a DIY wood screw, as these tend just to bore a hole in the cork, and end up pulling the centre out of the cork rather than removing it from the bottle. The most well-known style of corkscrew must be the 'waiter's friend', favoured by restaurant staff. I must admit to using this style myself, as it does the job well, and folds up so as not to cause injury in someone's pocket. The famous 'Screwpull' is the safest and most foolproof of modern corkscrews, and the top of the range 'Lever Arch' model (now with many lesser imitations) is a must for the devoted connoisseurs. The only model that I am still completely baffled by is the so-called 'butler's friend' which has two flattened prongs designed to be inserted between the cork and the bottle. Then, using a pulling/twisting action the cork is squeezed and extracted, unscathed! I am sure that butlers the world over can complete this task. I alas, cannot.

Opening a Bottle of Wine

It would be wonderful simply to write, 'Hold the screwcap firmly in your left hand and twist the body of the bottle with your right. Hey presto!' But sadly not all bottles are (yet) this easy to get into. While steaming through various wines you will inevitably come across many different shapes and styles of bottles. Some are a doddle to open, others a pain. A bottle of wine should not present too much of a challenge, but there is a right and wrong way to go about it. So, for those cork-sealed bottles, this is how you do it. First, take off the capsule (the plastic or metal casing over the top of the bottle). Some people like to cut around the capsule, leaving a neat skirt of colour, but I prefer complete removal, as I have sliced open my fingers and thumbs countless times on razor-sharp edges. If the wine has sediment and needs decanting, this elimination of the capsule also makes it easier to see through the neck of the bottle as you are pouring it. Next, screw in the corkscrew, vertically, straight, and all of the way. This sounds patently obvious, but screwing the corkscrew in at an angle, or only putting it in halfway, is encouraging the cork to break and that is a hassle that you really do not want to contend with. Then lever or pull, depending on the style of your corkscrew, using constant pressure as opposed to a nervous jerk. This will prevent the cork breaking and also avoid you elbowing someone into next week. Well done – have a rest and pour yourself a half-glass of wine. If the cork does break in two, and you are unable to chip it away or get a good grip with the corkscrew, push it into the bottle – just watch out for wine splurging out the top. You can always run the wine through a coffee filter if there are loads of pieces of cork dust left in it. Just remember to rinse the filter with water first to get rid of any cardboardy flavours in it.

Opening a Bottle of Champagne

Opening a bottle of Champagne is dead easy, but so many people make such a fuss about it and often cock it up completely. There are several basic points to grasp before showering your friends with a bottle of fizz. Make sure that nobody has shaken the bottle before you get hold of it – not funny! Always have a target glass nearby to pour the first gush into, and hold the bottle at forty-five degrees (this eases the pressure of the wine, which is desperate to get out). After the capsule has been removed, remember to keep your thumb over the end of the cork as the wire is taken out of the way, in case the cork attempts to fire out of the bottle and lodge itself in someone's eye. Twist the bottle (not the cork) slowly and point the bottle away from your mates. Ease the cork out gently and, just as it gets to the point where it is almost out, tilt the cork sideways and you'll release some of the gas inside the bottle. The noise of the gas emerging should be a hiss not an ostentatious pop, unless you are feeling particularly vulgar. Pour a small taste for you to nose, checking to see that the wine is in good condition. After it has been given the seal of approval, pour half of a glass for each drinker, then top the glasses up after the 'mousse' has subsided. This pouring procedure eliminates any chance of glasses overflowing and people getting a sticky champagne-hand.

Glasses

It is essential to have some good glasses in order to fully appreciate wine, as they are the medium through which the wine is transferred from the bottle to your mouth. There are many different styles of glassware on the market today and it is well worth investing in appropriate glasses. The finer the glasses, the less likely they will break when polishing and the better they will look on the table. Smart glasses can really show off a wine. If you are opening something particularly serious, don't expect it to shine out of a mass-produced Paris Goblet – it will always stand more of a chance from a Reidel, or other similarly beautiful glass.

It is possible to have a different glass-shape for every wine imaginable. It is, however, more sensible to have a white wineglass, a red wineglass, a champagne glass and a smaller glass that will accommodate sherry, port, sweet wines and digestifs (I use an ISO for this – see 'Setting up your own tasting'). If you are on a very tight budget, then one medium-sized glass will take care of any wine style (Champagne excepted). The main point to remember is that all glasses should curve in slightly at the top, in order that wine does not spill out when swirling it around. The rest of the decisions are purely personal and a matter of taste. Do try to avoid cut or engraved and coloured glass as they distort the hue of the wine. A popular question asked on the subject of glasses is, should you change glasses after every wine? The answer is, you should give your friends the option of using new glasses – but usually, people will rinse their own glass out with water and then just carry on. In a restaurant, you would expect new glasses for each wine.

Temperature

Be it red or white, the exact same wine poured at fridge, cellar or room temperature will taste completely different. Any wine served straight out of the fridge will be very cold (4°–7°C). Very few wines really need to be this chilly, as cold temperature inhibits fruit character, making the acidity taste much stronger. Generally, only sweet wines with huge, ripe flavours can handle these cold extremes. Champagne – traditionally an ice-bucket favourite – rarely needs to sit in ice for the duration, as the wistful, floral flavours are in danger of disappearing completely so that all you are left with on the palate is searing acidity. Light whites need to be a touch warmer than ice cold, and so it is a good idea to take the bottle out of the fridge and leave it on the side for a few minutes before serving – this will focus the fruit and pad out the palate. The majority of white wines ought to be served between 8° and 10°C, and finer whites like white Burgundy, and New World Chardonnays and Semillons can be drunk at anything up to 13°C. Vincent Leflaive, one of Burgundy's most venerable winemakers and now, sadly, no doubt keeping the sommeliers busy in heaven, taught me the best lesson in the effect of temperature on a wine. He kindly gave me a very expensive bottle of Montrachet, Burgundy's most famous white wine, to drink later that day with my dinner. He told me to give it to the wine waiter at the restaurant I was visiting that evening and tell him that M Leflaive says not to put it in a fridge or ice-bucket. Serve it 'warm' after dinner, instead of, as he put it, 'the British habit of a glass of port'. The wine was sublime, and it was possible to taste the thousands of layers of fruit and complexity that would have been masked by any form of chilling.

The opposite is often true about red wines. A 'room temperature' red can taste soupy and quickly lose its definition. A brief dunk in an ice-bucket can return a red to a tighter, more balanced state. Do not make the mistake of drinking red wine too warm. There are many reds that actually benefit from being drunk a bit colder than you might expect. All Beaujolais, many Pinot Noirs, most Cabernet Francs, Valpolicella, young Syrah and New World Grenache are but a few of the styles and grapes that appreciate a cooler environment. Even huge, blockbuster reds rarely need true warmth to open up, just air.

A popular expression in the world of wine is 'cellar temperature'. Short of measuring the actual temperature of a cellar, it really is a term for a point somewhere between fridge and room temperature that is the ideal for bottles of wine. If you are lucky enough to have a real cellar under your house, then you will not need to refrigerate many white wines. Some reds will require 'bringing up' to the house to acclimatise for half an hour or so prior to opening, but usually a cellar under a house is not only the best place for your clobber but also, not surprisingly, an excellent place to store wine.

The general rule is that fruity, young reds can be served cooler than big rich styles, and dry whites should not be as cold as sweet whites. The more concentrated a white wine the warmer it can be. Be prepared to leave a white out of the ice-bucket, and use ice for warm reds – topsy-turvy, but essential for the total enjoyment of the bottle from start to finish.

Decanting

Decanting is the process of pouring the wine from one container to another, often with the purpose of leaving any sediment formed in the first container behind. Racking (see Vinification) fulfils the same objectives as decanting, when the contents of one barrel are poured into a fresh barrel, leaving the lees behind.

As far as serving wine is concerned, decanting 'loosens up', warms and opens out red wine, as well as doing the more obvious job of getting rid of sediment. Most red wines that have 'thrown' a sediment require decanting before serving, as the sediment tends to billow in the wine if the bottle is disturbed and this can ruin the taste of the wine. A decanter is usually a glass-stoppered vessel into which wine can be poured for serving. There are many different shapes and sizes of decanter available and antique decanters are immensely collectable items. However, I tend to go for a simple, classic decanter that looks plain and does the job of aerating the wine. I am always terrified of breaking expensive glass and so, to date, my decanter is one of the cheapest as well as the most used gizmos in my kitchen.

In order to decant a bottle of red wine, first stand the bottle upright for at least a day, allowing any sediment to settle. Open the bottle of wine carefully, avoid shaking it, and remove the capsule completely. Get a clean decanter, or other container, for the wine. Then pour the wine slowly and evenly into it. Look through the neck of the bottle at a pale background – or, more traditionally, the flame of a candle – to watch the flow of the wine as it passes by. Stop pouring the second that the sediment, initially sitting at the bottom of the bottle, creeps near to the neck. This takes a little practice but, once proficient, there will only be a little wine left in the bottle with the sediment. If there is no sediment and the purpose of decanting is to let the wine breathe, then there is no need to be so careful, just whack it into the decanter.

Once in the decanter, the wine starts to 'breathe'. This aeration of both red and bigger white wines immediately improves the taste, as well as slightly warming the wine. Pulling the cork on a bottle of wine then letting it sit on the piano in the drawing room for two and a half hours is not always possible. Besides, decanting does the same job in a matter of seconds. Younger wines need to breathe more than old bottles, and very old wines can fall to pieces unless drunk quickly as they over-aerate and become too frail. Decanting is a great way to be able to enjoy wines that ideally, when opened and poured, would taste better the next day. Barolos, Zinfandels and hefty Syrahs are but a few of these monsters who could, if decanted, get the chance to open and approach their optimum flavours by the time you are ready to drink them. Do not be afraid of swirling the wine around the decanter a little, allowing as much surface area as possible to come into contact with the air. If a decanted white gets a little too warm then just pop it into an ice-bucket.

A nice trick along the same lines as ordinary decanting is 'double decanting'. This is decanting from a bottle into a decanter then back into the original bottle. Between decants wash out the sediment from the wine bottle with water. It is then possible to serve the wine in its original bottle, without the danger of any sediment clouding the issue, and it has also had the added benefit of a quick aeration. Double decanting enables the drinker to see the wine label instead of an anonymous decanter. Remember that old red Burgundy is *never* decanted. It is a sort of tradition, because Pinot Noir rarely throws a big sediment, and old Pinot Noir is a delicate sort that may collapse with too much air.

Order of Drinking

If you have lined up a diverse array of wines for dinner, it is important to get the order right, otherwise you may risk overshadowing a wine with the taste of the one drunk before. The order in which to serve wines is similar to that of an organised wine tasting: usually dry before sweet and light before heavy will do the trick. I do not necessarily subscribe to the school of thought that says that whites should be drunk before reds or that old wines should be drunk after young wines. There are many occasions when a light fruity red is a good precursor to a rich oaky white, and also many old bottles of red wine simply cannot follow the power and structure of a young red as the latter's flavour would be too dominant. The best solution to this dilemma is to think through the order of wines for a meal as if you were at a wine tasting (without any food) and ask yourself, would this mean that I could taste each wine one after the other without detracting from their flavours? Then look at your menu and guess at the food and wine compatibility and where the natural breaks for courses would be. Sometimes it may be necessary to drink a wine in between dishes (I fondly refer to this as 'inter-course') if it doesn't seem to work naturally with a dish, or if there is a break in style or grape variety. Good luck – this is a great challenge. Food and wine matching (dealt with later on) and menu planning is an art, and it is also good fun to try and test different combinations and flavours.

Wine Apparatus

None of the following wine paraphernalia is essential, and some are more useful than others – I'm sure you'll spot the silly ones!

Wine storage for expensive wines is often very tricky. Constant temperature, darkness and no vibration can rarely be found in cellarless houses unless you buy a **Eurocave** or other large wine storage cabinet. These not only protect the wines but also have separate sections that can be set at different temperatures. They are expensive but are a worthy addition for the serious collector, and are essential if you are storing fragile old wines. If you live in an apartment (without the luxury of a cellar), they are the only real way you can store wine perfectly.

Another luxury is a **Chilla** or quick-refrigeration machine that will bring down the temperature of a wine in a few minutes. If fridge space is limited, this machine proves invaluable, and is also useful for taking the edge off warm reds. There is a domestic version of this restaurant-designed machine available these days.

Decanting cradles seem to be inexplicably popular with wine lovers. They are very steady decanting machines, which pour a bottle slowly using a screw mechanism. Decanting cradles can be used for old wines or wines with heavy sediment, like port, but are no substitute for a confident, steady hand. They also take ages and look ridiculous.

Drip-stoppers are little collars that can be placed around the neck of a wine bottle, thus preventing dribbles of wine rolling down the outside of a bottle and marking the furniture. This is another crazy invention that does the job, but is no substitute for a little wipe with a cloth.

Wine thermometers are used to detect the temperature of a wine. Do not bother. Use your palate; it is far more sensitive and accurate to the relationship between taste and temperature than a thermometer will ever be. And people will think you are mad if you are seen taking a bottle's temperature.

Foil cutters are a neat gadget for removing the top of a capsule. As I have already mentioned, I prefer to remove the whole thing – but if you have one of these, at least there will be no jagged edges left.

HOW TO STORE WINE

Most wine bought nowadays is consumed within hours of actual purchase (I think the Aussies have the record – it is measured in minutes not hours!). Many people do not have the money or space to buy and store wine, and wine storage, conjuring up images of dark passageways lit only by candlelight, ending at a portcullis behind which piles of wooden cases sleep, is a rare sight. That does not mean that looking after several bottles, or even cases, of wine should be undertaken with any less care than in an imaginary cellar. Storage of wine is a rare art form. Looking after your wine, the stacking or racking of wine, in such a way as to maintain the condition of the wine and facilitate ease of location, is crucial. A cellar book can be used to record details of your collection and will also be useful when making tasting notes.

When finding a place at home to store your wine, bear in mind the following list of requirements. The storage area should be dark, have no vibration, be moderately humid, and have a constant temperature (7°–11°C is ideal). Under the stairs is usually the best place, unless the boiler is there. The cardinal sins are central heating, bright lights, overly dry conditions and lots of vibration – so next to a washing machine would rate as the worst, followed closely by a corner of the kitchen. If the room is light, then keep the wine in its cardboard or wooden case. Many people mistakenly think that their garage is a good place to store wine. However, the temperature range in a garage throughout the year could cause considerable damage to it. Always lie your bottles down to keep the corks moist. Wine racks are now available at any DIY shop or department store, or they can be custom built to fit into awkward places, making the most of your storage space.

It is sometimes possible to store wine with your local merchant, but storage charges will be payable, usually a year in advance.

RESTAURANTS

With such a large choice of wines available these days, it is amazing that so many restaurants have such dreary wine lists. Add to that creative spelling, dubious stock control and the exorbitant mark-ups that some restaurants insist on charging and this makes dining out an expensive and often disappointing pastime. It seems that restaurateurs have forgotten that greediness is all too transparent. With the huge selection of wine available in wine shops and supermarkets, and the consumer's price awareness, it is staggering that some restaurants manage to retain customers at all. The price of a wine on a restaurant wine list should never be more than two and a half times that of the same bottle retail. As a restaurant wine buyer myself, I try to avoid wines that could result in this sort of price comparison, preferring to sniff out more exclusive bottles.

Wine service in restaurants also tends to range from the enthusiastic and helpful to the rude and dismissive. Sommeliers (French for wine-waiters) are a crucial part of the fabric of a restaurant – in fact they will probably visit the table more times than any other member of staff, so it is crucial that a restaurant does not throw away an opportunity to impress customers by having one who is snooty and ill-mannered.

Wine provides the fundamental framework on which to hang the whole evening's event, and not just the food. From an aperitif with which to enliven the palate and peruse the menu, to deciding upon a nice bottle (or bottles) to complement your choice of food, finishing with a sweet wine or digestif, wine is the link between all aspects of the experience of eating out.

Great wine lists should show as much balance as the great

wines on them. From inexpensive to extravagant, light and fresh to huge and brooding, from Aligoté to Zinfandel, wine lists should try to cover as many flavours and styles as possible, taking care to complement the style of food of the establishment. This does not mean that all wine lists have to have hundreds of bins (choices). Far from it. I believe that five white, five red and a few fizzy and sweet wines can do the job, as long as they are chosen with care and represent good value.

Not all restaurants employ sommeliers, as they tend to be the flashy centre forwards of the restaurant world and command pretty stiff salaries. However, if a restaurant does, then the sommelier should be regarded as the salesman for the wine department. It is in their interest that you enjoy what you order, what they recommend. They should never push you into a sale that is inappropriate, and should try hard to match food to wine and keep the price of the bottles within your budget. Nothing is more embarrassing than a sommelier recommending a bottle and you have to admit that you would rather spend half that amount. The sooner you speak up the better. This will not dent your street cred. It should, in fact, galvanise the sommelier into trying to sell you another bottle later.

The most misunderstood part of eating out is the ritual surrounding ordering and tasting the wine. It should be a rock solid process, but sometimes can go horribly wrong. Here is the definitive checklist on what to do and when to do it.

1   Decide on a wine and then keep the wine list open in front of you. You can always point at it if the name looks unpronounceable, or the wine waiter looks a little slow. Sometimes restaurants have 'bin' numbers that help the staff locate the wine, so quote that if you are unsure. Remember the name of the wine and its vintage. There are occasions when a restaurant may have a few different wines with the same name, so check that you have the right one. Some wines can be red, white or rosé, like Sancerre, so again be clear on exactly which wine it is you want. If the list just says 'Sancerre £17.50', it is important to ascertain whose

Sancerre it is (which Domaine or estate) and from what vintage. It could be a young, fresh vintage from a top producer or a tired old Sancerre from Domaine Peint-Strippeur, and you don't want that. You are perfectly entitled to ask to see as many bottles as you like if the wine list does not show the relevant information.

2   The waiter will arrive with the bottle. Check that it is exactly the same one that you ordered before it is opened. If you let the sommelier open the bottle after you have only lazily checked the wine, later to find out that it is not the right one, then you are obliged to pay for it. For some wines you may decide to ask the wine waiter to decant it. Ask this now.

3   The bottle should then be opened carefully at the table. The person who ordered the wine will then be asked if they would like to taste it. Always say yes (even if it is a screwcap-sealed wine, you can still stick to the ritual). The wine waiter will pour a quarter of a glass and let you do your routine. See 'How to taste' for the full version, but usually in a restaurant, as you have ordered the wine and checked that it is the right bottle, there is no need to go into a full-blown ritual of snorting and slurping. Your dinner guests will be parched by now anyway. All that is needed is a quick sniff to check that the wine is not corked or out of condition. You do not even need to sip it. Once done, give a quick nod to the wine waiter to go ahead and pour. The staff will be impressed, as will your guests. If the wine appears to be corked, then reverse the situation and ask the waiter to taste it – this puts the pressure on them to act quickly and find another bottle. If there is any other problem, do speak up. If the bottle is a little too warm or a little too cold, tell the sommelier and they can make provisions.

4   It is important to note that if a second bottle of the same wine is ordered, before topping up the glasses, make sure you taste it in order to check that it is not corked. This way

you will avoid mixing a corked or faulty wine with a good glass, ending up with the whole lot thrown down the sink.

5 If you have enjoyed a sommelier's service, the nicest way to show your appreciation is to allow them to taste a small glass of the wine, particularly if it is an expensive or unusual bottle.

Remember that a wine list, if properly put together, can demonstrate the harmony between the kitchen and the cellar. To the trained eye it can show a degree of collaboration of styles, tastes and flavours. The best restaurants in the world pay as much attention to the wine as they do to their food.

Chapter 5

WINE AND FOOD

This chapter focuses on the wonderful and totally underrated skill of combining the flavours of wine and food. I could go into a huge preamble about not being a dyed-in-the-wool 'red wine with meat' and 'white wine with fish' kind-of-guy, but I won't. Suffice to say that it is totally up to you what you want to drink with your dinner, but some combinations really set off the wine and food partnerships perfectly. I have been a restaurant buyer for over fifteen years and have seen hundreds of cracking food and wine combos on the go. In this chapter I have noted down some of the most successful categories for you to enjoy.

Unusually, instead of listing dishes and their corresponding ideal wines, I have organised this chapter by grape variety. This is in the hope that it might make you choose your wine first and then see what food is available at the market, in order to design your menu. Backwards you say? Not at all – it is always good to get a different perspective, and it will undoubtedly encourage you to build a broader understanding of relationships in flavour between wine and food. Remember that wine and food are designed to go together. Very few wines are genuinely aperitif styles only.

RED GRAPE VARIETIES

Barbera and Pinotage

Both share ripe black fruit characters but an element of rusticity and perky acidity, so they love meaty dishes like **rabbit**, **beef**, **duck** or, perhaps, good quality **sausages** on a barbecue. Both can cope with **red wine gravy** and **roast vegetables** or indeed **pasta**.

Cabernet Franc, Dolcetto and Freisa

An unlikely trio, these grapes all share high acidity. They are all relatively aromatic, but not usually overly alcoholic. Cheeses like **Sainte-Maure de Touraine** or **Port Salut** would work well, as would **moussaka** or classic **roast chicken**. My favourite combination with a young Cabernet Franc from the Loire is **cauliflower cheese**.

Cabernet Sauvignon

Cabernet Sauvignon is a versatile variety and, bearing in mind it comes in all shapes and sizes, depending on the country or region, it can handle almost anything. Traditionally **roast beef**, **Beef Wellington** or **roast lamb** and red Bordeaux is a guaranteed success, making it a Sunday lunch regular. **Game** of all sorts also makes a nice match. However, avoid anything that smells too 'gamey', as there are other varieties that do this job better. Cabernet Sauvignon loves cheese, a young Bordeaux goes well with **Saint-Paulin**, and any 'Old World' Cabernet Sauvignon with **Cheddar**, **Camembert** and **Saint-Nectaire**. I say this, because the juicier and fruitier the wine becomes in hot climates, the less suitable for cheese and the more classically 'meaty' it becomes. **Toad in the hole**, **beef burgers** and **rare steak** are winners with New World Cabernet.

Gamay

Extraordinarily versatile, no wonder this grape is sold in practically every bar and brasserie in Paris. Beaujolais and Gamay de Touraine from the Loire both have pure red berry fruit and refreshing acidity, making food matching relatively straightforward. **Coq au vin**, **roast duck**, **roast chicken** or **turkey**, **ratatouille**, **steak and chips**, **croque monsieur** and 'meaty' fish like **cod** or **hake**, all work well with Gamay, and you can chill it down with a **curry**. Cheese-wise, with **Vacherin du Mont d'Or** is the unbeatable combination.

Grenache, Carignan, Cinsault, Malbec and Mourvèdre

The Rhône team, missing only a few members, are all on the spicy, firm side, save for a few light-coloured Grenache wines that more than make up for it in hidden alcoholic power. **Oxtail**, **full English breakfast** (or brunch!), **toad in the hole**, **cassoulet**, **goulash**, **shepherd's pie**, **Cornish pasty**, **steak-and-kidney pudding**, **casserole** and any other beef options all work in this company – but things get exciting when cheese is mentioned. **Saint-Marcellin** and **Chaumes** love Châteauneuf-du-Pape, Gigondas or, at the cheaper end, reds from the Côtes de Ventoux. Don't forget that Grenache has another side to its character – that of the sweet *Vin Doux Naturel* style. Blue cheeses like **Roquefort** and hard cheeses like **Mimolette** work well with both VDNs, Banyuls and Maury. These two wines also help out the age-old problem of chocolate. **Rich chocolate puddings** like Saint-Emilion au Chocolat, **chocolate truffles** or **chocolate cake** can all breathe a collective sigh of relief.

Merlot

The inbuilt fruitiness of Merlot cannot be ignored when matching it to food. **Beef burgers**, **roast duck**, **barbecued food**, even **chilli con carne**, wallow in the richness of juicy Merlot. But watch out when buying Merlots that you don't end up with a thin, green style, as it will not stand up to food as well as, say, a Chilean Merlot would. Cheeses like **Brillat-Savarin** and **Gratte-Paille** are Right Bank Bordeaux favourites.

Nebbiolo

With a tannic, acidic monster like Nebbiolo, there are very few dishes that can really talk the talk. **Cassoulet**, **venison**, **steak** and **wild boar** would get through unscathed. However, if you have an older bottle of Barolo or Barbaresco, the fruit will have tamed down and then you can follow the Pinot Noir section below.

Pinot Noir

Like Gamay this grape variety loves food, and rarely enjoys being drunk without. Inexpensive red Burgundy goes well with raclette, light Chalonnais wines with **roast chicken** and **coq au vin**, bigger New World offerings and Côte d'Or village wines with **game** (well hung), **beef** (Boeuf à la Bourguignonne – Burgundy Beef!) and **roast duck**. Don't forget rosé Champagne or red Sancerre with cheeses such as **Chaource**. Head back to the minerally Mâconnais and Chalonnais wines and cooler New World offerings, like Tasmania's finest, for **Emmental**, **Tomme de Savoie**, **Brie de Meaux** and **Reblochon**.

Sangiovese

What could be better than classic Italian cooking with the Chianti variety? **Lasagne**, **Spaghetti Bolognese** or **pizza**, as long as it is not a seafood selection, would all work well. Once again this variety has two sides to its character – that of the angry young rebel needing big red meat dishes, and the harmonious middle-aged gent, who complements **mushroom risottos** and **veal** as well as **Parmesan** and **Pecorino**.

Syrah/Shiraz

Another totally foody grape variety that can, this time, take on much heavier dishes. Best end of **lamb**, **steak au poivre**, **cassoulet**, **Stroganoff**, a traditional **mixed grill**, **venison** and **old game birds** – you name it, this grape is not scared. **Brie de Meaux** is the best cheese match.

Touriga Nacional

As this is the port variety, the classic winter combination is **Stilton**. In red wine form, it tackles an exclusively carnivorous diet.

Tempranillo

The Rioja variety behaves much like Pinot Noir when matching to food, so **beef** and **lamb** are the best places to start. It is also a surprising fan of **roast turkey**. The good thing about this grape is that it tends to have lower acidity than its Burgundian pal, so this time it doesn't need to be matched up to such demanding dishes.

Zinfandel

Chocolate once again finds a friend with dense fruit-packed styles of Zin. If you are feeling less ambitious, **duck**, **casseroles**, **crispy duck with hoisin** and any **beef** dish will work well. Follow the Sangiovese guidelines if you feel the need for a challenge.

WHITE GRAPE VARIETIES

Chardonnay

Another grape that has so many guises it can just about cover the whole menu singlehandedly. For **fish and chips** – what a great start – look no further than a crisp unoaked style to work with this favourite. On the fish theme, **fish cakes**, all white fish like **halibut** and **sea bass**, but also **poached salmon** are perfect matches for this versatile variety. Finer white Burgundies love lobster, but don't we all? New World Chardonnays are often on the oaky side, so make sure that the fish dish has enough sauce or at least some rice, pasta or potato to soak up some of this weight. Chablis and unoaked New World Chardonnays enjoy **roast chicken**, and oaked wines, albeit not too dominant, like **roast pork** or **goose**. The unlikely match is cheese. Cheeses such as the stinky **Epoisses** like white Mâconnais wines, **Vacherin du Mont d'Or** can go for Champagne and **Beaufort** loves a glass of Chablis.

Chenin Blanc

In its dry, Old World form, Chenin's acidity is perfect for cutting through any fish dish. New World Chenins, particularly lighter South African versions, lack power and are really only up to lighter **seafood** or **salads**. Richer, oaked styles behave like Chardonnay. When sweet, Chenin Blanc is honeyed and tropical and favours fresh **fruit tarts**, **pastries** and the unexpected classic French combination of a decadent **liver pâté with toasted brioche**.

Gewürztraminer

This lychee-imbued, spicy grape variety is tailor-made to take on the might of the Far East. **Chinese food**, unless it is too 'chilli-hot', is well served with this refreshingly fruity, but beguilingly weighty, variety. Dry Gewürztraminer is a good match with **Pacific Rim dishes**, and back home in Alsace, it is matched up to all manner of **fish** dishes, **terrines** and **savoury tarts**. Gewürz also finds a natural partner in cheeses like **Munster**.

Gros and Petit Manseng

Warranting a special mention, these highly individual oddities are stunning with **fish** dishes, fresh **seafood** and with local cheeses like **Tourmalet** and **Brebis**.

Melon de Bourgogne

The Muscadet variety would get the sack if it didn't complement its local industry – fishing. **Oysters** and *plateau de fruits de mer* including, **crab**, **langoustines**, **clams**, **prawns**, **crevettes**, **lobster**, **winkles** and **whelks** are luckily complemented by this relatively inexpensive white wine that takes the sting out of the bill.

Muscat and Muscadelle

Freezing cold Moscato d'Asti with **strawberries**, Orange Muscat with **chocolate mousse**, Muscat de Rivesaltes with **pear** and **almond tart**, liqueur Muscats for **Christmas pudding** and **sticky toffee pudding** – the huge Muscat family covers a load of bases on the pudding front.

Palomino and Pedro Ximénez

The two sherry varieties are real loners. Purists will tell you that dry sherry is a good match for various soups, whilst PX can only really be poured over **ice cream** or sipped with a caffeine-laden **espresso**. I favour a bowl of really nice **cashews** or **roasted almonds** for the former and a stretcher for the latter.

Pinot Blanc/Pinot Bianco

In the spirit of fair play the PB family does get some recommendations. **Scallops** and **pork** are my ambitious calls of the day, but they have to be twinned with good examples of the wines otherwise it just wouldn't work. If you can only find the light fresh styles then stick to **salads** and thin air.

Riesling and Albariño/Alvarinho

Putting these two together will cause a stir, but Riesling at its lightest is not dissimilar to Albariño and therefore is a good seafood and fish match. Beyond that, the similarity stops and Riesling gets into its stride collecting dishes as it goes: **chicken liver terrine**, **roast ham**, **onion tart**, **duck pâte**, **Chinese food** (although it doesn't go quite as well as Gewürz), lighter **Indian** cooking, any **creamy chicken** dishes, **chicken Kiev** and an all-time favourite *Assiette de Charcuterie* ('plate of meat' doesn't sound half as nice). **Pork** and **veal** are easily manageable. Sweet Rieslings like **fruity puddings** as well as, curiously, **pâté** again – but for my favourite, **rhubarb crumble** would win the award.

Roussanne and Marsanne

The weighty, ponderous white Rhône varieties can handle a surprisingly wide range of food. Following the footsteps of Chardonnay, but not quite as keen on the palate, these are main course wines that flounder a little. **Chicken**, **pork** and **veal**, as well as a large range of fish dishes including **fish and chips**, are all within their grasp. However, lacking the fruit definition of Sauvignon Blanc, they are not particularly refreshing unless Viognier is in the blend, in which case they can match up to a **cold chicken salad**, all **fish dishes** or a **goat cheese salad**. Speaking of cheese, they love **Maroilles**.

Sauvignon Blanc and Aligoté

Sauvignon Blanc makes great food wine that revels in the chance to expose its acidic zip and fresh citrusy flavours. Aligoté lacks the varietal extremes of its friend, but can almost keep up with the dishes. All manner of **pre-dinner nibbles** and **canapés**, **prawn cocktail**, **Caesar salad**, **quiche**, **artichokes**, **deep fried Calamari**, **fresh asparagus**, **avocado** and **corn on the cob** are all too easy. **Chinese** dishes, **Indian food** (hot stuff, too), **oysters**, **crab salad**, **sushi** and **Pacific Rim** cooking with ginger and spices are perfect combinations. New World Sauvignon Blancs, particularly from New Zealand, can really amaze the palate in their effortless handling of complex dishes. Sauvignon Blancs like Sancerre and Cheverny are the benchmark combination for goat's cheeses, like **Crottin de Chavignol**, **Selles-sur-Cher**, and for the good old favourite – a trusty **cheese soufflé**.

Semillon

In dry, Old World form this grape behaves like Chardonnay and so covers much the same ground, although perhaps not quite as competently. New World Semillon is a very different kettle of fish as it is far more tropical and lime-juicy and works well with kettles of **fish** among other things. The increased power and ripeness that the New World can offer, particularly as it is often blended with Chardonnay, means that Semillon is a useful and good value versatile grape. In sweet form Semillon eclipses all others. Sauternes and the like from Bordeaux are spectacular wines that can cope with everything from **foie gras**, through **terrines** of all sorts, to **every pudding** under the sun (except belligerent chocolate). Another surprise is that botrytised Semillon is a magical partner for blue cheese such as **Roquefort**.

Sylvaner

This refreshingly dull grape variety really doesn't like to be troubled with anything too testing on the food front, preferring to have light-weight opposition. Waxy cheeses or barely whiffy offerings like **Tomme de Montagne** will work; otherwise, you are banished to a life of salady obscurity.

Tokay-Pinot Gris/Pinot Gris/Tokay d'Alsace/Pinot Grigio

Think Gewürztraminer meets Riesling, gangs up on Chardonnay and has a fling with Semillon. Well that is what the first three grapes listed above can do in the food department (as they are all different names for the same thing). Pinot Grigio, despite being from the same family as the others, lacks the intensity and mouth-feel of T-PG and it behaves like a slightly skinny Pinot Bianco or Sauvignon Blanc. For that reason I would stick to **antipasti**, **lighter fish dishes** and **salads**. However, T-PG/PG/ Td'A, the Alsatian cruiser-weight, loves **smoked salmon**, almost all **starters**, **chicken**, **Thai food**, **creamy sauces**, cheeses like **Munster**, all **pâtés** and countless other delights. In sweet form, *Vendange Tardive*, it relishes the opportunity to work with cheeses like **Livarot**, and **fresh fruit puddings**.

Ugni Blanc/Trebbiano

The Mr Boring of the wine world still manages to crack a smile with some dishes, and the dryness and zingy character of both French Ugni Blancs and Italian Trebbianos are the mainstay café house wines in their respective countries. Good combos are **asparagus**, **tomato salads**, **cold chicken**, **goat's cheese**, and anything fresh and vegetabley.

Viognier

The sultry diva Viognier, despite an actively aromatic nose, likes **Asian-influenced dishes** if not quite the genuine article, cheese like **Pont-l'Evêque** and **fish dishes** that don't test it too hard. An all-round lunchtime winner, this grape can only start to cope with bigger and more flavoursome dishes when it reaches its upper end of the price scale. Condrieu and the like, from the Northern Rhône, are fiendishly expensive but are sublime with fish dishes. In the New World, Viognier is often blended with Chardonnay, or Marsanne and Roussanne when the weight of these three make it a bit more of an all-rounder – then **roast ham**, **goose** and **chicken** all work very well.

Chapter 6

WINE REGIONS OF THE WORLD

This is a massive chapter and one I hope you will flick through over and over again to find yet more estates, wineries and Domaines with which to challenge and reward your palate. Only by jumping around wines and keeping your dinner guests guessing can you really expand your wine knowledge and cater to your complex wine diet. This chapter is the key – use it!

ARGENTINA

There is one key region in Argentina where the vast majority of the best wines are made – Mendoza. It is here that the mighty red grape Malbec does its stunning thing. In fact, this is where the best Malbec is grown in the world. Indigenous variety Bonarda also pops up, making juicy, inexpensive, but interesting, blueberry-soaked reds. Of course, the world-famous stalwarts Cabernet, Merlot and Syrah also gatecrash this party. Tempranillo, the Rioja variety, loves Argentina's hot climate, presumably keeping its cool with an irrigated glass of Andes water in the evenings! White-wise, local favourite Torrontés makes tangy, fresh spritzy, early-drinking whites. Forward and inexpensive, these are great summer party wines. Chardonnay and a host of other world varieties are also planted, but I wouldn't venture too far off piste in search of these wines. My advice is to use Argentina for its three best suits – Malbec, Bonarda and Torrontés, as they are unique on the world stage. If you must drink Cab, Chard or any of the other international grapes, stick to the estates below and you should end up with a worthy 'New World' style wine (more often than not, lacking in true regional authenticity), but it won't necessarily trump equivalent wines from other countries. Argentina has come a long way in the last decade and full-bodied, carnivorous reds are definitely its strong suit. While many may currently appear coarse, a little too muscular and overoaked, this recipe will, I have no doubt, be refined in the near future. Couple this with some serious investment flooding into the country, and a host of smarty pants winemakers clocking up some serious air miles, and things are looking good. With cheap land and labour and perfect sun and soil, there is all to play for. Watch this space – there are already some cracking wines out there and there will be more and more coming on stream soon.

The best producers are: Anubis, Argento, Bodega Noemía de Patagonia, Catena Zapata (Catena), Clos de los Siete, Familia Zuccardi (La Agricola), Finca El Retiro, Norton, Santa Julia, Terrazas, Valentin Bianchi and Weinert.

AUSTRALIA

I travel to Australia two or three times every year, so crucial is this country's wine production to the world wine market and, more importantly, to my own wine writing (and consumption!). Australia is the number one wine supplier to the UK – a remarkable achievement in a very short space of time. This colossal business is driven by millions of cases of some of the most robust (price/quality ratio) wines in the modern world. These are made by some of the most professional, large brands – Jacob's Creek, Hardy's – on the planet. As a result of this success, Australia has an amazing base from which to launch more serious and interesting wines on the consumer. This must surely be the next stage of the Grand Plan. Getting a place on smart restaurant wine lists and pushing wine lovers up and over the five pound mark is paramount. Once wine lovers start to experiment with finer Australian wines, I am certain they will not look back. I believe that great Australian wine starts at as little as £6.99 on UK shelves – this is truly impressive. Very few countries in the world have the breadth of styles and quality of wines that Australia does at this level – but tweak the spend a touch more up to ten pounds, and I am certain I can blow your mind. At the very top end, however, France still controls the purse strings – prestige Champagne, red Bordeaux and red Burgundy are three areas where they reign supreme in people's minds. Granted Australia makes smart fizz, terrific Cabernets and increasingly elegant Pinot Noirs, but they are unlikely to worry the likes of Dom Pérignon, Château Latour and Domaine de la Romanée Conti in my lifetime. Having said this, if you put the very best Rhône varietals on the bench and stick them up against Shiraz or Shiraz blends from Down Under, or for that matter a handful of top white Burgundies versus a run of Aussie Chardonnays, you will be nothing short of amazed. Sauvignon Blanc is being perfected, Semillon is already there, and if you are serious about Riesling then you are in for a memorable ride. I believe that Australian Riesling is one of the strongest categories in the world.

Add all of this together and I am continually amazed at the breadth, quality and variety of wines on offer from this idyllic country. So how do they do it? The answer is that there is a drive and determination about Australian winemakers that is absolutely invigorating. In order to sell their wines they are obliged to travel all over the world. Their thirst for world food and wine culture is absolutely insatiable and, as a result, they head home packed with ideas, which they immediately implement and consequently make better and better wines. This passion and fervour is mesmerising. I don't see this hunger for improvement and development anywhere else in the world.

The current vogue in Australia is the emergence of wines from cooler climate regions. These embody finesse and elegance (copying the Old World models), so you can at last begin to wave goodbye to big, overblown, oaky Chardonnays of yesteryear. Even the famous, huge, porty red wines of the Barossa Valley are being pegged back for fine-tuning – lowering alcohol levels and endeavouring to introduce less barrel influence to the resulting wines. When century-old wine regions like Barossa listen, you can be sure the message is getting through.

You can now drink world-class Cabernet, Shiraz, Chardonnay and Riesling at reasonable prices from this winemaking utopia. What follows is a breakdown of the main regions, and for each a list of the wineries which will not let you down. I drink more Australian wine at home than wine from any other country, with France a close second. These two account for well over two-thirds of my wine diet. They should be up around this mark for you too.

Western Australia (WA)

With a superb climate, somewhat cooler than the rest of Australia but warm in European terms, Western Australia is a wine drinker's paradise. It is split into four main regions, the hottest and driest being the **Swan Valley/Perth Hill**s area. Situated inland from Perth, several wineries make good value wines here, with Houghton's being my favourite. Drive 90 miles south from Perth and you'll reach a new region, **Geographe**, which sits on top of its more famous neighbour **Margaret River**. Home to a handful of wineries, this region is centred on Bunbury, with Shiraz and Semillon being my picks of the grapes planted. World-class wines rear their heads in Margaret River (170 miles south of Perth, abutting Geographe). With a unique climate, on account of its curious oblong shape which juts out into the ocean, this is the place to be in WA. With bodies of water on three sides, the microclimates here range from positively hot in the north to chilly and windy in the south. Its climate is often mistakenly compared to that of Bordeaux, but, as Denis Horgan of the world-famous winery Leeuwin Estate so eloquently put it, 'The heat gets turned on earlier and off later.' This supposedly cool region is warm enough to make some of the nicest Cabernet Sauvignons in Australia. With over 100 wineries in Margaret River, it still only makes up less than 1 per cent of Australia's wine production. Having said that, in quality terms this is up there with some of the finest and most beautiful wine regions in the entire wine world. First planted in the early 1970s, most of the wineries are situated within five miles of the coast, around the various brooks that flow into the sea. As far as whites are concerned, Semillon (and Sem/Sauv blends) and Chardonnay do extremely well. Pierro, Cullen and Leeuwin make some of Australia's top Chardonnays, and in world terms these are fantastic value wines. Cabernet is the main red focus and these wines are very highly sought after. The flavours cover all of the bases that Bordeaux manages, but with the warmer climate the vintages tend to be more reliable and, accordingly, the wines are more approachable in their youth. Dripping with class, the top few estates make Cab that stands shoulder to shoulder with anything the New World can offer and can beat all but the very top echelon of red Bordeaux. Merlot, Cabernet Franc and Shiraz appear as well, but in much smaller quantities and only really serve to offer a bit of variety.

The Great Southern area of WA encompasses five particularly interesting sub-regions – **Mount Barker**, **Frankland River**, **Porongurup**, **Denmark** and **Albany**. With around fifty wineries, this is a busy part of WA, but there is very little volume here. The main thrust is Riesling for the whites and Cabernet and Shiraz for the reds. I have tasted very good examples of each of these varieties and a few Sauvignon Blancs look good, too.

There are two other regions of note on the southwestern tip

of Australia. Manjimup has a slightly more continental climate than Margaret River and it is also a little higher. Chardonnay, Cabernet and Merlot all perform well, but perhaps with less overt quality and vintage reliability than say Margaret River. **Pemberton**, south of Manjimup, is cooler and has more rainfall than its neighbour, and is better suited to Pinot Noir and Chardonnay, as well as the ever-present Bordeaux varieties.

All in all, WA is a region to follow.

> **The best producers in Western Australia are:** Alkoomi (F), Amberley (MR), Ashbrook Estate (MR), Brookland Valley (MR), Cape Mentelle (MR), Cullen (MR), Devil's Lair (MR), Evans & Tate (MR), Ferngrove (F), Forest Hill (D), Frankland Estate (F), Garlands (MB), Goundrey (MB), Houghton (S), Howard Park (MR), Juniper Estate (MR), Leeuwin Estate (MR), Millbrook (SP), Moss Wood (and second label Ribbon Vale) (MR), Picardy (M), Pierro (MR), Plantagenet (MB), Suckfizzle Augusta (and second label Stella Bella) (MR), Vasse Felix (MR), Voyager (MR), West Cape Howe (D), Wignalls (A), Willow Bridge (G) and Xanadu (MR).

> Key: (A) – Albany, (D) – Denmark, (F) – Frankland, (G) – Geographe, (MB) – Mount Barker, (MR) – Margaret River, (M) – Manjimup, (P) – Pemberton, (SP) – Swan Valley/Perth Hills.

South Australia

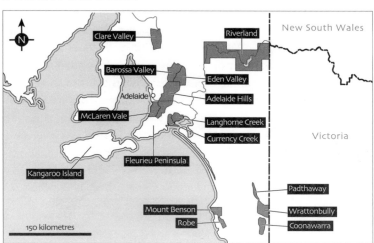

Nearly half of Australia's wine production comes from the state of South Australia. The headquarters of most of Australia's largest wineries are based here as well. The climate varies from region to region, with Riverland at one extreme being very hot, and Coonawarra and Adelaide Hills, among others, being much cooler.

The **Clare Valley**, in the far north of South Australia (75 miles from Adelaide), is our starting point. With over 150 years of continuous vine growing, Clare has a warm, sunny climate and refreshingly cool afternoon breezes. This, coupled with good altitude (around the 400–520m mark) and cold nights, makes Clare home to some of the finest wines in Australia. Clare does not have the starry profile and glitzy tourist allure of the Barossa Valley or the hippy chic of McLaren Vale and, being a bit of a hike from Adelaide, it doesn't have the footfall of visitors either. In essence Clare has an agricultural feel, with only a handful of hotels and restaurants. Having said this, it is a wonderful wine region where the people are close to the soil and work extremely hard at what they do. Cellar door tastings are, more often than not, hosted by family members and not corporate employees, and this authenticity, commitment and skill show in the wines. Home to Australia's most famous and awesome-value dry Rieslings, Clare provides wines that are a cornerstone in my wine diet. Magnificently balanced and age-worthy, and crackling with limejuice and verve, they drink beautifully in their youth but run and run if you let them – ten years is a doddle for these stunning wines. I also adore Clare Shiraz (and Cabernet for that matter), as it shows control, balance and complexity – this can't be said for your average Aussie Shiraz! This may be a region that flies under the radar but is an integral and essential part of any serious wine list or collection. Clare wines are fantastic value for money, exceptionally age-worthy and totally and utterly unique.

The best producers in Clare Valley are: Annie's Lane, Cardinham, Clos Clare, Crabtree, Eldredge, Grosset, Jeanneret, Jim Barry, Kilikanoon, Knappstein, Leasingham, Mitchell, Mount Horrocks, Neagles Rock, O'Leary Walker, Paulett, Petaluma, Pikes, Reilly's, Sevenhill, Skillogalee, Taylors (Wakefield in the UK), Tim Adams, Two Fold and Wendouree.

The **Barossa Valley** is one of the most famous wine regions in Australia. It's a warm region that produces powerful, spicy red wines, with a good capacity for ageing. The favoured grapes here are the meaty trio of Shiraz, Grenache and Mourvèdre. Ancient bush vines (many are well over 100 years old and unirrigated) abound in Barossa and it is these grandfathers of the wine world that have made these wines so intense and sought after. Cabernet Sauvignon is also widely planted and, while the spotlight is on the Shiraz wines and its SGM blends, Cabernet is responsible for some stellar wines, too. Most estates make a Riesling and Semillon as well, so it's not all blockbuster reds, and these can be sourced either from the valley itself or, more often than not, from the neighbouring, high-altitude region of Eden Valley. The inky, rich, high-alcohol Barossan reds, typified by the wines from Penfolds, Peter Lehmann and Yalumba, are legendary. However, things are changing – there is a move to lower alcohol levels through judicious viticulture; take the foot off the oak a little and allow the fruit to be heard and blend more – after all, Shiraz loves the company of Grenache, Mourvèdre and Cabernet. This all looks good for the future and, with a run of cracking vintages so far in the twenty-first century, the Barossa Valley is set to continue in its position of King of Oz.

> **The best producers in Barossa Valley are:** Barossa Valley Estate, Burge Family Winemakers, Charles Cimicky, Charlie Melton, Chateau Tanunda, Craneford, Elderton, Fox Gordon, Glaetzer, Grant Burge, Greenock Creek, Haan, Heritage, Hobbs, Kaesler, Leo Buring, Massena, Murray Street Vineyards, Orlando (Jacobs Creek), Penfolds, Peter Lehmann, Rockford, Rolf Binder Wines, Rusden, Saltram, St Hallett, Seppelt, Spinifex, Standish Wine Co., Teusner, Thorn-Clarke, Tin Shed, Torbreck, Turkey Flat, Two Hands, Willows, Wolf Blass and Yalumba.

The **Eden Valley**, which rubs shoulders with the Barossa and actually falls under its jurisdiction, is, geographically, a completely different proposition. Much cooler due to its altitude (380m at the warmer north end and 500m at the southern cooler end), Eden is, as the name suggests, a lovely place to grow grapes.

Riesling (running a close second to Clare's supremacy with this variety) favours the higher ground and its cooler evenings, and the reds (mainly Shiraz and Cabernet) are grown further north in the warmer areas around Keyneton, where Henschke's Hill of Grace vineyard resides. The big names in this pretty part of SA making stellar reds are Henschke, Irvine and Yalumba. Yalumba's own labels, Heggies and Pewsey Vale, are both top Rieslings along with Barossa-based Orlando's epic Steingarten and Penfolds' heavenly Leo Buring Leonay.

The best producers in Eden Valley are: Heggies (Yalumba), Henschke, Irvine, Mesh (Grosset & Hill Smith) and Pewsey Vale (Yalumba).

There are very few wine regions in the world as beautiful as the **Adelaide Hills**. Only twenty minutes out of downtown Adelaide, climbing up to a height of between 400 and 500m, this is cool-climate viticulture at its sexiest. Adjoining Eden Valley to the north, running into the northern tip of McLaren Vale in the south, and with views of the ocean and/or rolling hills from every vantage point, this is heaven. The difference in temperature between downtown and the 'Hills' can be over 10°C! This means that more sensitive varieties can be grown up here – Sauvignon, Chardonnay, aromatic varieties like Riesling and Pinot Gris, and Pinot Noir are the prime candidates. Warmer vineyard sites can handle Shiraz and even Cabernet – and they result in wines with elegance, herbal lift and definition. These are European-shaped wines and they inevitably find their way on to the smartest wine lists in Australia. With Chardonnay and Pinot Noir in the ground, it is no surprise that fizz is made up here, too. With over fifty small operations crammed into the folds in the Hills and only a short hop from the vibrant city of Adelaide, this is a wonderful place for a wine-tasting holiday.

The best producers in Adelaide Hills are: Ashton Hills, Barratt, Chain of Ponds, Geoff Weaver, The Lane (Edwards Family), Nepenthe, Petaluma, Shaw & Smith and TK (Tim Knappstein Lenswood Vineyard).

North-west of the Hills, heading towards the Gulf of St Vincent, are the **Adelaide Plains**. Home to one top-quality winery, Primo, and a handful of other lesser-known estates, this is a hot-temperature, low-rainfall region which, in general, makes rather ordinary wine.

> **The best producers in Adelaide Plains are:** Primo Estate and Wilkie.

Like Clare, **McLaren Vale**, keeps a relatively low profile considering its awesome quality wines. Half an hour south of Adelaide city and bounded on the east by the Adelaide Hills, McLaren Vale has a wonderful, moderating maritime climate (and some of the most beautiful beaches I have ever seen). Shiraz, Cabernet and Grenache are responsible for the best reds – and this is very much a premium red-wine region. Sauvignon, Semillon, Chardonnay, Riesling and Viognier (in the coolest sites) do quite well, too. With wonderful balance and less heat and power than most Barossa reds, McLaren Vale's finest really register on my Richter scale. The chassis is European and the fruit New Worldy, and it is this wicked balance that ensures I drink a load of these reds over the course of the year. They are still underrated (price-wise). Follow my list of estates below and you will be in for a real treat.

> **The best producers in McLaren Vale are:** Bosworth, Cascabel, Chalk Hill, Chapel Hill, Chateau Reynella (Hardys), Clarendon Hills, Coriole, d'Arenberg, Fox Creek, Gemtree, Geoff Merrill, Hardys Tintara, Hastwell & Lightfoot, Hoffmann's, Kangarilla Road, Kay Brothers Amery, Koltz, Linda Domas, Mitolo, Noon, Oliver's Taranga, Pertaringa, Pirramimma, Richard Hamilton, Rosemount (McLaren Vale), Simon Hackett, Tatachilla, Ulithorne, Wirra Wirra and Woodstock.

Heading further down the Fleurieu Zone (40 miles from Adelaide), you come across four more wine sub-regions – **Langhorne Creek**, **Currency Creek**, **Southern Fleurieu** and **Kangaroo Island**. Langhorne is stuffed with big company money, grinding out Shiraz and Cabernet to blend into varietal wines. There are also a few smaller operations making nice enough wines, but I am more of a McLaren Vale fan. Currency Creek, surrounding the holiday destinations of Goolwa and Port Elliot, is a mini version of Langhorne. Unless you're living in or on hols in Oz, the Southern Fleurieu and Kangaroo Island won't be part of your wine diet yet.

Miscellaneous estates of quality are: Ballast Stone (Currency), Bleasdale (Langhorne), Brothers in Arms (Langhorne), Heartland (Limestone Coast/Langhorne) and Zonte's Footsteps (Langhorne).

Further afield, some 230 miles south of Adelaide, you'll find **Coonawarra** – the founding father (and big daddy) of the group of Limestone Coast regions. Famous for its 'terra rossa' (red earth) soils and its terrific Cabernet Sauvignons, Coonawarra is a must if you are a fan of this noble red grape. Intense blackcurrant flavours and a eucalyptus and mint nose are the hallmarks of Coonawarra Cabernet. Shiraz is also grown to a very high standard and there are even a few worthy whites down here as well. **Padthaway**, **Mount Benson**, **Robe** and **Wrattonbully** are the names of four other regions here and each of them is championed, in some way, by a large company (Lindeman's, Stonehaven, Hardys, Yalumba etc.) and a handful of smaller ones. There are few unmissable wines from these regions, as the majority of the fruit ends up in multi-regional blends. One noteworthy exception to this is the stunning debut 2003 vintage from Tapanappa in Wrattonbully, which shows that, if you pick the right vineyard site and work extremely hard, you can make a world-class wine.

The best estates in Coonawarra are: Balnaves, Bowen, Brand's, Highbank, Hollick, Jamiesons Run, Katnook, Ladbroke Grove, Leconfield, Lindemans, Majella, Parker, Penley, Redman, Wynns and Yalumba.

Riverland is worthy of a short mention, as it is the baking hot region 140 miles inland from Adelaide on the banks of the Murray River. This is where tons of bulk wines are made. Banrock Station and Angoves are here, among others, and it is no surprise that Chard, Shiraz and Cab are the most-planted varieties.

Victoria

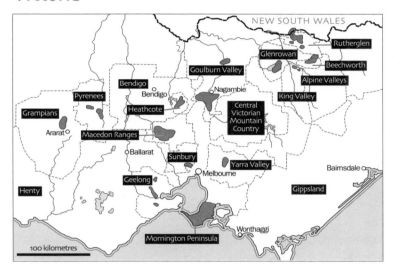

Extraordinarily complicated and with more wineries than South Australia, Victoria takes a while to get your head around. The list of my favourite wineries tacked on to each of its regions should ease the pain.

The **Yarra Valley**, 25 miles from Melbourne, where Pinot Noir and Chardonnay are king and queen, is a very popular tourist destination for city daytrips. With a climate somewhere between Burgundy and Bordeaux, this is regarded as a cool-climate region. I have a suspicion that, given time, its Pinot will not quite hit the heights of some of the other regions in Victoria, but that the Shiraz will do extremely well in coming years. The Yarra also makes some great fizz and a wide range of other varieties (Cabernet, Roussanne, Marsanne etc.), usually championed by artisanal, perfectionist wineries.

Mornington Peninsula is a very chichi region, packed with massive houses and helicopter landing pads. This is where loaded Melbournites head for the weekend. Once again, this is a cool-climate region and so Pinot Noir, Chardonnay and Pinot Gris all do very well here. There is a slight element of Emperor's New Clothes about Mornington, as there are more than seventy producers packed into this small region, but only a handful make my top selection.

It is just a short ferry ride across the water from the Mornington Peninsula to the Bellarine Peninsula and the **Geelong** wine region. This region is the other 'jaw bone' that makes up Melbourne's mouth – Port Philip Bay. On a clear day you can see the city glinting in the distance. Not surprisingly this is another windy, maritime-influenced wine region. Once again, because it's cooler, Chardonnay and Pinot Noir are the grapes of choice. Shiraz (and even Cabernet) does much better here than in Mornington, particularly in sheltered vineyards and with warmer vintages.

Go 30 miles northwest of Melbourne and you find the **Macedon Ranges**. Famed for Chardonnay and Pinot Noir, and in particular for its sparkling wine production, this is a hilly, relatively high-altitude region and it is peppered with interesting, small, boutique wineries. As always Shiraz pops up and this time makes a Rhôney, peppery style.

> **The best producers in the Macedon Ranges are:** Bindi, Cobaw Ridge, Domaine Epis, Hanging Rock and Virgin Hills.

The tiny region of **Sunbury** is about a quarter of an hour past the airport (Tullamarine) on the way out of Melbourne – it is the closest wine region to the city centre. There is only one winery here that has rocked my world – Craiglee. With a superb Chardonnay and a stunning Shiraz, Pat Carmody leads the pack, showing that fully ripe, totally complex, age-worthy wines can be made at moderate alcohol levels.

In the western Victoria zone, **Grampians** is the new name for the Great Western region. This is a beautiful region with three amazing wineries. Shiraz is the main deal here, but not big bold Shiraz, rather peppery, herbal, black-fruit-soaked wines. Best's, set up in 1867, is one of the iconic wineries in Australia. The original plantings still produce wine, and I was amazed at the ancient cellar, where the wines still age today like they did back then.

> **The best producers in Grampians are:** Best's Great Western, Mount Langi Ghiran and Seppelt Great Western.

Just to the east of Grampians is the **Pyrenees** region. Small, perfectly formed and blessed with some star estates, this is a cool but sunny red-wine region, focusing on Shiraz, Cabernet Sauvignon, Merlot and Pinot Noir. For the record, I think that Dalwhinie is one of my favourite estates in the world – small, dramatic vineyards, an awesome, one-room, space-age winery and sensational wines!

> **The best producers in Pyrenees are:** Dalwhinnie, Redbank and Taltarni.

Henty is a region I have not yet visited, but I know the wines from one of its most famous estates – Crawford River. In the far southwestern corner of Victoria, with Coonawarra not that far away over the border in SA, the plantings are tiny but, it is said, the potential is enormous. The aforementioned Crawford River makes unmissable wines – try and find the dry and sweet Rieslings.

Bendigo is situated to the east of Pyrenees and it has, in the past, happily surfed along nurturing a growing reputation for fine wines. That was until Heathcote was granted its own autonomy and a few of the star estates were lost. The remaining estates continue to make Shiraz, Cabernet, Chardonnay and Riesling to a high standard.

The best producers in Bendigo are: Balgownie, Passing Clouds, Pondalowie and Water Wheel.

Next door, stand alone **Heathcote** has been the proud owner of some serious street cred since 2003, when it broke away from Bendigo, and a few very smart wineries now carry the banner for this region, making wondrous, peppery, moreish styles of Shiraz.

The best producers in Heathcote are: Heathcote Winery, Jasper Hill, Mount Ida, Tyrrell's (Heathcote Shiraz) and Wild Duck Creek.

The **Goulburn Valley** and its **Nagambie Lakes** sub-region are home to some superstar estates. Here Tahbilk has its world-famous 1860 vineyard which, I have to say, looks in very good nick to me – and the wine is phenomenal, too. Shiraz, Cabernet, Chardonnay, Riesling and the Rhôney white varieties Marsanne, Roussanne and Viognier are all doing well here. The vast majority of these wines are also very good value because they haven't attracted the label hunters yet.

The best producers in Goulburn and Nagambie Lakes are: David Traeger, McPherson, Mitchelton and Tahbilk.

Rutherglen is a northeastern Victorian wine region that gives me goosebumps just thinking about it! It is home to the most hypnotic of after-dinner tipples – Liqueur Muscats and Tokays. There are three levels of fortified wine in Rutherglen – Rutherglen

Muscat, Classic and Rare. You simply must taste these wines. They make port, sherry and Madeira look positively sheepish. With phenomenal power and length on the palate, and very good value for money bearing in mind just how old some of these wines are, this is a name to remember. **Glenrowan** is a separate region, but it does exactly the same thing (all bar the obvious one below are from Rutherglen).

The best producers in Rutherglen are: All Saints, Baileys of Glenrowan, Campbells, Chambers Rosewood, Morris, Rutherglen Estates and Stanton & Killeen.

The **King Valley**, in northeast Victoria is home to one very famous name, Brown Brothers. It is also a great source of fruit for sparkling wines as some of the vineyards are very high indeed. **Beechworth** to the east of the King Valley was put on the map by Giaconda. This superstar estate makes one of Australia's finest Chardonnays. They also make a stellar Pinot, an awesome Cab, a frightening good Shiraz and a very sexy Roussanne! Sorrenberg, just up the road makes excellent Chardonnay, too, and one of Australia's funkiest Gamays. Battely's and Castagna's Shirazes and Savaterre's Chardonnay are another three great Beechworth wines. Oh, by the way, all of these are terrifyingly expensive!

We have almost completed our clockwise (albeit disjointed) circuit around Victoria and **Gippsland** is the last of the main regions worthy of a mention. It is here that the delightful Phillip Jones, of Bass Phillip, fashions the most extraordinary and collectable Pinot Noirs.

The only other region is way up in the northwest corner of Victoria, straddling the state boundary with New South Wales. **Murray Darling**, centred on Mildura, is another huge area, and combined with **Swan Hill** to the east they make up nearly 40 per cent of the country's crush. Names like Andrew Peace, Deakin Estate, Lindemans' Karadoc winery, Trentham, Zilzie, Simeon, McWilliams, Mildara Blass and Hardys are all up here.

This might not be a beautiful part of the world, but it is a very important one.

Tasmania

Tasmania is split into two distinct regions – northern Tassy around the delightful town of Launceston and southern Tassy surrounding the main city of Hobart. Chardonnay and Pinot Noir are the stars here, with Riesling, Pinot Gris and Gewürz doing a good job, too. Tasmanian sparkling wines – clean, dry, complex and very affordable – are doing awfully well in the world market, but it is the Pinots that we are all obsessed with. Victoria may do a good job with this variety, as do a handful of winemakers in the Adelaide Hills, but with the chilly Tasmanian climate, ample rainfall and fleeting moments of sunshine, Pinot must think it's back home in Burgundy, it's performing so well here! For every rule there is an exception and the Coal River area in the south is home to Domaine A who make awesome Cabernet and Merlot – just proves you can do anything if you select the correct site and work like a demon!

The best producers in Tasmania are: Andrew Pirie, Apsley Gorge, Bay of Fires, Chatto, Clover Hill, Craigow, Domaine A (and Stoney Vineyard), Elsewhere, Freycinet, Grey Sands, Jansz, No Regrets, Pipers Brook (and Ninth Island), Providence, Spring Vale, Stefano Lubiana, Tamar Ridge and Touchwood.

New South Wales

The **Hunter Valley**, 80 miles north of Sydney, is NSW's most famous region. For the past decade, the Hunter has been a massive tourist destination and New South Wales's more important wine producer. However, there are a few other very smart areas that are rapidly challenging Hunter's divine right for the limelight – but before I tell you about these, let's get stuck into the venerable old dear herself.

The **Lower Hunter** is a bizarre place. It is a very marginal wine region – bloody awful weather more often than not! – but despite this, it churns out one of Australia's most famous and multi-award-winning wine styles – dry Semillon. There is some useful Shiraz here, if the rain holds off at harvest time, and a few other grapes (Chard and Cab) are planted, too, with varying success. Now golf courses, hotels, restaurants, and some of the world's most important studs (horses!) all rub shoulders with acres of picturesque vineyards. Hunter Semillon is a must in your wine diet. It is more often than not unoaked and eminently age-worthy. Think nothing of opening up a ten-year-old wine.

> **The best producers in the Lower Hunter are:** Allandale, Bimbadgen, Brokenwood, Glenguin, Keith Tulloch, Lake's Folly, Lindemans, McGuigan, McWilliam's/Mount Pleasant, Meerea Park, Tempus Two, Tower Estate and Tyrrell's.

The **Upper Hunter Valley** is famous for one winery only, and it is a biggy – Rosemount. I could not believe the size of the tank farm at Denman when I first visited Rosemount a few years ago. In **Mudgee**, where Rosemount also sources grapes (actually it takes them from all over Oz), there are loads of smaller wineries, who, on the whole, don't see much action on the export market. Not surprisingly Chardonnay, Semillon, Shiraz and Cabernet are responsible for the main action. Huntington Estate and Simon Gilbert are my two picks from this 'nest in the hills' – the Aborigine translation for Mudgee. I will rather rudely jump over **Cowra** as I have never been particularly wowed by any of the wines from this region. Warmer and lower than Mudgee or Orange, this region's wines shouldn't be troubling your wine rack in the near future. One region which is causing a huge stir is **Orange**. This is high-altitude winemaking – 600–1,000m. As the expression goes, 'Orange starts where Adelaide Hills stops.' This is what the Orange dwellers are singing and they are insinuating that, not only is the region closer to God – literally – but they think the wines will end up being finer, too! Chardonnay, Sauvignon Blanc, Shiraz, Cabernet and Merlot are all looking smart up here. The higher you go the less likely the reds will ripen, but if you push the vines and have a magical touch, the resulting wines will be more edgy and elegant. This is a beguiling region that I am following closely. Certainly top end restaurants in Sydney are snapping up small estate wines like Smarties.

> **The best producers in Orange are:** Bloodwood, Brangayne, Cumulus and Logan Wines.

Riverina – also known as **Griffith** and the **Murrumbidgee Irrigation Area (MIA)** – is 400 miles southwest of Sydney, 200 miles west of Canberra and only 300 miles north of Melbourne (i.e. in the middle of nowhere!) and this is where a load of the big companies make some of the bottom end, supermarket wines. Casella, Cranswick, McWilliams, Miranda, Orlando and Southcorp all hang out here. There are only two smaller companies to send a search party out for: Lillypilly Estate with their superb Tramillon (a Traminer/Semillon blend) and De Bortoli's sensational, Sauternes-style, botrytised Semillon: Noble One – this is Australia's most-celebrated and, more often than not, finest sweetie. **Canberra District** is somewhere I have yet to visit, so I can't give you the lowdown on the topography, but I will definitely be heading there soon, as they have two stunning estates making sensational wines – Clonakilla (Shiraz and Viognier experts) and Lark Hill (Pinot and Chardonnay).

We are not finished yet, but in a way we have already covered all the significant bases, because **Shoalhaven Coast**, **Tumbarumba**, **Hilltops**, **Cowra**, **Hastings River**, **Southern Highlands**, **Gundagai**, **Perricoota** and even Queensland's **Granite Belt**, **South Burnett** and **Queensland Coastal** regions may be up and running, but they don't trouble the top scorers at the moment. However, there are murmurings – every time I head down to Australia, I hear that the next big thing is just around the corner, and who am I to argue with that?

This country is moving at such a pace that I am blown away every time I get off the plane. This is what makes Australia such a wondrous wine producer and an essential part of my wine diet.

AUSTRIA

Austria somehow always seems to come up smelling of roses (or Riesling, or whatever). Despite scandals, minuscule production (as far as the wine world is concerned) and astronomic prices (as far as the known solar system is concerned), they nonchalantly crack on regardless. Austria is blessed with wave upon wave of funky Riesling and Grüner Veltliner, now shipped abroad in relatively meaningful quantities. The old gripes still exist – namely, distribution is poor and prices are terrifying – but if you are into fit, energetic dry Rieslings and spicy, floral Grüner Veltliners, then you will have to spend some money here. I drink a few botts every so often, just to fulfil my insatiable thirst for gorgeous Riesling. Lately there have been a few cheaper, second labels emerging from some of my chosen producers, so I am able to impress my friends with a Grüner or two. The question is, do they rush out the next day and try to buy one? I am not convinced.

> **The top producers are:** Alois Kracher, Bründlmayer, Emmerich Knoll, Feiler-Artinger, Franz Hirtzberger, Fred Loimer, Freie Weingärtner Wachau, Graf Hardegg, G & H Heinrich, Helmut Lang, Hiedler, Höpler, Josef Pöckl, Jurtschitsch, Manfred Tement, Paul Achs, F X Pichler, Polz, Prager, Salomon, Schloss Gobelsburg, Sepp Moser, Velich, Wieninger, Willi Opitz and Dr Wolfgang Unger.

CANADA

Canada has two main winemaking regions, **Ontario** and **British Columbia**. While very few examples of Canadian wine are readily available outside Canada, some do creep through. Steer clear of red wines in general, as they tend to be green and lack fruit. Light whites are well made, particularly Chardonnays and Pinot Blancs, and ice wines are a special favourite. Unlike in Germany, where the required climatic conditions (snow and freezing temperatures) only happen in certain vintages, the icy weather in Canada arrives like clockwork. Don't go for the Vidal grape varieties though (it always has a funky nose in my opinion), stick to Riesling.

The top producers are: Burrowing Owl, Cave Springs, Château des Charmes, Daniel Lenko, Henry of Pelham, Inniskillin, Mission Hill, Paradise Ranch, Quails' Gate, Southbrook Farms, Sumac Ridge and Tinhorn Creek.

CHILE

I am a little bemused by Chile's performance in the world wine market. There is no doubt that around the £4 to £5 mark the big brands have taken over from Australia as the engine room of the budget wine spend. Chile's average bottle price on UK shelves is way under £4 and I have to admit, when Australia was doing this a decade ago I didn't ever really go a bundle on those wines either. Not surprisingly, Australia has moved onwards and upwards and Chile must do this too, to encourage people to experiment. It is worth mentioning that Concha y Toro, Chile's biggest wine producer, is a phenomenal outfit. If you drink wines from the Casillero del Diablo range (now nudging up over a fiver) and ranges above this, you will be extremely impressed. Below this level, however, I believe it is impossible to make decent wine, and this is Chile and other New World countries' inherent problem. So, my advice is to cut out Chilean cheapies and concentrate on the quality. Big brands tend to lead the way but, as every year passes, more boutique estates find their way into the export market. Chile is also expanding its winemaking into more marginal (cooler) regions. This will help complexity and balance in whites, and allow Pinot Noir and other more sensitive reds to get a foothold. For far too long Chile has been planting vast vineyards in the Central Valley and allowing them to grow like weeds – hence the dull wines on our shelves.

Chile is split into three regions, the Northern, Central and Southern Zones. In the Northern Zone it is generally too hot and dry, in the Southern Zone it is too wet, but surprise,

surprise, in the Central Zone it is perfect (too perfect really). The Central Zone is split further into wine regions. From north to south, the **Aconcagua**, 100 miles north of Santiago, is the prime site for Cabernet Sauvignon. This is where Errázuriz make their mega-expensive Seña. **Casablanca**, on the coast near Valparaiso, attracts cool, early morning Pacific Ocean fog that makes it perfect for Sauvignon Blanc, Gewürztraminer and Chardonnay, rather like a Chilean version of Carneros in California. The **Maipo**, just south of Santiago, is half red, half white, with Cabernet Sauvignon, Merlot, Carmenère, Sauvignon Blanc and Semillon doing the work. **Maule**, which includes the Curicó and Rapel Valleys, plants Cabernet Sauvignon, Sauvignon Blanc and Semillon again, and this is where Miguel Torres, of Catalonian fame, has his successful operation. The last main region in the south is **Bío-Bío**, where much of the bulk wine is made for local consumption. I have tasted wines from new regions like the **Limarí Valley** in the far north, where Chardonnay and Pinot Noir are looking smart. I have seen Syrahs from single vineyard hillside sites that rival some of the best in the world, but most of these wines are experimental and are designed to keep industrial winemakers amused while they do their day job of making millions of cases of duller wines. This will change, but it can't happen quickly enough. I don't drink much Chilean wine at home, but I suspect some people pile through it. When I do pick out a bottle, it is from one of the producers below and it will generally be a smarter wine. This is the safest territory. My advice is to avoid the bottom end wines, as they are inevitably disappointing – and do what I do: careful, informed research!

The best producers in Chile are: Alvaro Espinoza, Amayna, Casa Lapostolle, Concha y Toro, Cousiño Macul, De Martino, J & F Lurton, Michel Laroche & Jorge Coderch, Miguel Torres, San Pedro, Valdivieso, Veramonte, Viña Errázuriz, Viña Haras de Pirque, Viña Leyda, Viña Montes, Viña MontGras, Viña Morandé, Viña Pérez Cruz and Viñedos Organicos Emiliana.

FRANCE

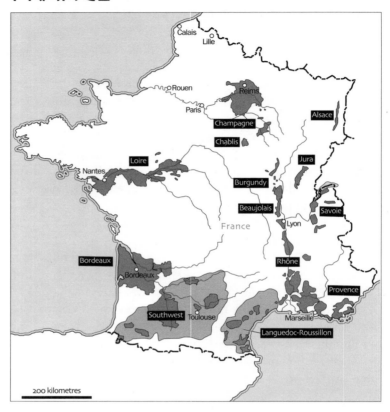

I will try not to sound too biased in my introduction to France, but if I had to make a list of my all-time favourite ten wines, they would all be French. If it were a top twenty, Australia would have five or six of the balance and Italy the rest. These three countries run my palate. Why is this? And why is France so important to me, you, and our wine diet? I have already explained how Australia strides like a colossus in the sphere of New World wines, and Italy gets a go in a few pages' time, but, for now, the most important and fascinating wine-producing country is France, and I suspect it will be for many, many years to come.

My very first tastes of wine were French and my cellar, albeit of the limited under-stair variety, holds a lot of French wines.

For me, France is the spiritual home of winemaking and, while I recognise that many other countries make outstanding wines, and I love drinking them, my wine brain has always made a mental comparison of any non-French wine to its French 'yardstick'. I just can't help it. My palate has always been used to European levels of acidity and tannin. When you start to taste wine, you have to decide where on earth to kick off. It is useful to have in your mind a definitive style, a sort of blueprint, for each grape variety. It just so happens that most of my model grape variety flavours are French. If I gave you a glass of wine and asked you your opinion, you would be assessing it in comparison with other wines you have tasted. I wonder which country's wine styles you would be using for your judgement?

I am not alone in this way of thinking. Leaving aside Germany, Italy and Spain, as they have their own definitive grape variety styles, the rest of the winemaking world has, in the past, looked to the French 'classics' for inspiration. Californian Cabernet Sauvignons try to emulate the complexity of the great wines of Bordeaux; Australian Chardonnays strive for Burgundian longevity and complexity, and New Zealand Sauvignon Blancs aim to capture the refreshing quality and zestiness of the Loire Valley's finest.

It is as if there is a one-way rivalry between New World winemakers and France. The 'young', new world of wine wants to play with old father France, but France just shrugs its shoulders and turns away. The French are usually caricatured as intrinsically arrogant, never showing any signs of concern about the wine challenges emerging from abroad. I suspect that inwardly the French need this pressure to thrive, and it is certainly clear that wine technology and grass roots viticultural skills have had an enormous collective kick up the derrière over the past twenty years. This concern came about as a result of thousands of cases of varietally pure wines flooding the export market from Australia, New Zealand, Chile, Argentina and, latterly, South Africa, with low prices and high-impact commercial fruitiness with which the French could not compete. Add to that the celebrations that take place every time a New World wine beats glorious, venerable Château 'La Tour Eiffel' in a blind tasting. This competition is fierce. Personally, I think that this style of taste comparison makes no sense. Surely wines should be considered like with like. I love finding out which is the best in a line-up of Gevrey-Chambertins. However, if a Central Otago Pinot Noir was thrown into the tasting, it might sweep the board if the tasters identify with the atypical, exceptional ripeness of fruit. The two styles are poles apart, the only similarity being the grape used. I also like to balance the equation by conducting a similar tasting of Kiwi Pinots, then at least I know the best wines of the two different worlds (this is, of course, what I do virtually every day). It is important to remember that one wine is no 'better' than the other and can't really be judged on the same playing field. Thankfully, after well over a hundred years of New World winemaking, some New World estates have realised that there is no need to try to beat the French, but instead to join them on the great wine lists of the world.

All winemaking countries have vastly different cultures and climates. The world's greatest winemakers taste regularly and widely, and they inevitably have a passion for all things European. They like to buy, collect and drink the wines – don't we all? The private cellars of many New World winery owners tell the tale. It is not unknown to find as many bottles of wine from France, Italy and Spain (as well as the obligatory bottles of port and Madeira) as their own country or estate's wines. Aspirational young winemakers travel to France to work with their heroes, hoping that some of the mystique will rub off, as well as learning the old-fashioned ropes at the same time. I know for a fact that French vignerons love meeting keen New World wine students. They wouldn't admit it out loud, but they learn a ton from these highly trained youths as well.

Having said all this, the fact remains that the French have something that much of the winemaking world has not, or has not yet found, and that is a true 'sense of place'. By that I mean that they grow a vast array of grape varieties, each one focusing in on its precise favoured area. These areas have been shown, over centuries, to be the best ones to extract the maximum potential and character from their chosen varieties.

The reason for this terrific sense of place is the strict application of French wine laws. The *Appellation Contrôlée* (AC) system was set up to preserve the regional character of the wines and is the envy of the entire wine world (as well as, unfortunately, having the flip side of stifling any creative innovation at the same time). I will touch on other countries' wine laws in due course, but for a country where the ACs can be anything from a tiny single vineyard to a whole region, the organisation and implementation is amazing. AC rules cover all of the exact vineyard plots allowed to be planted, their minimum vine density, pruning and training systems, maximum yields, winemaking processes, including alcoholic strengths and the permitted grape varieties, and include a mandatory independent analysis by the region's enforcers. Irrigation is banned (in most places), as is the blending of multi-vintage wines to help boost the poorer years. Spain, Italy and Portugal all based their own systems on this model. Germany's system is loose knit and certainly less clear by way of a guide to its best wines. The AC system is by no means perfect, as the regulatory bodies seem to be a touch too lenient on some substandard wines that are awarded the AC seal of approval. The other problem is that AC laws are to some degree a straitjacket on experimental winemakers, forcing them to release any wines made from 'unacceptable' grape varieties on the lowly Vin de Pays classification, despite their obvious appeal. There is no doubt, however, that the overall idea is sound and the results speak for themselves. As in any governing body there are a number of anomalies, but this pioneering regulator has worked well enough to influence the rest of the winemaking world.

So what, where, how and when should you drink great French wine? This section is the most intricate and complex in the entire book, so take it slowly. When you've finished you will have a lifetime of wine to track down and enjoy. However, remember France is a world of wine in its own right, but it is

...not THE world of wine. A French-only wine diet would lack pizzaz and dynamism at the lower end, and you would quickly go broke trying to keep up with some of the stellar labels that you will inevitably fall in love with. My advice is simple – balance is key, in life and wine, and France has a romance about it that is essential to your vinous happiness.

Bordeaux

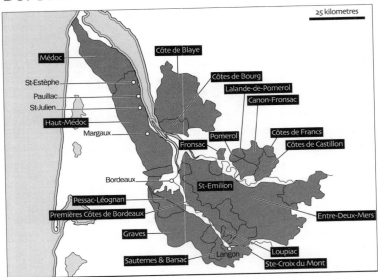

Our first port of call is just that, a port. Bordeaux gives its name to the huge surrounding wine region and is situated on the Garonne River that leads to the Gironde estuary on the west coast of France. Bordeaux is the biggest single wine region in the world, covering more than 115,000ha and producing a mighty 750,000,000 bottles of wine per year. Red Bordeaux is one of the mainstays of France's wine economy. However, the grand Châteaux of the Médoc, Graves, St-Emilion and Pomerol only account for 5 per cent of the overall production. Some 13,000 producers struggle along, making this mighty region worth about a quarter of all of France's AC wine. The immensely important grape varieties grown in this region are: reds – Cabernet

Sauvignon, Merlot, Cabernet Franc and Petit Verdot; dry and sweet whites – Semillon, Sauvignon Blanc and Muscadelle. Here, blending is the key skill followed by maturation in oak barrels – a very classic style of winemaking.

The greatest advertisement for Bordeaux must be that Richard the Lion Heart was a regular consumer of its wines. When Henry II married Eleanor of Aquitaine in 1152, Bordeaux became British for three centuries. King John actively encouraged shipments of 'clairet' (pale red wine) to British shores, on account of a favourable tax deal – nothing changes! The consumption in those days was nothing short of outstanding. When, in 1453, the English left and Gascony, including Bordeaux, reverted to French rule, wine was France's leading export and Britain its most important customer.

Britain remained a strong export market, even after the Dutch took over as the most important economic power in the seventeenth century. The Dutch brought an important skill to the low-lying banks of the Médoc, that of their home-grown talent for drainage. Dutch engineers cut the ditches that still criss-cross the Médoc today, allowing the marshy land to be reclaimed and exposing the famous gravel beds that form the basis of some of the world's greatest red wines.

Meanwhile, in 1703, England signed a deal with Portugal – the Methuen Treaty. This raised taxes on French wines to exorbitant levels, thus favouring the wines of Portugal. However, the British, knowing a good wine when they taste it, continued to access the finest wines of Bordeaux, and built up a steadfast following in the cellars of the English aristocracy and the emerging wealthy industrial middle class.

The French Revolution was but a tiny disturbance for the Bordelais, and only a few rich Château owners got the chop. The region was relatively unscathed and remained intact, only to be struck by a 'one-two' from a blight of oidium in 1852, followed by the demon Phylloxera vastatrix in 1869. By 1882 almost all of the vineyards had been destroyed. Only by the early twentieth century had everything reverted to normal. Bordeaux entered the AC system in 1936.

Another point of interest is that in 1855 the Bordeaux Official Classification was drawn up. Sixty châteaux in the Médoc and one from Graves, as well as twenty-six Sauternes and Barsac châteaux, were classified into two ranking systems, rather like football league tables. The reds were put into five classes or 'growths' known as *Cru*, from 1st to 5th (*Premier* or *1er Cru* to *Cinquièmes* or *5ème Cru*). The sweet wines were divided into two classes, *1er Cru* and *2ème Cru*, although Château d'Yquem was elevated to its unique title of *1er Cru Supèrieure*. These tables were created using the latest (1850s) market prices of the various wines. With only a handful of exceptions, they still have remarkable accuracy today. The Graves region was classified in 1959 and the Right Bank area of St-Emilion was classified in 1955, updated in 1985 and finally re-updated in 1996. Pomerol has no classification whatsoever.

In the Haut Médoc, below the classed growth system, there operates another series of classifications. This splits up the remaining châteaux in terms of their *Cru Bourgeois* status: from the top, *Cru Grand Bourgeois Exceptionnel* followed by *Cru Grand Bourgeois* and lastly *Cru Bourgeois*. This system is a bit of a mess, as there currently exist two versions of the same classification. These titles rarely indicate increasing levels of quality. However, you would be advised to opt at least for a *Cru Bourgeois* grade wine rather than ungraded when buying Médoc wines. For my part, I just think of them as one big classification – *Cru Bourgeois*.

Bordeaux is split into two parts, the Left and Right Banks (not North and South or East and West). They each have distinctly different soils and produce different styles of wine.

THE LEFT BANK
Médoc

The striking aspect of Bordeaux is the sheer size of the region and its properties. Driving out of Bordeaux, northwest up the region of Médoc, the city gradually disappears and the châteaux gradually appear. At first the names seem a little obscure, but the further you progress along the main road, the grander the names and the properties become. Unlike Burgundy, where a single

Domaine might produce two or three thousand cases of wine covering seven or eight different labels, a large Left Bank châteaux like Lafite-Rothschild produces as much as 20,000 cases of its main wine and a further 20,000 cases of its second wine. Not only are these châteaux big, but their wines are also expensive, making the Bordelais some of the richest wine producers in the world.

The Médoc is split into two parts, the Haut-Médoc and the Bas Médoc or just plain Médoc. The Haut-Médoc is further split into several different *communes*: Margaux, St-Julien, Pauillac and St-Estèphe being the big four, with two other less fashionable areas, Moulis and Listrac. A *commune* is a village and its surrounding land, and it is in the big four *communes* that almost all of the classed growth clarets exist.

The Left Bank is sandwiched between two bodies of water, the Atlantic Ocean and the Gironde estuary. This makes the climate very firmly maritime. The region gets mild winters and long, warm summers, and is protected from the harsh westerly Atlantic breezes by a line of pine forests that run between it and the ocean. All of the wines on this side of the river tend to be Cabernet Sauvignon dominant. Here the Cabernet Sauvignon grape develops amazing blackcurrant, leather and cedarwood aromas – the international hallmarks of a great Cab Sauv.

Margaux

The biggest of the communes is home to its namesake Château Margaux and the first of the five *1er Cru* wines that we come across. The style of the wines from this commune is said to be lighter and more 'feminine' (a tasting note that I don't really understand or use). The classic Margaux hallmarks are a violet scent, 'rounder' fruit on the palate and less aggressive tannins on the finish than can be found in the meatier offerings from the neighbouring communes. Margaux has five little parishes, Labarde, Cantenac, Arsac, Margaux itself and Soussans, and they each have their own well-made châteaux offerings. Just south of Labarde are two properties that are outside of the Margaux appellation, but whose wines I have always enjoyed: Châteaux d'Angludet and Cantemerle. Whenever discussing Margaux, I automatically include these two in the frame, as they make similar-styled wines. If there were ever a tweaking of the boundaries or a re-classification, I would vote for them as full-blown Margaux members. Not only are their wines sublime, they would make it into my favourite châteaux section below, if they were not already resplendent in the best value section.

My favourite Châteaux are: d'Angludet, Brane-Cantenac, Cantemerle, Durfort-Vivens, Ferrière, d'Issan, La Lagune, Margaux, Palmer, Pavillon Rouge du Château Margaux and Rausan-Ségla.

The best-value Châteaux are: d'Angludet, Cantemerle, Ferrière, Haut-Breton Larigaudière, Kirwan, Monbrison and du Tertre.

Moulis and Listrac

These two little-known appellations are next door to Margaux, and south of St-Julien. They contain some remarkably good finds, between them producing 600,000 cases of wine, of which 88 per cent (Moulis) and 66 per cent (Listrac) are of *Cru Bourgeois* status. It would be foolish not to take a peek, and what you discover are some very good taste-alikes of the real thing farther up the road. If you are trying to get into classic red Bordeaux but find that the prices are too punishing, then there is no better place to look than here. Generally these wines are a little lighter and earlier maturing than the classed growths, so they tend to be less expensive and more forward. Some of these châteaux are very reliable sources of well-made wine and they are beginning to step on the toes of one or two of the big names nearby.

My favourite Châteaux (they are all relatively good value) are: Chasse-Spleen, Clarke, Fourcas Loubaney, Maucaillou and Poujeaux.

St-Julien

Drive a few miles north out of Margaux, up the D2, and St-Julien appears in front of you. This small commune is jam-packed with incredible names. Keep your eyes on the road as you pass the grand Châteaux gates and your passengers shout out a constant stream of sign posts indicating the impossibly famous properties. Here the wines have an elegance, balance and breeding not found in any other area of Bordeaux. St-Julien has a tangible feel of wealth and aristocracy in the air. In wine tastings, time after time, wine lovers prefer the charm and harmony of this *commune*'s wines to any other. St-Julien seems to embody all of the other *commune*s' best qualities – Margaux's subtlety and balance, Pauillac's power and longevity and St-Estèphe's old-fashioned, blackcurrant and cigar-box nose. There are no 1st growth châteaux in St-Julien but a bevy of 2nd growths. These are often referred to as super-seconds, on account of their concentration and excellence. There is also a run of 3rd, 4th and *Cru Bourgeois* wines worth sniffing out. All of these properties make luscious, gentleman's clarets that have the classic hallmarks of leather, cassis, old library books and fresh tobacco on the nose. If you think I'm getting a little carried away, it is because this is my favourite *commune* in the whole of Bordeaux. St-Julien borders the heavy-weight *commune* of Pauillac, and one château is worth giving a special mention as it treads the boards between the moreish St-Julien style and the monster intensity of neighbouring Pauillac – Château Léoville-Las Cases. These vineyards actually sit next to those of Château Latour (*1er Cru*). Léoville-Las Cases is an awesome wine, often needing a minimum of ten years to lose its tannic coating, but when up to racing speed this wine, for me, epitomises the enormous pleasure that Bordeaux wines can bring.

My favourite Châteaux are: Branaire-Ducru, Clos ou Marquis, Ducru-Beaucaillou, Gruaud-Larose, Lagrange, Langoa-Barton, Léoville-Barton, Léoville-Las Cases, Léoville-Poyferré, St-Pierre and Talbot.

The best value Châteaux are: Clos du Marquis (second label of Léoville-Las Cases), Gloria, Lalande-Borie and Moulin-Riche (second label of Léoville-Poyferré).

Pauillac

Magnificent texture, opulent black fruit and staggering longevity are the hallmarks of great Pauillacs. Three of the five *1er Cru* wines are from within these hallowed boundaries. Pauillac is the most famous of the Haut-Médoc appellations, with Mouton-Rothschild, Lafite-Rothschild and Latour the jewels in its crown. Here the wines, brutally tannic in their youth, are long-lived and exhibit cedarwood, intense blackcurrant fruit and masses of spice on the nose. They are generally deep, rich and full-bodied on the palate and monumentally long on the finish. While most of the châteaux are out of the price range of normal mortals, there are some good *Cru Bourgeois* wines and second labels that can give a glimpse of what the *commune* can do. If, however, the chance to drink, or even taste, one of the great *1er Cru* or super-second Pauillac wines arises, drop everything and line up with a pint glass.

My favourite Châteaux are: Batailley, Les Forts de Latour, Grand-Puy-Lacoste, Haut-Bages-Libéral, Haut-Batailley, Lafite-Rothschild, Latour, Lynch-Bages, Mouton-Rothschild, Pichon-Longueville Baron, Pichon-Longueville-Comtesse de Lalande and Pontet-Canet.

The best value Châteaux are: Haut-Bages-Libéral, Haut-Bages-Monpelou and Lacoste-Borie (second label of Grand-Puy-Lacoste).

St-Estèphe

At the end of the line of the famous *communes* is St-Estèphe. Just a few steps from the Pauillac vineyards of Château Lafite, the extraordinary looking pagoda of Château Cos d'Estournel, towers over the landscape. The wines of St-Estèphe have a reputation for being the tightest, most reserved and slowest of the bunch to mature, with Cos, the snail, leading the pack. This may have been true in the past but, since the mid eighties, the percentage of Merlot in this Left Bank Cabernet Sauvignon dominant recipe has been increased a bit to soften off these brooding beasts. Not perceived as remotely 'commercial', unless a super-ripe vintage comes along (like 2003), St-Estèphe wines suffer from a sub-soil with a high proportion of clay. This makes the ripening process that bit more difficult and often results in wines with noticeably more acidity than those from the rest of the gravelly Médoc.

Having said that, they tend to age gracefully and numerous *Cru Bourgeois* châteaux live much longer than is usually the case. This means that laying down cases of relatively inexpensive St-Estèphe clarets can be enjoyable and rewarding as the wines creep towards their long-awaited period of drinking. There are more underrated châteaux here than in any other *commune*, but remember you need to exercise a fair degree of patience before you uncork them.

My favourite Châteaux are: Beau-Site, Le Boscq, Calon-Ségur, Cos d'Estournel, Cos Labory, Haut-Marbuzet, La Haye, Lafon-Rochet, Montrose, Les-Ormes-de-Pez, de Pez, Phélan-Ségur and Ségur de Cabanac.

The best value Châteaux are: Beau-Site, Le Boscq, La Haye, Lavillotte, Les-Ormes-de-Pez and de Pez.

Haut-Médoc and (Bas) Médoc

Lumped together in a single section, the two appellations Médoc and Haut-Médoc cover all of the gaps in the Left Bank tapestry. They contain hundreds of properties that don't fall within the strictly controlled boundaries of the grander *communes*. This is where the bargain hunter must look for up-and-coming, over-achieving properties. In good vintages, the lower prices asked for these wines, lacking grand *commune* postcodes, are the true deals to be had in Left Bank Bordeaux. From the (Bas) Médoc, beyond the northern tip of St-Estèphe, all of the way back down to the outskirts of Bordeaux itself, this region covers some 22,000 acres of vines. There is no one particular style of wine produced under these two AC labels, as the sprawl of châteaux cover such a vast array of soils and microclimates. One thing is certain – the blend will favour Cab Sauv and the warmer the vintage the better the wines.

The pick of the Châteaux bunch are: Arnauld, Cambon la Pelouse, de Lamarque, Malescasse, Patache d'Aux, Potensac, Rollan de By, Sociando-Mallet, Tour du Haut-Moulin and Villegeorge.

Graves

The other main red and, for the first time, white wine region of Bordeaux's Left Bank is Graves. Graves is situated southeast of the city of Bordeaux. It also has the fifth remaining *1er Cru* château, that of Château Haut-Brion. In 1987, a separate appellation of *Pessac-Léognan* was created within the Graves area to encompass the most famous properties, lying on the best 'Graves' (gravel) soils. It is here that the finest wines are made. The dry white wines of Graves epitomise the power and poise of the classic Semillon/Sauvignon Blanc partnership (sometimes including Muscadelle). Many red wine châteaux make a white wine, and these wines have started to be fashioned in a more Burgundian manner. By that I mean a pre-fermentation maceration, then cold fermentation followed by a spell in new oak barrels (or indeed full-blown barrel fermentation). This change of tack not only broke the mould but also attracted worldwide interest in these wines which, until recently, could best be described as dowdy. The red wines of Graves often lack the power of the big four Médoc *communes*' wines, but make up for it with stunning texture and aroma. They tend to mature a little earlier and have a distinctive mineral character that truly reflects the composition of their gravelly soils.

My favourite red Châteaux are: Bahans-Haut-Brion, Carmes-Haut-Brion, Chantegrive, Domaine de Chevalier, de Fieuzal, Haut-Bailly, Haut-Brion, La Mission-Haut-Brion, Pape-Clément, Picque-Caillou and Smith-Haut-Lafitte.

The best value red Châteaux are: Bahans-Haut-Brion (second wine of Haut-Brion), Chantegrive, La Garde, La Louvière and Picque-Caillou.

Recommended white Châteaux are: Carbonnieux, Clos Floridène, Domaine de Chevalier, de Fieuzal, Haut-Brion, Laville-Haut-Brion, Pavilion Blanc de Château Margaux, Smith-Haut-Lafitte and La Tour Martillac.

Sauternes and Barsac

A forty-minute drive south of Bordeaux brings you to the capital of the world's sweet wine production, Sauternes. This area, although known collectively as Sauternes, includes the five little *communes* of Sauternes, Barsac, Fargues, Preignac and Bommes. It accounts for the decadently sweet white wines that grace the most discerning dinner tables. It is bizarre that, year after year, these properties pray for gloomy weather that brings on the onset of 'noble rot', Botrytis cinerea. This rot turns a regular late harvest into the nectar of the gods, albeit of minuscule proportions. The fact that these climatic conditions only really happen three years in ten, means that the life of a Sauternes producer must be a stressful one. Fashion also plays a big part in the appeal of these wines. While Port and Madeira never seem to be in vogue, thankfully sweet wines like these have always caught our eye and palate. As a single half-bottle of this heavenly wine can serve eight people with a more than adequate glassful, it is a mystery to me why more people are not using Sauternes (or other sweet wines for that matter) to finish off an evening's merriment. It seems such an abrupt end to stop with a big red and then just launch into coffee. I certainly need to wind down after the workout a huge *rouge* gives my taste buds, and a glass of Sauternes is the vinous equivalent of an icy plunge pool.

As Sauternes enjoys misty, mild, humid weather, the exact opposite of a red wine's wish list, it is not uncommon for Sauternes to have a great vintage when the rest of Bordeaux has a turkey. If you have never tasted a wine from these parts, I strongly urge you to track one down. I promise it will be worthwhile.

> **My favourite Châteaux are:** d'Arche, Bastor-Lamontagne, Broustet, Climens, Coutet, Doisy-Daëne, Doisy-Dubroca, Doisy-Védrines, de Fargues, Filhot, Gilette, Guiraud, Les Justices, Lafaurie-Peyraguey, de Malle, Nairac, Rabaud-Promis, Raymond-Lafon, Rayne-Vigneau, Rieussec, Suduiraut, La Tour Blanche and d'Yquem.
>
> **The best value Châteaux are:** Broustet, Doisy-Daëne, Filhot, Les Justices, Nairac, Rabaud-Promis and Rayne-Vigneau.

The Rest

Before we cross to the Right Bank, there are a number of miscellaneous areas that are worth a quick mention. Between the Right and Left Banks there are a few named regions that produce fairly simple wines that can provide an everyday style for Bordeaux-philes. **Cadillac**, **Loupiac** and **Ste-Croix du Mont** all make everyday sweet styles that rarely match even the most basic of Sauternes, but can provide a pleasant summery wine for picnics or for big parties. Domaine du Noble is a nice property to track down. **Entre-deux-Mers** is the area between the Garonne and Dordogne rivers that separate the Left and Right Banks. This region is responsible for vast quantities of often-bland red and white wines that usually go into supermarket 'own label' wines, or are used for 'house' wines in bars and restaurants. **Bordeaux** and **Bordeaux Supérieur** wines account for the general, wide appellation surrounding these smaller areas; the Supérieur label indicates a higher alcohol wine, made with stricter rules on yields. Here also we find the slightly more upmarket region of **Premières Côtes de Bordeaux**, where some properties make fairly useful reds and whites, particularly in good vintages. The trick with all of these wines is to try to wangle a taste before you buy.

Recommended whites are: Bauduc – Les Trois Hectares, Bonnet, Thieuley and La Tour de Mirambeau.

Recommended reds are: Fontenille, Grand-Mouëys, Jonqueyres, Lezongars, Méaume, Reynon, Plassan, de Sours (who make a wicked rosé, too), Thieuley and de la Tour.

THE RIGHT BANK
St-Emilion

This part of Bordeaux is really beautiful, unlike the flattish land of the Médoc. The town of St-Emilion itself nestles in the hills, some twenty miles east of Bordeaux. The best vineyards in the area are perched on top of a limestone plateau and its surrounding hillsides, or on a gravel outcrop near the border with Pomerol. Here the classic Bordeaux *cépage* (grape content) is reversed. Merlot is the dominant grape followed by Cabernet Franc, with Cabernet Sauvignon bringing up the rear. The wines of St-Emilion are widely enjoyed on account of their fleshy, forward fruit (high Merlot content) and lack of searing tannin in youth (low Cabernet Sauvignon content). The number of châteaux in this relatively small appellation is huge, producing some three million cases a year. The range of styles is fairly diverse as the differences in soil play a major part in the equation. This means you should endeavour to follow a property that you like, rather than simply relying on the appellation as a whole. St-Emilion is also responsible for a fascinating trend in winemaking – the advent of micro-wineries, where the wines are often made from single vineyard plots that are harvested very late, at painfully low yields, which gives rise to super-ripe fruit. Coupled with lashings of new oak treatment the results are awesomely impressive, if showy wines. The problem is that this phenomenon is relatively new (fifteen years is a short time in Bordeaux) and nobody can truly predict how these wines will age in the long term. Most of these 'fashion victim' wines have high Merlot content and show incredibly well when very young. They already command much higher prices than say the majestic Château Ausone or the celestial Château Cheval Blanc (the top two estates in St-Emilion). It is remarkable that until the late eighties/early nineties nobody would have considered making such a ridiculously narcissistic style of wine. The American market, spurred on by a succession of good vintages, sought more and more over-the-top flavours similar to the naturally ripe wines of the Napa Valley and the like. One or two entrepreneurs obliged and now the trend has spread like wildfire. I sound sceptical because I am. The prices and allocations for single bottles of these wines sound like the equivalent case quantities from the old-fashioned estates. How long can it last before the bubble bursts and people buy with their palates as opposed to their wallets?

My favourite Châteaux are: Angélus, L'Arrosée, Ausone, Beau-Séjour Bécot, Belair, Canon-La-Gaffelière, Le Castelot, Cheval Blanc, Clos Fourtet, Dassault, La Dominique, Figeac, Larmande, Magdelaine, Monbousquet, Tertre-Rôteboeuf, La Tour-du-Pin-Figeac, Troplong-Mondot and Valandraud.

The best value Châteaux are: Bellefont-Belcier, Chauvin, Dassault, Haut-Sarpe, Larmande, Quinault, Tour Baladoz, La Tour-Figeac and La Tour-du-Pin-Figeac.

The St-Emilion Satellites

Lussac St-Emilion, Montagne St-Emilion, Puisseguin St-Emilion and St-Georges St-Emilion are all tongue-twistingly named areas orbiting around St-Emilion itself. They offer wines of similar *cépage* to St-Emilion proper, but lack their impressive longevity. These wines are a good way of tasting the Right Bank style without paying ludicrous prices. Usually, they must be drunk over the first five to six years of life.

Recommended Châteaux are: Bel-Air, Croix-Beauséjour, Durand-Laplagne, Haut-Bernat, Lyonnat, Montaiguillon, Roudier, St-Georges and Teyssier.

Pomerol

With no classification system you might think it is difficult to navigate your way around this tiny, exclusive region, but do not despair. There are but a handful of magnificent châteaux making incredible wines – most, sadly, in tiny quantities. The most famous of all is Châteaux Pétrus, a byword for excellence. Pétrus is one of the only wines in Bordeaux to be made from virtually 100 per cent Merlot (a small slice of Cabernet Franc usually finds its way in). Most Pomerols are very high in Merlot content, approaching 80 per cent in most cases. Therefore when the vintage is favourable, the wines cannot fail to be flattering, exuding exhilarating, plummy, chocolaty and spicy overtones. With such high proportions of Merlot, the wines tend to drink well when they are in their youth, so no matter how grand the wine, it is always possible to enjoy a glass, even if the optimum drinking time might be a further ten years off. These wines are highly sought after and, on account of the limited volumes, the prices of Pomerols tend to be fairly punitive. Collectors line up every year, cap in hand, hoping for allocations. Once again, a chance to enjoy a top flight Pomerol can be rare, and should never be passed up as this little region is single-handedly responsible for global Merlot fever!

Lalande-de-Pomerol

Like St-Emilion, Pomerol has a piggyback appellation, in the
shape of Lalande-de-Pomerol. Lush styles, lacking in true cellar
potential, that shape up early on in their lives is the name of the
game here. In top vintages the wines can be very intense, but
still manage to drink relatively young. Look out for much lower
prices than in Pomerol itself – it is well worth keeping an eye on
this part of Bordeaux. Perhaps the strange fact about this region
is that it is actually bigger than Pomerol.

Recommended Châteaux are: Bel-Air, Belles-Graves, La Fleur de Boüard
and Laborde and Siaurac.

The Rest

Surrounding these main areas is a collection of lesser-known
regions, all producing reliable versions of claret. **Canon-Fronsac**
and **Fronsac** are areas several miles to the west of Pomerol
producing increasingly more competent wines. The style is a
little more chunky and robust than their more famous neighbour,
and in good vintages can resemble a more Left-Bank-flavoured
wine. The best reason to shop here is the price. Very few
châteaux have managed to command a regular global audience
and so the price tags are refreshingly affordable.

Recommended Châteaux are: Canon-Moueix, de Carles, Fontenil, du Gaby,
Hervé-Laroque, Mazeris, Moulin-Haut-Laroque and La Vieille-Cure.

The **Côtes de Bourg** and **Blaye**, almost directly opposite Margaux and St-Julien on the other side of the Gironde, are two large, ancient areas of vineyards where several committed winemakers make some very impressive wines. Here, once again, the prices are reasonable, but demand for the top wines will increase due to the huge price rises in the more classic regions. The Côtes de Bourg is the finer of the two appellations. Here, Roc des Cambes is worthy of a special mention. This property is owned by a talented St-Emilion winemaker who, in his wisdom, recognised the huge potential of this unfashionable region. His wines are truly spectacular. Others will follow his lead, watch these areas closely.

Recommended Châteaux are: Bel-Air La Royère, Fougas, Garreau, Haut-Bertinerie, Haut-Grelot, Haut-Sociando, Les Jonqueyres, Mondésir-Gazin, Peybonhomme, Roc des Cambes, Segonzac, Tayac and des Tourtes.

The **Côtes de Castillon** is situated east of Puisseguin St-Emilion, and produces chunky, workhorse wines, with relatively little complexity but at reasonable prices. They tend to be Merlot dominant, but have a fair degree of muscle and can often require a few years in the cellar to soften. Not beautiful, but they do the job well.

Recommended Châteaux are: d'Aiguilhe, de Belcier, Cap de Faugères, Pitray, Puyanché and Robin.

The **Côtes de Francs** is another of these little-known appellations, except that this time it is a relative newcomer. In the past it formed part of St-Emilion, but now operates under its new name. Here, wealthy St-Emilion winemakers have taken to buying run down estates and, after injecting a bit of skill, in most cases make lovely wines.

Recommended Châteaux are: de Francs, Laclaverie, La Prade and Puygueraud.

Burgundy

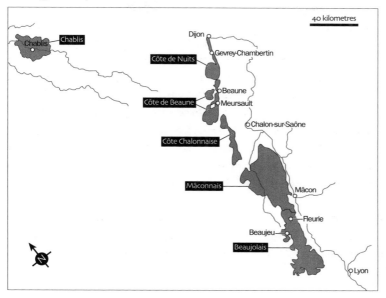

The next major French wine region to tackle is Burgundy. In comparison with Bordeaux, this region is relatively small in production terms, making half as much wine. Take Beaujolais out of Burgundy's production figures and the volume of wine made plummets to only a quarter of that of Bordeaux. Despite its smaller size, this does not mean it is easier to get to know: far from it, for if Bordeaux has two dimensions to consider – the château and the vintage – then Burgundy has three. Imagine first, if you will, a mathematical graph representing Bordeaux – one axis lists the châteaux names and the other lists the vintages. When you next taste a wine from Bordeaux, you could run your finger down the side of the table, locate the château name then run your finger across the table until you found its corresponding vintage. Then write in your tasting note. OK, this may end up being a large table and it would certainly take several years of constant tasting to fill it in well. (And there would be the added problem that in a few years' time every wine would have to be re-tasted, as they would all have aged and developed.)

Now, however, consider the shape of Burgundy's graph. It would have to have three dimensions. Once again, vintage would be on one axis, but instead of the Château name, substitute the name of the specific village and/or vineyard the wine came from. Now here comes the third dimension – the name of the producer who actually made the wine! Whereas in Bordeaux, Château Latour comes from one estate, owned by a single owner, a Burgundian vineyard – for example Echézeaux – is owned by no less than eighty or so smallholders. So, the third dimension is the owner or winemaker who has access to the grapes from a specific *climat*, or plot in a vineyard. In theory eighty different people could make Echézeaux! Imagine if we had that many different Château Latours to contend with.

So there, in a nutshell, is the beguiling and challenging aspect to this wonderful region. It is essential to get to know the individual domaines or producers who look after each separate plot of land – and that, obviously, takes some doing – but I will make it easier by recommending my favourites as we travel the length and breadth of Burgundy, giving you solid pointers to the better areas and, of course, suggesting ways to remember this oh-so-complicated bastion of the wine world.

Location

Situated in the centre of France, Burgundy's regions stretch all the way from **Chablis** in the north (100 miles south of Paris), via the **Côte-d'Or**, **Côte Chalonnaise** and **Mâconnais**, down to **Beaujolais** in the south, just a few miles north of Lyon. Burgundy has a continental climate, unlike Bordeaux's maritime one, with colder winters and cooler summers, and suffers from the awkward problem of spring frosts and unwanted October rain, which can cause havoc at harvest.

It is undoubtedly the most complicated wine region in the world – the sort of place where 'local knowledge' is worth its weight in gold. Within its boundaries the wines range from downright boring to mind-blowingly sensational. There are a number of rules to remember to help make sense of this region, but first, before divulging my hot tips, here are a few details regarding the history of Burgundy that explain why it is such a patchwork of small plots of land.

History

Prior to the French Revolution most of the vineyards in Burgundy were owned by the church. After the uprising, the church lost out in favour of the people. Each delighted villager was given a plot of land to work and these plots further fragmented when inheritance law changed from primogeniture to giving equal shares to all sons and daughters of the vineyard owners. Ownership of land only increased in size if one villager married another and they combined their little parcels. This would account for the predominance of double-barrelled names in Burgundy. There were family agreements and the inevitable buying and selling of land but, on the whole, very few families owned entire vineyards – just a few rows of vines here, and few more over there.

Some sites, like the white Montrachet vineyard and the red Chambertin vineyard, produced such amazing wine that they became very well known – so well known, in fact, that villagers decided to borrow these names and tack them on to the name of their local village. This broadened the appeal of wines made from the whole village area and not just the famous vineyard itself. And so Puligny and Chassagne, two villages which both lay claim to the fame of the Montrachet vineyard, were henceforth known as Puligny-Montrachet and Chassagne-Montrachet. Lucky old villagers – this has done them a massive favour when selling their wines. Likewise, the unknown hamlet of Gevrey became Gevrey-Chambertin, raising its street cred instantly. These double-barrelled versions at least let the outside world know that the style of the wine might in some way resemble that of the top quality, single vineyards.

So, in the end, Burgundy came to have a remarkably complicated ownership system and impossibly fragmented vineyards. On the up side, at least each vineyard has its own unique name.

Appellation Contrôlée Rules

The wines of Burgundy are classified into four different AC quality levels, and each and every vineyard belongs to one of these categories. These AC rules were set out in the 1930s and were awarded to each vineyard depending on its potential quality. The Côte-d'Or region alone is divided up into over a hundred different *appellations* (village names). The lowest level of Burgundian wines is known as **Regional**. These wines are labelled Bourgogne Rouge (Red Burgundy) or Bourgogne Blanc (White Burgundy). The grapes for these wines could come from anywhere within the boundaries of the entire region. The range in quality of these wines is understandably huge. A reputable producer will inevitably make a sound wine, whereas a cowboy company will just bottle the dregs. Almost every Domaine makes this style of wine and it is usually used for home consumption or sold locally to restaurants. Regional wines usually contain below-par grapes that could have ended up in higher-quality level wines but were deemed unsuitable, or they are made from grapes that are grown outside named village boundaries. More often than not, however, an excellent Domaine's lesser grapes will eclipse a duff Domaine's best grapes so there are bargains to be had once you know who's who. Other wines that fall within this category are more specific regional wines. These are made from grapes sourced from a number of approved villages within a specified area: for example, Beaujolais-Villages or Côte de Beaune-Villages and Côte de Nuits-Villages. If wines from more than one of the villages in Beaujolais, the Côte de Beaune or Côte de Nuits are blended together, then they are entitled to these names. These wines are generally of higher quality than 'straight' Bourgogne level, as they focus on more precise areas within Burgundy as a whole. They should also reflect the flavour of the wines made from these sub-regions. Once again, the producer is the crucial factor when buying this style of wine – Domaine name is all!

Climbing up the quality ladder, the next level for Burgundian wines is the *Village* classification. If a wine is made from grapes harvested within the boundaries of one village alone, and not blended with grapes from further afield, it is entitled to use its village name. These wines' labels will indicate the village name and the Appellation Contrôlée designation, which also includes the village name as well. For example, a wine made from grapes entirely from within the boundaries of the village of Volnay will state this village name and also say *Appellation Volnay Contrôlée* on the label.

Restricting the source of the grapes even further, the two remaining levels of classification refer to the individual quality status of wines made solely from specific named vineyards. Each plot of land is precisely mapped out and awarded its own quality status and some reach the level of **1er Cru** or **Grand Cru**.

Within the boundaries of the village of Meursault, vineyards such as Les Tillets and Les Luchets are classified as *villages* status. While a wine made from these vineyards can be labelled Meursault Les Tillets or Meursault Les Luchets, they are not *1er Cru* status, just a specific vineyard-designated wine. The French term for this is a *climat* or a *lieu dit*. These wines are of an undoubtedly higher quality than say an ordinary, 'straight' Meursault, but not as fine as a Meursault *1er Cru*, from a higher-rated vineyard such as Les Charmes.

Sometimes a village might possess several *1er Cru* vineyards and even the highest level of all, a *Grand Cru* vineyard as well. The red wine village of Vosne-Romanée has no less than six *Grand Cru* vineyards, and these need not include the reminder that they are in Vosne-Romanée on the wine label, as their individual degree of fame is assumed. The only name needed on the wine label is that of the vineyard itself – of which La Romanée is one of the six.

The Grape Varieties

I have waited until now to introduce you to the Burgundian grape varieties and, boy, are they famous. The world-renowned white wonder Chardonnay and its equally starry red companion Pinot Noir feature in the leading roles and are ably supported by the zingy white grape Aligoté and much derided red Gamay.

Remember this – all Chablis, all Côte-d'Or whites, all Côte

Chalonnaise whites and all white Mâconnais wines are made from Chardonnay. The only exception to this, and it will declare itself on the label, is our friend the Aligoté grape. Similarly – all Côte-d'Or reds, all Côte Chalonnaise reds and all Mâconnais reds are made from Pinot Noir, except for the wines of Beaujolais which use Gamay, and a rarely seen, weird and wonderful blend called Bourgogne Passetoutgrains, that has to include a minimum of one-third Pinot Noir to two-thirds Gamay.

Domaines and *Négociants*

The word 'Domaine' is used in Burgundy to mean an estate. A Domaine owns its own vineyards and makes its own wines. Look out for this word on a wine label as it is an indication that the winemaker has total control over the growing of his grapes and didn't just see them for the first time when they arrived at the winery door. A Domaine-bottled wine should be a sign of quality. A *négociant*, a French word meaning 'merchant', on the other hand, is the term used for a winery that buys grapes (or wine) from various different sources, then makes, blends or ages the product, bottling it and selling the finished wine under its own label. The problem lies in the quality of the component parts of a *négociant*'s wines – these often vary considerably. Different farmers use different vineyard management techniques and this gives rise to superior and inferior crops. The blending of these grapes together rarely equals the sum of the parts. It is easy to understand why so many of Burgundy's wines are sold under the *négociant* umbrella as most of the smallholdings are too tiny to be able to afford winemaking equipment, and selling the crop is the easiest way to make some money. *Négociants* not only buy grapes, but can also undertake to blend finished wines together, as some small wineries lack the marketing skills or distribution network necessary to do this job on their own. Once again the problem of blending together inferior wines can lead to dreary finished products.

Having said this, over the last twenty years, the word *négociant* has gone from a good reason to avoid certain bottles of Burgundy, to a very good reason to reconsider the finer *négociant* houses. As bad press was heaped on these merchants on account of their total lack of care over the wines they sold, some *négociants* introduced contracts with their growers. These contracts set out terms for tending the vines and ensured minimum levels of ripeness at harvest time. The best *négociants* work very closely with their grape suppliers. This close contact led to a quantum leap in the quality of fruit and therefore resulted in outstanding wines being made. Producers like Louis Jadot, Nicolas Potel, Bouchard Père et Fils and Faiveley are at the forefront of this new wave of newfound *négociant* confidence. Incidentally, many of these 'houses' own their own vineyards as well as buying in grapes – these wines are bottled under Domaine labels.

A relatively new, 'old' trend is re-emerging in Burgundy, and that is the renaissance of the purist *éléveur*. In English, this means individuals who buy 'finished' wine and then take on the ageing responsibilities themselves, often in flashy, 100 per cent new oak barrels, bottling the wines without fining or filtration. Ex-pastry chef Dominique Laurent was one of the first people to kick-start this vogue.

I have to declare a particular interest in Burgundy. For me this is one of the most beautiful and romantic places in the world. I adore the Pinot Noir and Chardonnay grapes and the regional cuisine is also sublime. Every year I spend two or three weeks tasting through hundreds of bottles of wine in search of the most celestial Pinots and Chardonnays on the planet. They are here, my job is to find them, and it is one of the annual highlights of my career. If you have the chance to visit Burgundy, then go for it. You will, I am certain, be bitten by the bug.

CHABLIS

Visiting the Burgundy regions, moving from the far north to the south, we start with Chablis, a region producing steely dry white wines made from the Chardonnay grape variety (remember Ch- for Chablis, Ch- for Chardonnay!). It is easy to forget this, as a big, oaky New World Chardonnay has no apparent similarity to these lean, focused, high tensile beauties, but it is important to remember that they are made from the same grape. I have heard many people in wine bars say, 'I don't want a Chardonnay, but I'll have a glass of Chablis,' unaware of their gaffe. It just goes to show how much climate can affect the flavour of a wine. Up in these far northern reaches of Europe's vineyards, it is very cold and frost is the biggest worry for viticulturalists. In Chablis, one severe snap can ruin an entire vintage.

Chablis is a remarkably famous name in the wine world. In days gone by, the New World would use this place name on any bottles of dry white wine, but today, Chablis guards its name and its style of wine fiercely.

Like other parts of Burgundy, Chablis uses a 'Regional, *Village*, *1er Cru*, *Grand Cru*' system, established in 1938 to indicate increasing levels of quality. *Village* Chablis can vary from dull, insipid, watery white wine, to green-hued, pinpoint accurate Chardonnay with invigorating, zesty and refreshing fruit. Once again the Domaine-bottled wines are worth favouring, but there are some good *négociants* as well. Below *village* Chablis is the little-known Petit-Chablis appellation. These wines are usually lean, green and disappointing, and as Chablis is a relatively inexpensive wine, saving only a small amount by buying a Petit-Chablis doesn't make sense. Going in the other direction, of the forty famous *Premier (1er) Cru* vineyards, names like Fourchaume, Montée de Tonnerre (Thunder Mountain), Montmains, Vaillons and Vosgros, among others, have the ability to produce great wines. However, like the rest of Burgundy, it is the responsibility and skill of the winemaker that transforms the crop into a great wine. *Premier Cru* Chablis can live for anything up to ten years, getting more complex and developing more flavour nuances as time goes by. Only when you get up to *Grand Cru* level do the wines take on any sort of true richness, weight and structure. The seven *Grand Crus* to look out for are Blanchot, Bougros, Grenouilles (literally 'frogs'), Les Clos, Les Preuses, Valmur and Vaudésir. All of these vineyards are grouped together on top of a hill overlooking the town of Chablis, hogging the best soil and sunlight. *Grand Cru* Chablis can happily last the course for fifteen years, although they usually get gobbled up long before they reach their peak.

Stainless steel is the order of the day when making these wines, although increasing numbers of producers use oak barrels to give their wines more flavour characteristics. The old boys regard this as a little bit offside, but most people these days have some oak in their wineries. *Premier* and *Grand Cru* level wines can usually handle a fair degree of oak so, if it is in balance, I do not see why winemakers shouldn't use it.

> **My favourite Chablis Domaines are:** Billaud-Simon, A & F Boudin, Daniel Dampt, des Genèves, Jean Durup, Jean-Paul Droin, Laroche, Laurent Tribut, Louis Michel, Raveneau, René & Vincent Dauvissat and William Fèvre.

Before we move on to the rest of Burgundy there is a region called the **Côtes d'Auxerre** stuck on the bottom of Chablis, where we find a village called **St-Bris-le-Vineux**, which makes a few interesting Sauvignon Blancs and Chardonnays. It was a VDQS level wine region (one lower than AC) until 2002 when it was given full AC status. However, because the grape name Sauvignon Blanc is not allowed to be written on the label of a bottle of white Burgundy, the name has been changed from Sauvignon de St-Bris to just Saint-Bris. This wine is a sort of cross between a Sancerre and a Chablis in style. The best winemaker based here is Jean-Hugues Goisot, whose wines are incredibly good value. He makes a good Aligoté, a great Sauvignon and a stunning *Corps de Garde* Chardonnay. Also here is a village called Chitry, where Christian Morin makes lovely Chablis-style but cheaper Chardonnays. However, it is not all good news in this little region, as I have yet to taste a decent red from **Irancy**. They are made from Pinot Noir, and also benefit from newly awarded AC status, but are generally too thin and lean. I would stick to hot vintages for fear of losing the fillings in your teeth!

THE CÔTE-D'OR
(Côte de Nuits and Côte de Beaune)
This is the collective term for the two main areas of vineyards

situated at the heart of the Burgundy region: the Côte de Nuits and the Côte de Beaune. Stretching thirty miles from the vineyards of Marsannay in the north to Maranges in the south, the Côte-d'Or is a near-continuous skinny slope of vineyards facing east. The village names you pass as you travel down the main road that follows this hill form a roll call of the greatest Pinot Noirs and Chardonnays in the world. The finest vineyards are situated in the middle of the slope itself, and the lesser wines are made on the flatter land at the bottom, or on the hilltops. The patchwork of vineyards is mesmerising to look at. This is the most mystical and captivating wine region I have ever visited – the concepts of *terroir* and microclimate are felt in the soil, air and wines so clearly that all of the complexities of the region seem to make sense in an instant.

The **Côte de Nuits**, the northerly of the two main regions in the 'golden slope', is the red-wine dominant half. Here the Pinot Noir grape reigns supreme, making blockbuster styles from this sensitive variety. It is also here that all but one of the red *Grand Cru* vineyards are situated. Before I run through the villages themselves, it is worth noting the regional wines that can be found in this part of the Côte-d'Or. Côte de Nuits-Villages comes from the vineyards on the northern (Fixin and Brochon) and southern (Comblanchien, Corgoloin and Prissy) extremes of the Côte de Nuits. These wines can offer very good-value drinking if you stick to reputable producers. Bourgogne Hautes-Côtes de Nuits wines are made from the hills above and behind the Côtes, where some fine estates have planted mainly red and a few white grapes to expand their production. Here also, the wines can be much cheaper than the Côte proper, but finding a good producer is a priority, as this will guarantee expert winemaking and therefore a good wine.

NB – My favourite Domaines listed are in the villages where they are based. It is worth remembering that most of these make wine from other neighbouring villages, too.

The villages of the Côte de Nuits (from north to south) are:

Marsannay-la-Côte and Fixin

Granted full AC status in 1987, Marsannay reds can sometimes resemble neighbouring Gevrey-Chambertins when made by the best producers. And, for that reason, winemakers based in nearby Gevrey often make the best Marsannays. The wines are usually meaty and robust, often lacking elegance. Marsannay can be found in white and rose form but these wines are very rare. I have never tasted a truly charming Fixin (pronounced 'Fiss-an' as opposed to 'Fix-in'). There are some *Premier Crus* here, but they only make even more backward and muscular wines for those with immense patience and cellar space to enjoy.

> **My favourite producers of Marsannay are:** Bruno Clair, Charles Audoin, Fougeray de Beauclair and René Bouvier.
>
> **My favourite producer of Fixin is:** Pierre Gelin.

Gevrey-Chambertin

Burgundy proper starts here in Gevrey, the largest of the Côte-d'Or villages (it is a small town really, with a few nice hotels and restaurants). These wines have the deepest colour of the red wines in the region, although there is a vast variation in the quality of Gevrey produced. Here, more than anywhere, must the thirsty buyer exercise caution. Gevrey has eight *Grand Crus*. I have listed them in order of my favourite and most intense to the lightest and fruitiest – Le Chambertin, Chambertin Clos de Bèze, Mazis-Chambertin, Latricières-Chambertin, Charmes-Chambertin, Ruchottes-Chambertin, Griotte-Chambertin and finally Chapelle-Chambertin (did you spot the link? It is no surprise Gevrey hijacked the name). Gevrey also possesses some terrific *1er Cru* vineyards. In the right hands, Les Cazetiers and Clos St-Jacques often out-perform the Grand Crus. Aux Combottes, Les Goulots, Combe au Moine and Champeaux are a few of the other all-star cast of *1er Crus*. Finally, *1er Cru* Craipillot is worth finding for dinner parties – and not just because of the comedy name!

Morey-St-Denis

Morey-St-Denis seems to suffer from being wedged in between two more famous neighbours – Gevrey-Chambertin and Chambolle-Musigny. The wines here seem to be lighter, but more sinewy than Gevreys, but more tannic and blunt than Chambolles. For this reason, they often fail to wow the taster early on in their lives, and then sometimes turn out to be a little bit four square when they are mature. Morey likes warmer vintages, when the Pinot fruit can reach full, physiological maturity on the vine. There are four *Grand Crus* here – Clos de la Roche, which is among the best red wines of the entire Côte-d'Or, Clos St-Denis, Clos de Tart and Clos des Lambrays. These are all worth tracking down in great years. The *1er Cru* vineyards worthy of note are Clos de Monts Luisants, from which Ponsot makes an amazing and rare white wine, and La Bussière, Les Faconnières and Clos des Ormes.

Chambolle-Musigny and Vougeot

The wines of Chambolle-Musigny are characterised by a sexiness and voluptuousness unlike any other red wines in the region. The scent of these wines is alluring (crushed strawberries and wild cherries) and they tend to be approachable when fairly young on account of the layers of fruit. Underneath the stunning chassis, Chambolles have considerable power but are easier to appreciate than, say, the wines of neighbouring Vosne. It goes without saying that top Domaines must be chosen for these hedonistic pleasures. *Grand Crus* in the village are Bonnes Mares and Musigny. Bonnes-Mares actually straddles the boundary between Morey and Chambolle – so if the plot of vines used for a wine is at the Morey end you can expect a darker, heavier wine. Conversely, the end nearest the village of Chambolle produces more aromatic styles of wine. Musigny itself is on the southern end of the village, sharing a boundary with Vosne. Stunning *1er Crus* are Les Amoureuses (an unforgettable wine and one that wins the prize for the most romantic vineyard name – to be enjoyed with your lover?) and Les Charmes (another beauty, not surprisingly), as well as Aux Beaux-Bruns, Les Véroilles, Les Baudes and Les Fuées. Le Musigny makes some white wine, the only white *Grand Cru* outside the Côte de Beaune, but I have never seen any! This village, for me, really shouts Pinot Noir from the rooftops, so perhaps it is the place to start if you haven't encountered these wines before.

Clos de Vougeot is an enormous, tourist-trap château with an accompanying large, walled, *Grand Cru* vineyard owned by no less than eighty or so different proprietors. Given the diversity of ownership and sheer size of the vineyard, it is not surprising that the quality of Clos de Vougeot wines ranges from dull to cosmic. Confusingly, alongside this plot of land is an area known as Vougeot, which has some *Premier-Cru*-rated vineyards. These often eclipse their grander namesake. Some white is made here, too.

> **My favourite producers of Chambolle-Musigny and Vougeot are:** Christian Clerget, Comte Georges de Vogüé, Ghislaine Barthod, Jacques-Frédéric Mugnier, Pierre Bertheau, G Roumier and de la Vougeraie.

Vosne-Romanée and Flagey-Echézeaux

These two villages have it all – relatively inexpensive Domaines, all of the way up to the extortionately priced but, thanks to their stellar quality, somehow completely reconcilable wines of Domaine de la Romanée Conti (DRC). From Bourgogne Rouge to Richebourg, this village covers a lot of ground on the palate. One thing is certain: that when tasting one of this village's *Grand Crus*, you have to remind yourself it is the medium-weight, aromatic Pinot Noir we have here. The wines are absolutely massive, with stunning aromas and structure only really reserved for grapes like Cabernet Sauvignon. The top producers' wines always amaze me, as they have the capability to age forever. This is where I have tasted my greatest ever red Burgundies, and just the thought of a glass of any of the wines on this page makes my heart race. First the big names: the *Grand Crus* in Vosne are Romanée Conti and La Tâche (these are *monopoles,* vineyards exclusively owned by one Domaine, in this case the aforementioned DRC), Richebourg, La Romanée, Romanée-St-Vivant and La Grande Rue. Echézeaux and Grands-Echézeaux are two situated in Flagey, where any village or *1er Cru* level wines are sold under the name of Vosne-Romanée. *Premier Crus* worth looking out for are Les Beaux Monts, Aux Brûlées, Aux Malconsorts, Les Chaumes, Les Gaudichots, Cros Parentoux and Les Suchots.

My favourite producers of Vosne-Romanée are: Anne Gros, Emmanuel Rouget, Jean Grivot, Lamarche, Leroy, Méo-Camuzet, Mongeard-Mugneret, René Engel, Robert Arnoux, de la Romanée-Conti and Sylvain Cathiard.

Nuits-Saint-Georges and Prémeaux-Prissey

Nuits-Saint-Georges is a very long vineyard area (5km) bisected by the town of Nuits itself. The vineyards are split into two distinct areas and those closest to Vosne, at the northern end, have more elegance, texture and fruit (I tend to prefer these). The southern end vineyards, near the hamlet of Prémeaux, are planted on very stony soils that were once considered infertile, but in fact give rise to rich, earthy, long-lived wines. Nuits has twenty-seven *1er Cru* vineyards and not one *Grand Cru*. The best of the *1er Cru* vineyards are Les Cailles (stones), Les Vaucrains (good-for-nothings) and Les St-Georges itself at the southern end, and, Aux Murgers, Aux Boudots, Les Damodes, La Richemone and Aux Chaignots at the juicy Vosne end. The wines of Nuits are usually fairly robust and take several years to become approachable.

My favourite producers of Nuits-Saint-Georges are: Alain Michelot, Bertrand Ambroise, J-C Boisset, Daniel Chopin-Groffier, Daniel Rion, Dominique Laurent, Faiveley, Henri Gouges, Jean Chauvenet, Jean-Jacques Confuron, Lécheneaut, Nicolas Potel and Robert Chevillon.

The **Côte de Beaune** section of the Côte-d'Or runs south of the town of Beaune and is further split into a red grape (Pinot Noir) dominant northerly section and a white grape (Chardonnay) dominant south. It is here that all but one of the white *Grand Cru* vineyards are situated. Before I run through the villages themselves, it is again worth noting the regional wines that can be found in this part of the Côte-d'Or. Surprisingly, Côte de Beaune-Villages wines are all reds, despite being situated in a strong white wine region. These wines again offer good value drinking, but stick to well-known producers. Bourgogne Hautes-Côtes de Beaune is also a red wine dominant appellation, with the same rules applying as regards buying.

The villages of the Côte de Beaune are:

Aloxe-Corton and Ladoix-Serrigny

It is here that we find the last remaining red *Grand Cru* vineyard, Corton. The wines of Corton tend to be more reminiscent of a Côte de Nuits style, having power and firm acidity in youth. They may not have the stuffing of a Vosne-Romanée, but are unlike the other fleshier red wines made in the Côte de Beaune. Corton can be simply labelled 'Corton', or can attach a named vineyard site to its title. The best *climats* (named vineyards) within Corton to look out for are Le Clos du Roi, Les Bressandes and Les Perrières. Aloxe-Corton ('xe' pronounced 'ss') wines, both *village* and *1er Cru*, are found on the lower slopes of the hill of Corton. These wines are scaled down versions of the big red wine itself. The great white wine of this area is the *Grand Cru*, Corton-Charlemagne, which can be found nestling beside its red namesake on the panoramic hillside above the village. Austere, powerful and mineral in youth, Corton-Charlemagne is the long-distance runner of the white

Grand Crus. They tend to broaden out after a few years, but if drunk too early seem to lack definition despite their considerable weight. The appellation Ladoix is a mystery to me as I have tasted many bottles of this village's red wines and have remained distinctly underwhelmed by them all. I suspect that most of them are sold under a Côte de Beaune-Villages (CdB-V) label.

> **My favourite producers of Aloxe-Corton and Ladoix-Serrigny are:** Bertrand Ambroise, Bonneau du Martray, Coche-Dury, Edmond Cornu, Dubreuil-Fontaine, Louis Jadot, Michel Juillot, Louis Latour, Maurice Rollin, Tollot-Beaut and Michel Voarick.

Pernand-Vergelesses

If you sneak around the hill of Corton to its northwest side, then plunge down into the valley below, the vineyards of Pernand-Vergelesses lie in wait. Tucked away in a valley off the main Côte-d'Or hillside, Pernand's problem is one of exposure. The hill of Corton blots out the sun for much of the day. However, the better vineyards on flatter land do receive adequate sunshine. Many of the vineyards in Pernand harvest late on account of their sunshine deficit and consequently in tricky vintages are at the mercy of the elements. I prefer the white wines of Pernand, as good examples have a 'baby-Corton-Charlemagne' feel about them, only you do not have to wait ten years to enjoy them. The reds often lack ripeness and fruit and, like Ladoix, I suspect a lot of the wine here ends up in CdB-V! However, in good vintages they can be very good value, so don't tell anyone and take advantage of one of the few bargains in this expensive region. The best *1er Cru* vineyards to look out for are Ile de Vergelesses and Vergelesses.

> **My favourite producers of Pernand-Vergelesses are:** Germain and Maurice Rollin.

Savigny-lès-Beaune

Savigny-près-Beaune (old French for 'near Beaune') became

Savigny-lès-Beaune in 1863. Here, well-made white wines again resemble diminutive Corton-Charlemagnes in the mineral, nutty fruit they exude. In good years the reds can be sublime, with the wines treading a taste tightrope between the flavours of Nuits and Beaune. My favourite growers make a vast range of styles of red Savigny, from light, fresh, strawberry cocktail *villages* wines, via tight, mouth-watering, damson-infused *1er Crus* like Tollot-Beaut's Les Lavières to brooding, monster *1er Crus* like La Dominode from ever reliable Jean-Marc Pavelot.

> **My favourite producers of Savigny-lès-Beaune are:** Chandon de Briailles, Jean-Marc Pavelot and Maurice Ecard.

Chorey-lès-Beaune

Chorey is the forgotten village of the Côte de Beaune. Only awarded AC status in 1974, and without a single *1er Cru* vineyard, this village is on the wrong side of the road (RN74), but is worth a mention because in good years the red wines have pure, red cherry appeal. They are precocious and require little cellaring. Stick to my two producers and you won't go wrong.

> **My favourite producers of Chorey-lès-Beaune are:** Jacques Germain and Tollot-Beaut.

Beaune

Beaune is the capital of the southern section of the Côte-d'Or. Once an encampment of wine-loving Julius Caesar, Beaune's wines are almost all red and, invariably, the Leslie Phillips of the red Burgundy charm school. Calm, collected, forward and fruity, these wines have style and yet rarely live as long as those of their two southerly neighbours, Volnay and Pommard. There are a huge number of *1er Cru* vineyards in Beaune curling around the northwest corner of the town, and here is a small selection of the finest sites: Les Cent-Vignes, Les Bressandes, Les Grèves, Clos du Roi, Les Montrevenots, Les Epenottes and Les Teurons. There is a smattering of white made here, too, and Les Clos-des-Mouches, by Drouhin, is one of the more collectable versions.

Pommard

Pommard is only a few kilometres south of Beaune, but the wines could not be more different. I absolutely adore this style of Pinot Noir. Lacking the brawn of the Côte de Nuits, but possessing more structure and length than most wines from Beaune, Pommard is an attractive prospect for Pinot-philes. There are so many good winemakers and vineyards in this village that if you combine the following *1er Crus* with the producers below the results are nothing short of epic. Les Pézerolles and Les Epenots on the Beaune side often have more power and require a few more years to soften than Les Rugiens, Les Fremiers and Les Jarolières on the Volnay side, which have a silky, velvety dimension to the taste.

Volnay

Volnays are sexy, silky-smooth, welcoming wines, which somehow feel like red wines planted on white-wine soil. In fact the Volnay vineyards touch the reds of Pommard on one side and the whites of Meursault on the other. The best Volnay Domaines make heavenly wines that will appeal to all red-wine lovers (and most white). No *Grand Crus* needed here as a host of outstanding *1er Crus* do the job admirably. Taillepieds, Clos des Ducs, Champans, Clos des Chênes, Les Caillerets and Les Mitans are all first class, and even a *1er Cru* red vineyard in neighbouring Meursault is sold under the Volnay appellation, that of Les Santenots. *Village* level Volnay made by any one of the names below will always impress, and will give you a superb idea of what a classic Côte de Beaune red should taste like.

Monthélie

Bordering Volnay and Meursault, this little village might be expected to make excellent wines. However, the reality is that the minuscule white production does not get anywhere near even moderate Meursault, and most of the red wine is presumably sold as Côte de Beaune-Villages. The best reds that I have tasted have been notable but not amazing – there must be more out there? You have to wait for a warm vintage to really get the most from Monthélie, and then you will find them better value than many Volnays if you stick to the best estates. There are eleven *1er Crus,* but I will not bother listing them, as the Domaine name is by far the most important factor.

Auxey-Duresses

Passing Monthélie and heading down a valley off the main drag, you come across Auxey (say 's' for 'x'). Again, like Pernand, being tucked up in a valley facing the wrong way has its ripening problems, but some vineyards have good aspects, like the best *1er Cru*, Les Duresses. A handful of famous Domaines from nearby villages own vineyards here – Coche-Dury makes a good red, but the only locals of note are listed below. About a quarter of Auxey is white and it can do a passable impression of a Meursault in the right hands. The reds tend to be lean and green in youth, unlike their neighbour Volnay, needing a few years to iron out tannins. Do stick to good vintages, otherwise the fruit will never really come around.

St-Romain

At the end of this valley, beyond Auxey, sitting high up on a cliff, is the town of St-Romain. I am not usually keen on their wines but, once again, in good vintages (warm ones) decent wines can be made.

My favourite producers of St-Romain are: d'Auvenay and Christophe Buisson.

Meursault

The first, and largest, of the serious white wine villages back on the Côte-d'Or proper is Meursault. A utopian Chardonnay community, this village is a lovely place to stay, situated in the middle of a carpet of stunning, picturesque, old vineyards. There are no *Grand Crus* here but a few *1er Crus*, of which Les Charmes, Les Genevrières and Les Perrières are the cream of the crop. Some red Meursault is made, but don't worry about it – that is not the point of this village. Honey, nuts, lime, brioche, mouth-filling richness and heroic length are the hallmarks of great Meursault – this is Chardonnay firing on all cylinders, and it is this style of wine that is the reason why Chardonnay is planted all over the world. Meursault is a village that uses a lot of *lieu-dit* names on bottles. These indicate the name of the vineyard the wine comes from because, even though it may not be a *1er Cru*, it may have a worthy track record nevertheless. Some of the most well known are: Les Tillets, Les Luchets, Le Tesson, Les Meix Chavaux and Les Grands Charrons. *Village* Meursault is usually drinking two or three years after the harvest, making these wines the most forward of the three great white villages.

My favourite producers of Meursault are: des Comtes Lafon, Henri Germain, Jean-François Coche-Dury, Jean-Michel Gaunoux, Jean-Philippe Fichet, Marc Rougeot, Michel Tessier, Patrick Javillier, Roulot and Vincent Bouzereau.

Puligny-Montrachet

This is the village that boasts the greatest concentration of white *Grand Cru* vineyards, as well as no less than twelve *1er Crus*.

Chevalier-Montrachet and Bienvenues-Bâtard-Montrachet are in Puligny, while Le Montrachet and Bâtard-Montrachet have vineyards in Puligny and Chassagne. These tiny vineyards (Montrachet is only 100 yards wide) are supposedly the most expensive real estate in the world (including downtown Tokyo!). As these wines are phenomenally expensive it is usually best to try to search out *1er Crus* wines in order to get a glimpse of what the mighty Grand Cru wines taste like. Top *1er Cru* vineyards are the superbly placed Le Cailleret and Les Pucelles (next to the big boys) and the rich, heady Les Folatières, Les Perrières, Champ Canet, Clavaillon, Les Referts and La Truffière. It is hard to explain just how amazing these wines can be without lapsing into convoluted wine-speak and personal gibberish – except to say that there are few Chardonnays in the world that at ten years old are just starting to drink well, retain their freshness and complexity, as well as layers of fruit flavours capturing every element of your concentration and hypnotising your taste buds.

> **My favourite producers of Puligny-Montrachet are:** Domaine Leflaive, Etienne Sauzet, Louis Carillon, Olivier Leflaive and Paul Pernot.

Chassagne-Montrachet

Village Chassagne tends to be more impressive than *village* Puligny for some reason. Perhaps better value has something to do with it – there is a lot more of it around, too. Chassagne shares two *Grand Crus* with Puligny (see above), but also has one of its own, Criots-Bâtard-Montrachet. The white wines made in this village are superb, and there are a number of fabulous reds as well. In fact, over half of the wine made in this village is red. (Always watch out when you are ordering Chassagne in a restaurant.) The reds from Chassagne are very underrated and they provide a great source of early-drinking, great-value Pinot – once again, stick to the best producers. The *1er Crus* (both red and white) hug the side of the hill, while the village or *lieu-dit* vineyards are on the flatter land. Good white *1er Crus* are: La Boudriotte, Les Chaumées, En Cailleret, Les Champs Gains and

Vide Bourse. Strangely, white Chassagne usually outlives red by a few years.

> **My favourite producers of Chassagne-Montrachet are:** Bernard Morey, Blain-Gagnard, Fontaine-Gagnard, Gagnard-Delagrange, Guy Amiot, Jean-Noël Gagnard, Marc Colin, Marc Morey, Michel Colin-Deléger, Michel Niellon and Ramonet.

St-Aubin

Like Chassagne this little village is planted with both white and red grapes. Tucked away behind Chassagne, St-Aubin's wine is often released as CdB-V. However, as more and more drinkers discover these Chassagne-style wines at much lower prices, the interest in St-Aubin is increasing. There are a handful of *1er Crus* here, of which Sur le Sentier du Clou and Les Frionnes are the best reds and Les Murgers des Dents du Chien, En Remilly, Le Charmois, Les Combes and La Chatenière are the best whites. As some vineyards touch both Puligny and Chassagne, the best whites tend to be situated along these boundaries. My favourite two producers of St-Aubin are both based in the village, but some outsiders make wines worth looking out for; Chartron & Trébuchet and Jadot are two excellent *négociants* and Domaines Bernard Morey and Marc Colin are based around the corner in Chassagne.

> **My favourite producers of St-Aubin are:** Gérard Thomas, Henri Prudhon and Hubert & Olivier Lamy.

Santenay

The last main village on the Golden Hillside is Santenay. Here, the charm and fruit that is found in the rest of the Côte de Beaune is somewhat lacking. Red Santenay is usually a rugged creature, lacking in elegance. Luckily there are bargains to be snapped up from reputable Domaines. I am only keen on Girardin as far as local talent is concerned, preferring to look further afield for winemakers who are used to handling finer fruit. White Santenay is a relative rarity and in the right hands it can provide good, classy drinking for less cash than its near neighbours' wines. The best *1er Cru* vineyards are La Comme, Clos-de-Tavannes, Les Gravières and Beauregard because they follow on the hillside border with Chassagne.

My favourite producer of Santenay is: Vincent Girardin.

Maranges

This *really* is the last village on the Côte, or rather the last three villages all sharing the name Maranges – Cheilly, Sampigny and Dezize. The wine is usually released as CdBV; there are very few fine wines to be found in this outpost. Mainly utilising Pinot Noir, only the mercurial Bernard Morey (in Chassagne) manages to set my palate alight with enthusiasm. You are better off jumping over these three villages and heading straight for the Côte Chalonnaise.

CÔTE CHALONNAISE

Wedged between the Côte-d'Or and the Mâconnais area is a region known as the Côte Chalonnaise. Here there are three distinct islands of vines set in rolling hills. Starting just south of Santenay, in the town of **Bouzeron**, we find the other famous white grape of Burgundy – Aligoté. 'Bourgogne Aligoté de Bouzeron' is the only appellation specifically set up for this refreshing, zingy white grape. A & P de Villaine make the finest version of Aligoté in the world, and they can achieve a surprising depth of flavour from this simple little grape. Just a few kilometres down the road is the village of **Rully**, where white and red grapes are grown. This time we are back in Chardonnay and Pinot Noir territory, but I rarely come across truly juicy red wines from this appellation. Chardonnays are the order of the day and, apart from the Château de Rully, Paul & Henri Jacquesson, Eric de Suremain, de la Folie and Vincent Dureuil-Janthial, I prefer to buy wines from outside producers. These Chardonnays often have finesse and will benefit from short-term ageing, and, at half the price of a Puligny-Montrachet, they are worth searching for. There are a number of *1er Cru* vineyards here and it is definitely worth trading up to them to ensure more fruit intensity in the glass. **Mercurey**, the biggest village in the Chalonnaise, is the next on the list, and it is dominated by the Pinot Noir grape. Years of tasting, showing fair play to all, has left me with only a handful of producers to recommend: Antonin Rodet, Bruno Lorenzon, Luc Brintet, Michel & Laurent Juillot and J & F Raquillet. The best *1er Cru* vineyards sites are Clos des Barraults and Les Champs Martins. The style of wine to look out for is medium-weight Pinots, with medium-term ageing capacity. There is a small amount of white here, too, and the best Chardonnays also come from my recommended producers.

There is then a break in the vineyards before coming to the village of **Givry**. Locals such as Domaine du Clos Salomon, Joblot and François Lumpp make fine reds that have less body than the wines of Mercurey but are preferable to gambling with red Rully. In this unfashionable village, there is a small amount of white produced from Chardonnay, but I would wait until the exclusively white appellation of **Montagny**, a little further south, before choosing any wine. Montagny wines have Chablis-style acidity, with a depth and nuttiness more commonly associated with the Côte-d'Or. The good news is that they are fortunately much cheaper than both of those regions. All of the wine from this village is classified as *1er Cru*, as long as the alcohol level reaches 11.5 per cent, which makes it hard to differentiate between them unless you are armed with a producer's name. So here they are, just two – Bertrand and Stéphane Aladame. Other producers from further afield make Montagny, and if you find someone useful from the Côte-d'Or proper, then take a punt!

MÂCONNAIS

Neatly fitting like a jigsaw piece into the southern end of the Côte Chalonnaise is the Mâconnais. This is 'white wine central' for Burgundy, as the Mâconnais pumps out three times more white wine than all the rest of Burgundy put together. This is also the transition point for red grapes, where Pinot Noir's dominance gives way to Gamay. A quarter of the vines planted here are Gamay and there is a little Pinot Noir as well – but I would ignore these wines! Red Mâconnais, 'pah', we have not got to Beaujolais yet where Gamay does its thing and, if you want Pinot Noir, go back up north, this is Chardonnay country.

There are three main types of Mâcon blanc: Mâcon plus a village name, Pouilly plus a village name and St-Véran. There are apparently forty villages that can attach their name to a Mâcon blanc but Lugny, Cruzille, Prissé, Fuissé, Uchizy and Davayé are probably the best known. Back in 1999, Viré and Clessé broke free from this rule and set up their own elite AC called *Viré-Clessé*. It is widely believed that these are the finest of the white Mâcon wines. Pouilly on the other hand has only three main attachments to its prefix – Loché, Vinzelles and the far superior Fuissé. St-Véran has only one – St-Véran, of course. One tricky but worthwhile point to pass on is the pronunciation of Pouilly-Fuissé. There are so many mangled versions of this lovely wine it is now time to get it right once and for all – 'Pwee-Fwee-say'.

As with the rest of Burgundy, it is not where the vineyard is but who makes the wine that is the most important factor in the Mâconnais. This is a huge region and there are a number of outstanding Domaines. The beauty of the wines from the Mâconnais is that they range from crystal clear, rapier-sharp fruit to oaky, honeyed, decadent beauties. Most of these wines have the ability to age, although not for as long as their Côte-d'Or counterparts. The 'best value Chardonnays in the world' is how many of my contemporaries rate this region. Stick to the estates below and that statement will not be wrong.

> **My favourite Mâconnais producers are:** André Bonhomme, Château de Beauregard, Château Fuissé (Jean-Jacques Vincent), Daniel Barraud, des Deux Roches, Goyard, Guillemot-Michel, Héritiers du Comte Lafon (from Meursault fame), Jeandeau, Jean Thévenet, la Croix Senaillet, la Sarazinière, Michel Forest, Robert-Denogent, Talmard and Verget (Guffens-Heynen).

BEAUJOLAIS

Gamay is the grape of the region. This purple-coloured, super-juicy grape is responsible for the buffoonish Beaujolais Nouveau as well as the most underpriced *Grands Vins* imaginable.

Beaujolais makes approximately 15 million cases of wine per year, compared to the rest of Burgundy's total of only about 9 million, so there is always enough to go around. A scary fact is that more than half of Beaujolais's production is sold as Beaujolais Noweau – the cheapest and nastiest incarnation of this style. There are three different styles of wine made here: Beaujolais, Beaujolais-Villages and Beaujolais Cru. Straight Beaujolais is frankly worth avoiding, as it could come from anywhere within the region and most of it is sold as Nouveau. Beaujolais-Villages is a blend of wines from two or more villages. This style of wine can be well made, depending on the Domaine or the person who makes it. The third level is Beaujolais Cru, where the wine must be entirely made from within the boundary of any one of the ten approved villages. It is said that each village has its own flavour nuances and style, and this in part is true. However, it is always up to the individual winemaker whether or not the final wine is light or heavy, forward or tannic, so I tend to follow winemakers or Domaines as opposed to village names. There is a tiny amount of white and rosé made in Beaujolais, but skip the white as a Mâcon Blanc is usually a better bet, while the rosé can be delicious if it's from a decent name. When on top form, the red wines of Beaujolais can range in style from the chillable crushed-red-fruit flavours, indispensable on a picnic, to rich, gamey, blackberry fruit and pepper and spice on the nose, a worthy accompaniment to roast chicken or beef stew. Beaujolais offers the most food-friendly, affordable wines in the world. Reacquaint yourself with this much-derided region.

The ten Beaujolais *Cru* Villages are: Saint-Amour, Juliénas, Fleurie, Moulin-à-Vent, Brouilly, Côte de Brouilly, Régnié, Chénas, Chiroubles and Morgon.

The top producers are: Alain Passot, André Cologne, Aucoeur, Bernard Mélinand, F & J Calot, Champagnon, Château de Pierreux, Coudert, Georges Duboeuf (domaine-bottled wines only), J-L Dutraive, J-F Echallier (des Pins), Hélène & Denis Barbelet, Henry Fessy, Jacky Janodet, Jean-Charles Pivot, Jean Foillard, Louis Jadot (Château des Jacques), Marcel Lapierre, Maurice Gaget, Michel Chignard, Pascal Granger, Patrick Brunet, Paul Janin and Vissoux.

Champagne

Champagne is the one wine region where image counts above everything. It is the world's most bulletproof wine brand – no other world wine region has protected its image and lofty price so cleverly over the years.

As you can probably tell, I am a slightly jaded Champagne lover. This is because the region and its wines split neatly down the middle. On one side sits the mass-produced, overpriced, mean-tasting fizz destined to be hosed down at parties, weddings and other functions, where the taste is second to the fact that it says Champagne on the label. On the other side, there are beautifully crafted, elegant wines with finesse and longevity – worth every penny of their not-inconsiderable price tags.

I will, not surprisingly, concentrate on the latter category. First, however, we must look at how this enigma is made, and also run down the different styles found in the region.

Before we start, it is important to remember that Champagne is the most northerly of France's wine regions so the grapes are barely ripe when harvested. The capital of Champagne, Reims, and the other main town in the area, Epernay, are in fact northeast of Paris. There would be no point making still wines here – they would simply be far too dry and harsh to drink. And yet, this style of grape as a base for sparkling wines is fantastic. *Voilà* – the capital of the world's finest fizzies.

HOW TO MAKE CHAMPAGNE

Champagne is usually made from Chardonnay, Pinot Noir and Pinot Meunier. The colour pigments in the skins of the two red grapes could colour the juice, so, once the harvested grapes are crushed, the skins are quickly removed from the must. The must is then fermented in stainless steel tanks, or occasionally oak barrels. The alcoholic fermentation is followed by malolactic fermentation in an effort to soften the searingly high levels of acidity. This results in a bone-dry, searingly acidic (rather unpleasant, it has to be said) white wine. It is now that the magical blending process occurs. Non-vintage Champagne is not only a blend of two or three of the above grape varieties from many different vineyard sites, but also a mix of different vintages of wine (hence NV = 'not one vintage'). The most skilled job in this region is that of the blender who assembles infinitely variable combinations of base wine into a completed *cuvée*. The aim is to produce a 'house' style that remains the same despite the variations in vintage etc. For instance, NV Billecart-Salmon Brut Réserve should always taste the same, no matter where you are in the world. If you like it once, you should like it again and again – this is the main aim of NV Champagne. Once the blend is decided and the acidic white wine bottled, a small amount of *liqueur de tirage* is added to each bottle. This contains, sugar, yeast and 'still' Champagne. The bottles are sealed with a cap, like a beer bottle, and banished to the cellars for a second alcoholic fermentation. The carbon dioxide generated from this is trapped in the bottle and dissolves into the wine, later to be released in the form of bubbles when the day of uncorking arrives. The next process, *remuage*, is a gradual twisting and jiggling of the bottle in order to shake the lees (the dead yeast cells) down to the neck behind the cap. This is done by stacking the bottles in an A-frame wooden contraption, drilled on both sides with sixty holes. The neck of the bottle is put into this *pupitre*, with the bottle lying horizontally. Over the course of eight or so weeks a man called a *remuer*, with wrists like a gorilla, twists and gradually inverts the bottles into a vertical, upside-down position, with the sediment ready to be ejected. The bottle tops are plunged into a frozen brine solution and the neck section of the bottle freezes, capturing the sediment in a champagne ice cube. This is gently popped out of the bottle (*dégorgement*) and replaced with a *liqueur d'expédition* (a wine with a touch of sugar depending on the style). A cork is banged in, a wire is fastened around it to prevent any unwanted explosions and the bottle is labelled, ready for the off.

Sounds easy? It is not surprising that Champagne is a fairly expensive wine style – the winemaking process is complicated, the equipment costs a bomb and the wine must be aged for a minimum of one year (the best houses usually aim for three) before it is sold. Having said that, mechanisation has made these processes a lot easier than in monk Dom Pérignon's day. When he spotted some of his wine popping its corks in the monastery cellar and, legend has it, he invented Champagne, everything was done by hand.

CHAMPAGNE STYLES
Non-Vintage
This style is blended across different vintages (usually three), endeavouring to capture a 'house style'. Non-Vintage Champagne accounts for three-quarters of all Champagne produced. The style ages well in the short term, and most wines will improve after a year of extra cellaring. This is the least expensive style of Champagne and marketing managers strive to get their customers to remain 'brand-loyal' to it.

Vintage
This is made entirely from one year's harvest, so will only be conceived in particularly good vintages. Vintage wines tend to be more expensive than Non-Vintage by about half as much again (unscrupulous houses release a vintage as often as possible). This is not the point and reputable houses will stick to the five or so years in ten when the weather is favourable and the wine worthy.

Rosé
Non-Vintage or Vintage, these wines are made by blending a little red wine with white. Most rosé Champagnes also have a higher percentage of red grapes in the blend to help marry the tastes together. Rosé fizz tends to suffer from the vagaries of fashion and I suspect the majority of bottles of this delicious style of wine get consumed on St Valentine's Day. This is a shame because its unique flavour does, in fact, complement many dishes well and I reckon it should be drunk whenever you get the urge (as often as possible really!), as opposed to on only one day of the year.

Blanc de Blancs
This style can also be Non-Vintage or Vintage and, as the name suggests, it is white wine made from white grapes only. As we are in Champagne, that means 100 per cent Chardonnay. The

name also translates to suggest white wine from the Côte des Blancs, which is a predominantly Chardonnay-planted area of Champagne. Either way it means the same thing. BdBs are usually much tighter on the palate initially (lacking Pinot Meunier's palate-softening characteristics) and need some time in the cellar to soften; these wines can be amazingly concentrated with very long finishes.

Blanc de Noirs

White wine from black (red) grapes – in this case the two Pinots, Meunier and Noir. This is a relatively rare style of wine that can, in certain cases, have a delightful pink tinge to its colour. BdNs tend to be fruitier than other styles of Champagne, perhaps even tasting red – if you've got your eyes shut. Non-Vintage and Vintage styles are made.

Crémant

Crémant is a very rare style that is so called on account of its frothing, or 'creaming' character. The wine is less aggressively fizzy than normal Champagne, and usually made from the finer Chardonnay grape.

Préstige Cuvées

At the top of the ladder, these styles are usually Vintage wines, although there are some notable exceptions. The finest vineyards' crops are put aside in excellent vintages then handcrafted into these beautiful wines. It is not unknown for this style of Champagne to last for twenty or more years, making them some of the longest-lived, dry-white-wine styles. Super expensive, usually drunk by fictional secret agents and the like, they should always reward the drinker with unbeatable complexity and heroic length. As always, it is necessary to select certain houses over others.

TOP CHAMPAGNE HOUSES AND THEIR FINEST *CUVÉES*

Billecart-Salmon *NV* Brut Réserve, Brut Rosé, Blanc de Blancs and Demi-Sec. *Vintage* Blanc de Blancs, Le Clos Saint-Hilaire, Cuvée Nicolas-François Billecart, Elisabeth Salmon Rosé and Grande Cuvée.

Bollinger *NV* Special Cuvée. *Vintage* Grande Année, RD and Vieilles Vignes Françaises Blanc de Noirs.

Deutz *Vintage* Blanc de Blancs and Cuvée William Deutz.

Gosset *NV* Brut Excellence, Grande Réserve Brut and Grand Réserve Rosé. *Vintage* Célébris and Grande Millésime Brut.

Alfred Gratien *Vintage* Brut.

Charles Heidsieck *NV* Mise en Cave and Rosé. *Vintage* Brut Millésime.

Jacquesson *Vintage* Avize Grand Cru Blanc de Blancs, Dégorgement Tardive and Grand Vin Signature.

Krug *NV* Grande Cuvée. *Vintage* Vintage and Clos du Mesnil.

Laurent-Perrier *NV* Cuvée Rosé Brut, Grand Siècle 'La Cuvée' and Ultra Brut.

Moët & Chandon *Vintage* Brut Impérial and Cuvée Dom Pérignon Brut.

Pol Roger *NV* Brut 'White Foil'. *Vintage* Brut Chardonnay, Brut Rosé, Brut Vintage and Cuvée Sir Winston Churchill.

Louis Roederer *NV* Brut Premier. *Vintage* Blanc de Blancs, Brut Millésime, Brut Rosé, Cristal and Cristal Rosé.

Ruinart *Vintage* Dom Ruinart Blanc de Blancs and 'R' de Ruinart Brut.

Salon *Vintage* Blanc de Blancs.

Taittinger *NV* Brut Réserve and Prélude. *Vintage* Comtes de Champagne Blanc de Blancs.

Alain Thiénot *Vintage* Brut and Grande Cuvée.

Veuve Clicquot *NV* Brut 'Yellow Label' and Demi-Sec. *Vintage* La Grande Dame Brut, La Grande Dame Rosé and Vintage Réserve.

SMALLER HOUSES WELL WORTH TRACKING DOWN

Albert Beerens, André Jacquart, Bertrand Robert, Château de Boursault, Claude Carré, Delamotte, J Dumangin, Edouard Brun, Egly-Ouriet, Fernand Thill, Fleury, Gatinois, Gérard Dubois, J-M Gobillard, D Henriet-Bazin, Jacques Selosse, Larmandier-Bernier, Leclerc Briant, Legras, A Margaine, Le Mesnil, Paul Déthune, Pertois-Moriset, Pierre Gimonnet, Pierre Moncuit, Pierre Vaudon, Roger Brun, G Tribaut and Vilmart.

> **NB** – Do not waste your money on cheap champagne; for just a few pounds more the experience can be ten times as pleasant. Use the above list, find your 'house' style and stick to it!

Alsace

I have said that Champagne is a long way north in winemaking terms. Well, Alsace is up there as well, and it ought to suffer the same climatic, ripening problems – but it doesn't.

There is a reason why, and it is the magnificent Vosges Mountains. These form a classic 'rain shadow' – one slope acts as a shelter from wind and rain for slopes on the opposite side. This results in some of the lowest rainfall statistics in France, coupled with superb sunshine hours. So it is not all doom and gloom in Alsace – far from it: twelve million bottles of mainly dry, white Alsace wine are produced in a good year, and that is a lot for a region that seemingly has a bit of an identity crisis.

The main obstacle Alsace that has to deal with is the public's perception of its wines. The wine trade's love of these wines has never quite crossed over to the consumer. Perhaps it is because the wines are bottled in the traditional 'flute' shaped bottle and look dangerously German? Maybe the grape varieties written on the wine labels are not that familiar? Whatever the reason, the only way to bring these uniquely delicious wines to the attention of the drinking public is to talk about them and increase communication channels. A recent PR push has focused on the compatibility of Alsatian wines and Asian/fusion food. I would encourage you all to taste the wines.

Alsace is one of France's easier regions to understand: the rules and regulations are relatively straightforward, and all of the wines are AC quality level. If the grape variety appears on the label, it must contain 100 per cent of the variety stated. If it is blended, then a brand name may be used or else the term *Edelzwicker* will be mentioned. Some sparkling wines are made using the traditional method and these are known as *Crémant d'Alsace*. Again, if they contain 100 per cent varietal fruit, this grape variety will be noted on the label.

The best fifty vineyards in Alsace have been designated *Grand Crus*, and when the grapes from one of these vineyards is used, the label will read *Alsace Grand Cru* followed by the name of the vineyard and the grape variety. Only four of Alsace's grape varieties have *Grand Cru* quality status: Riesling, Gewürztraminer, Tokay-Pinot Gris and (for some reason) Muscat.

Vendage Tardive (VT) and *Sélection des Grains Nobles* (SGNs) styles can be made, weather permitting, by leaving the grapes on the vines late into the picking season, then harvesting them with higher than normal sugar levels, or when they are botrytis-affected. These two styles of wine are generally very rich and usually sweet. VT styles last in the bottle for ages, gradually drying out as time marches on. SGNs usually remain sweet and can be very syrupy and decadent. These are both pretty expensive and relatively rare.

The grapes used for making Alsace wines are the aforementioned Riesling, Gewürztraminer, Tokay-Pinot Gris and

Muscat, as well as Sylvaner, Pinot Blanc and Pinot Noir (see the Grape Varieties chapter for details).

I absolutely adore the wines from this region. They act as thirst-quenching aperitifs and skilful food-matching wines (from pâtés, salads, all fish dishes, chicken, Chinese, Asian, French, English ... whatever, to puddings, and after dinner sippers) – oh, they do everything. And they are such good value.

The one golden rule is, as always, to know not what the grape variety is, or what the vintage is like, or which Grand Cru vineyard the grapes came from, but who made the wine.

The top producers are: Albert Boxler, Albert Mann, André Thomas, Bott-Geyl, Ernest Burn, Hugel, Josmeyer, Marc Kreydenweiss, Marcel Deiss, Mittnacht-Klack, Ostertag, Paul Blanck, Rolly Gassmann, Schlumberger, Schoffit, Trimbach, Weinbach and Zind-Humbrecht.

The Loire Valley

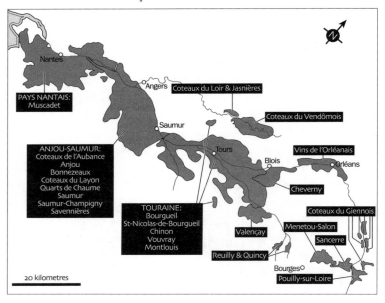

This is a picturesque and historic wine region to tour around, not least because it is home to some of the most beautiful châteaux in France. Its hotels and restaurants are fabulous value as well. Starting on the Atlantic coast in the town of Nantes, then slicing east and south through over 600 miles of verdant French countryside, the Loire river and its tributaries cover a myriad soil types and dozens of microclimates. In fact, this one region has it all, from light aperitif sparklers and all manner of whites including some superb sweeties, through Beaujolais-challenging, fruit-driven gluggers, to dark, deep, brooding, cellar-demanding red wines. The greatest single incentive to demystify this region as soon as you possibly can, is that, for some reason, the wines made here lag a long way behind other classic French wine in terms of price. It is near impossible to spend more than £15 on a bottle of Loire wine and most can be snapped up, including the top Domaines' wines, for between £5 and £10. So save some cash and prepare for a taste-bud challenge.

The four main regions in the Loire are (starting on the coast):

NANTES

The *Pays Nantais* or Nantes countryside is famous for one main white wine – **Muscadet**. You might think this an inauspicious start to our tour. After all, even the finest Muscadet is hardly a *Grand Vin* – but they are worth tracking down. They are all inexpensive and thirst quenching, and this dry, tangy wine is the perfect match for salads and fresh seafood. This is the definitive garden glugger that should be drunk young, ice cold and by the flagon. The Muscadet grape (also known as Melon de Bourgogne) is at its best in the Sèvre-et-Maine region to the southwest of the town of Nantes. There are two rules to remember when buying Muscadet. First, make sure that the label specifies that the wine comes from this superior sub-region. Second, that the style of wine made is *sur lie*, meaning that the wine sits on its lees, or sediment, during its production – this results in more flavour and depth on the palate.

The best Muscadet producers are: Château de Chasseloir, Chéreau, Luc Choblet, de la Mortaine and de la Quilla.

ANJOU-SAUMUR

This is a large region covering the land between the towns of Angers and Saumur. Forget Anjou Rosé (the watered-down, sweet cranberry juice of the wine world), this fine region sports the champion white grape of the Loire, Chenin Blanc. Remarkably age-worthy, dry Chenins, the finest of which are **Savennières**, are made well in this region. A couple of Domaines produce wines that can live for twenty or thirty years, so perfect are their balance and acidity. The other styles of Chenin Blanc made here are the sweet wines of **Coteaux du Layon** (which can add one of six village names to this prefix on the label), **Coteaux de l'Aubance**, **Bonnezeaux** and **Quarts de Chaume**. Late-picked and often botrytis affected, the wines are unctuous, oily and dripping in honeyed fruit. These wines can live for as long as top Sauternes, but represent much better value.

Saumur is the capital of the sparkling wine industry in the Loire Valley, where traditional-method wines are made from Chenin Blanc, Chardonnay and Cabernet Franc. It is said that Chenin makes a lumpier, 'sweeter' style of fizz than its noble, northern French competitors, but with the Champenois owning several properties here, and the much lower price tag, these wines are worthy of a place in your wine diet. Perhaps not as showy or downright celebratory as Champagne, they are great for summer parties or used to make sexy cocktails.

The first glimpse at the red wines of the Loire comes in the shape of **Saumur Rouge** and the often superior **Saumur-Champigny**. Here, where the Vienne river meets the Loire, the gravel soils are perfect for the Cabernet Franc grape to thrive. The top estate is Domaine Filliatreau, where they make several *cuvées*, from a light, purple-coloured, blackberry-scented Saumur, Château Guiraud, to an ancient Saumur-Champigny *Vieilles Vignes* selection that needs five years to be approachable and is a perfect example of Cabernet Franc's depth of fruit and black-cherry-infested finish. This wine is about the same price as a bottle of supermarket own-label Champagne!

The best producers of **Savennières are:** des Baumard, Clos de la Coulée de Serrant and La Roche-aux-Moines.

The best producers of **Coteaux du Layon, Coteaux de l'Aubance, Bonnezeaux and Quarts de Chaume are:** des Baumard, Château de Fesles, Château Pierre-Bise, Didier Richou, Moulin Touchais, de la Roulierie and Vincent Lecointre.

The best producers of **sparklers are:** Domaine des Baumard, Bouvet-Ladubay, in particular their Cuvées Saphir and Trésor (owned by Champagne Taittinger), and Gratien & Meyer (associated with Alfred Gratien Champagne).

The best producers of **Saumur and Saumur-Champigny are:** du Hureau, Filliatreau, Langlois-Château and Nerleux.

TOURAINE

Touraine, around the town of Tours, is home to some of the Loire's best-known wines and best-kept secrets. With its western-end bang next to Saumur, the region starts with three heavy-weight reds. In fact, these are the last big reds in the entire region, so make the most of them. **Chinon**, **Bourgueil** and **Saint-Nicolas-de-Bourgueil** are meaty Cabernet Francs that generally drink well between two and six years old. Having concentrated, rich, blackberry fruit in good vintages, these wines are nice substitutes for red Bordeaux, as they are always good value and can have considerable complexity. They are delicious served chilled in warm weather, but work like a Bordeaux if you want a wintry treat. The famous white wines of **Vouvray** can be dry (*sec*), medium-dry (*demi-sec*) or sweet (*moëlleux*) and, once again, the Chenin Blanc grape fulfils these tasks admirably. The only criticism of dry Vouvrays are that, in youth, they have massive acidity (the inbuilt battery pack, which allows it to age so gracefully) and need food to balance the dryness. **Montlouis** is the little-known next-door neighbour to Vouvray, copying its styles and often offering even better value for money. However, there are less stellar producers here. Surrounding these river-hugging regions is the Touraine countryside where two bargain wines can be found – **Sauvignon de Touraine** and **Gamay de**

Touraine. This is a white and red double act, and both styles are best drunk young. They offer a cut-price Sancerre and Beaujolais taste so beloved of the Parisian café society. Stick to the best producers and you can't go wrong. Finally, there are two sneaky, secret little areas nearby called **Jasnières** and **Cheverny**. In hot years, Jasnières can give Savennières a run for its money at half the price, and white Cheverny, made from Sauvignon Blanc (occasionally with Chardonnay or Chenin blended in), can out-perform many lesser Sancerres for a fraction of the cost.

The best producers of Chinon: Bernard Baudry, Charles Joguet, Couly-Dutheil and Desbourdes.
The best producers of Saint-Nicolas-de-Bourgueil are: Jean-Paul Mabileau and Max & Lydie Cognard-Taluau.
The best producers of Bourgueil are: Joël Taluau, Lamé-Delille-Boucard, de la Lande (Delaunay) and Pierre-Jacques Druet.
The best producers of Vouvray are: Bourillon-Dorléans, Gaston Huet and Philippe Foreau.
The best producer of Montlouis is: Michel & Laurent Berger.
The best producer of Sauvignon de Touraine is: Alain Marcadet.
The best producer of Gamay de Touraine is: Henry Marionnet.
The best producers of Jasnières are: Joël Gigou and Jean-Baptiste Pinon.
The best producers of Cheverny are: de la Gaudronnière and Salvard.

CENTRAL VINEYARDS

This is surely the most fashionable section of the river, as it includes the mega-famous darlings **Pouilly-Fumé** (*fumé* meaning gun smoke which is often found on the nose of the wine) and **Sancerre**, whose wines feature in every media lunch and catwalk launch, as well as the less well-known (and often much better value) **Quincy**, **Menetou-Salon** and **Reuilly**. Of the last three, Menetou is the finest Sancerre taste-alike, with Reuilly and Quincy being a little more rustic. We are now so far along the Loire that we're within spitting distance of Chablis, where the climate is far from maritime and more continental. This is the worldwide home of the Sauvignon Blanc grape variety. With chalky soils and Sauv as far as the eye can see, these five villages produce variations on a central theme – and that theme is a combination of fresh, dry, zippy, citrusy, green, tangy, nettley, crisp, floral, elderflower, asparagus and gooseberries flavours. This famous quintet of villages acts as the role model for all of the Sauvignons on the globe and, if you follow the list below, you will see why. Once in a while, ambitious winemakers use a degree of oaking to augment the flavour of their Sauvignon Blancs. One of these mavericks is eccentric M Didier Dagueneau. His Pouilly-Fumé, Cuvées Silex and Clos des Chailloux, have a strong oak element. I find these wines interesting, expensive and unusual, but rarely does the dominant oak flavour knit perfectly with the freshness that Sauvignon Blanc embodies.

The local rosés and reds are made from Burgundy's Pinot Noir grape, resulting in a cross-dressing style of wine: definitely Pinot underneath, but with a sheer, floaty, off-the-shoulder number on top. This is a good way of tasting well-made, feather-light French Pinot without having to spend Côte-d'Or prices – but stick to warmer vintages.

The best producers of Sancerre are: Alain Gueneau, Alphonse Mellot, André Dézat, André Vatan, Bailly-Reverdy, Christian Lauverjat, Cotat, Daulny, Henri Bourgeois, Henri Natter, Merlin-Cherrier, Pascal & Nicolas Reverdy, Philippe de Benoist, Serge Laloue, Sylvain Bailly, Vacheron and Vincent Delaporte.
The best producers of Pouilly-Fumé are: André Dézat (Domaine Thibault), Cedrick Bardin, Château du Nozet (de Ladoucette), Château de Tracy, Didier Dagueneau, Hervé Seguin, Jean-Claude Chatelain, Michel Redde, Serge Dagueneau and Tabordet.
The best producers of Menetou-Salon are: de Chatenoy, Henry Pellé and Jean Teiller.
The best producers of Reuilly are: Henri Beurdin and Gérard Cordier.
The best producer of Quincy is: Jacques Rouzé.

MISCELLANEOUS

There is a handful of outlying areas that fall under the Loire jurisdiction, many of which are closer to other, major wine regions as the crow flies, but it just goes to show how long this river really is. My picks of the group start with the VDQS region **Haut-Poitou**. (VDQS stands for *Vin Délimité de Quantité Supérieure*, and is higher than a Vin de Pays.) It is 50 miles southwest of Tours around the town of Poitiers, making Bordeaux-blend reds and some useful Sauvignon Blancs and Chardonnays. **Saint-Pourcain** is a VDQS region whose best wines come from the local co-operative, the *Union des Vignerons*. Gamay blended with Pinot Noir makes up the red, and Sauvignon, Chardonnay and Aligoté, the white – giving away that this region is between the Loire and Burgundy. Last is the AC region of the **Côte Roannaises**, which, despite being on the Loire's banks, is only one range of hills west of Beaujolais. Gamay is the call of the day, making wines similar to Beaujolais in style and taste, only cheaper. This region is making a comeback after an apocalyptic decline in business in the early twentieth century.

The Rhône Valley

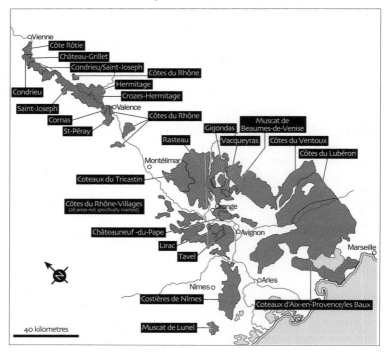

Situated in the southeast corner of France, this hot region stretches 200 kilometres from Vienne in the north to Avignon in the south. The Rhône Valley is neatly split into two distinct regions, the Northern and Southern Rhône. There is a lot of talk about the value afforded by the fabulous wines made in this region. Sadly, some of the best wines are already out of reach of mere mortals, but if it is moderately spicy, meaty reds you are after, then this is a great place to be.

THE NORTHERN RHÔNE

The bruiser of the red-grape varieties, Syrah, dominates all of the red wines of the Northern Rhône – and by way of a change, the whites favour the Cinderella grape, Viognier and the ugly sisters, Marsanne and Roussanne. The northern Rhône Valley is a craggy, steep-sided, narrow strip of vineyards following the river south. The climate is continental; however, the mistral, a wickedly bitter wind, whistles up the valley at over 100kph, endangering shoots and leaves without warning. The great wines of this region sit firmly at the top of the world's best wine lists, with their Syrah and Viognier occasionally equalled but rarely bettered outside this collection of famous appellations.

From north to south, the Northern Rhône areas are:

Côte Rôtie

Some of the most monumental wines I have ever tasted have come from this relatively small appellation. Up on the hillside where the English translation, 'roasted slope', really hits home, the vines cling to the terraces by the skin of their grapes. One man, Marcel Guigal, is single-handedly responsible for making these wines so famous. His vineyards, or cliffs of vines, are situated in an amphitheatre-shaped hollow above the town of Ampuis. Single vineyard bottlings of La Turque, La Mouline and La Landonne, are indefinably majestic. Côte-Rôtie can be made with the addition of up to 20 per cent Viognier that tempers the violets and spice on the nose and calms slightly the roar of Syrah's cassis, smoke and leather on the palate. Top Côte-Rôtie can usually live happily for up to twenty years.

Condrieu

From one of the most impressive red wines to one of the most celestial whites – Condrieu is an exotic concoction made from the beguiling Viognier grape variety. Very few serious white wines demand to be drunk young, but Condrieu doesn't want to waste any time and hits the ground running, or, should I say, sashaying. The opulent peach kernel, nutmeg and apricot blossom characters make this wine one of the most attractive white grape varieties on the nose. The lack of mouth-drying acidity makes it all too easy to drink. This is the wine that made the Viognier grape world-famous, but there is one factor that naturally slows the sales down – the price. Condrieu tends to be as expensive as Côte-Rôtie – and that is a lot of dosh to fork out for a puppy-fat white wine. The only bargains to be had in this part of the world are the 'de-classified' Condrieus, made from young vines, reject *cuvées* or vines grown above the officially permitted AC altitude. Stick to the producers below and you may find a few that tickle your fancy – if not it's off to the South of France or Australia for a bit of solace.

Château-Grillet

This preposterously overpriced, tiny, single estate AC (the only one in France) is supposedly the pinnacle expression of Viognier. Blame Thomas Jefferson; he started it all off and, whereas his taste in Bordeaux was exemplary, he got this one wrong. Apparently it ages well, but I have tasted many vintages of dull, confusingly variable wines. Steer clear and save yourself a fortune.

Saint-Joseph

Both red and white wines are made in this appellation, and they offer a good-value alternative to white and red Hermitage, Cornas and Côte-Rôtie. The reds are made from Syrah plus up to 10 per cent of white grapes Marsanne and Roussanne. The white wines are Marsanne and Roussanne blends. The style is that of a slightly more rustic version of the grander names – lacking finesse but making up for it in sheer balls. Both styles should be drunk within six years of the vintage. I love these two styles as they are honest, have chunky fruit, and they really do represent a genuine taste of the region and its *goût de terroir*.

> **The best producers of Saint-Joseph are:** Bernard Faurie, Delas, Jean-Louis Chave, Jean-Louis Grippat and Pierre Gonon.

Hermitage

Hermitage is a tiny appellation that has the most famous of the Northern Rhône's red wines. A small amount of Marsanne and Roussanne may be added to the red, but they are usually 100 per cent Syrah. They have deep, plummy, chunky, peppery fruit with a full-bodied ripe and grippy finish. The whites are fairly bosomy numbers, with Marsanne and Roussanne bursting out everywhere in the form of peachy, nutty, oily fruit. Of all the Northern Rhône whites, these last the longest (up to fifteen years usually). The reds age at a snail's pace and rarely show their full hand until they are at least five years old, and can survive happily until twenty-five.

> **The best white Hermitage producers are:** Chapoutier, Jean-Louis Chave, Grippat and E Guigal.
> **The best red Hermitage producers are:** Chapoutier, Delas, Grippat, Jean-Louis Chave, Michel Ferraton, Paul Jaboulet Aîné, Sorrel and Tardieu-Laurent.

Crozes-Hermitage

Scaled down versions of Hermitage are available here, both in red form and white, and made from the same grapes. Situated around the town of Tain, this largish appellation (ten times that of Hermitage) requires a careful hand when selecting fine wines. Best drunk young, and even chilled a touch in the summer, the red wines can be unbelievably peppery on the nose and very juicy and fleshy on the palate. White Crozes needs only be one year old to reach its peak – use it to wash down some grilled or poached fish, or a mushroom or goat's cheese salad.

The best producers of Crozes-Hermitage are: Alain Graillot, Albert Belle, du Colombier, Domaine Pochon, Gilles Robin and Olivier Dumaine.

Cornas

There are only reds here, all made from 100 per cent Syrah. Unapologetically full-bodied and carnivorous, these wines can be heady and often over-intense in their youth. Lacking in finesse, and quite often lacking in balance, they require a few years to soften before they have the courage to attempt the huge amount of brooding fruit on offer. These powerful, tannic wines can last for up to fifteen years in a good vintage. They represent good value on wine-shop shelves; put your seatbelt on and go for it.

The best producers of Cornas are: Alain Voge, Auguste Clape, Jean Lionnet, Noël Verset, Robert Michel, Thierry Allemand and du Tunnel (Stéphane Robert).

St-Péray

This is a white-wine-only village, with some fizz produced as well, and it's the last in the line of appellations from the Northern Rhône. I wouldn't really bother, because the Loire makes better sparkling wine and I've already listed some cracking whites above.

While we are on the subject of wines to miss, there are two regions off the bottom of the Northern Rhône that you can cross off your shopping list as well – Clairette de Die, a sparkling wine made from the unspeakably dull white grape variety of the same name, and the reds and whites of Chatillon-en-Diois. If you have to drink something, just to say you've at least tried it, then have a go at Clairette de Die Tradition, a fizzy Muscat-dominant wine that is France's answer to Italy's Moscato d'Asti.

THE SOUTHERN RHÔNE

Where the Northern Rhône relied on Syrah to do the legwork, the Southern Rhône is a heavily blended region, with Grenache grabbing the lion's share of the reds. This region is huge in comparison to the Northern Rhône and it has a much more Mediterranean climate. The mistral is still present, but it helps occasionally by drying out the vineyards when conditions are too humid.

This is the land of **Châteauneuf-du-Pape**, **Gigondas**, **Vacqueyras**, **Lirac** and gallons and gallons of **Côtes-du-Rhône** – a generic appellation that covers the entire Rhône region, although the vast majority of the wine comes from the Southern end. There is also an enormous variation in quality of these wines, from disgraceful, chemistry-set reds to 'baby-Châteauneuf-style' wines; the best are always from well-known producers. There are seventeen villages in the Southern Rhône that are allowed to use their names on the label if the contents of the bottle are exclusively from within their boundaries. These wines are known as Côtes-du-Rhône-Villages, of which the best known are – **Gigondas**, **Vacqueyras**, **Cairanne**, **Rasteau**, **Valréas** and **Sablet**. These wines are a big step up in quality over basic Côtes-du-Rhône as the permitted yields are lower, and the minimum alcoholic strength is 12.5 per cent. In 1971 Gigondas broke away from the *Villages* list and became an appellation in its own right. Vacqueyras followed in 1990. These two represent the finest wines to come out of the Southern Rhône save for Châteauneuf itself.

The red wines from this region are usually complicated blends and can include anything up to thirteen varieties (in the case of Châteauneuf). Grenache, Syrah, Mourvèdre and Cinsault always grab the first places on the bus, with Picpoul, Terret Noir, Counoise, Muscardin, Vaccarèse, Picardin, Clairette, Roussanne and Bourbelenc usually somewhere behind. Incidentally, the last three of these are white. Very few winemakers actually follow the letter of the law and use all thirteen – most rely on the first four. Southern Rhône reds are usually drunk between two and eight years old, although Châteauneuf-du-Pape should be allowed at least three years to become approachable and can last for a further twenty.

White wines are made from Grenache Blanc, Clairette and Viognier, with the reliable Roussanne variety lending its weight to the blend. Châteauneuf-du-Pape Blanc is the only really serious white from down here, and it is very rare. Rosés are popular, especially the overrated **Tavel**, whose tannin and alcohol levels are quite something.

Sweeties are produced in the Southern Rhône from the Muscat Blanc à Petits Grains grape via the *Vin Doux Naturel* process. These light, fresh wines are reminiscent of peaches, coconut, apricots (and grapes). Drink them very cold in order to appreciate them fully, as they get a little sickly when they warm up.

The best Côtes-du-Rhône (and -Villages) producers are: Brusset, Château du Trignon, Clos Petite Bellane, Coudoulet de Beaucastel, Domaine Gramenon, E Guigal, Marcel Richaud, Piaugier, Rayas (Fonsalette) and Tardieu-Laurent.
The best Lirac, Rasteau, Tavel and Vacqueyras producers are: Château des Tours, Clos des Cazaux, des Espiers, de la Mordorée, La Soumade and du Trapadis.

The best Gigondas producers are: Château du Trignon, Font-Sane, R & J-P Meffre (Saint-Gayan), Saint-Cosme and Santa-Duc.

The best Châteauneuf-du-Pape producers are: de Beaucastel, Les Cailloux, Chapoutier, de la Charbonnière, Charvin, Clos du Caillou, Clos des Papes, de Ferrand, Fortia, de In Janasse, de Marcoux, de la Mordorée, du Pegaü, Rayas, Versino and Le Vieux Donjon.

The best Muscat de Beaumes-de-Venise producers are: Chapoutier, Domaine de Durban and Paul Jaboulet Ainé.

There is a host of miscellaneous regions tacked on to the bottom and sides of the Rhône. Here is a summary of what to hit and what to miss.

The **Côtes du Ventoux** on the south-eastern fringes of the Southern Rhône between the **Coteaux du Tricastin** and the **Côtes du Luberon**, makes light quaffing reds in a mini-Côtes-du-Rhône style. The best labels to look out for are La Vieille Ferme and Claude Fonquerle's Château Valcombe. The aforementioned Tricastin makes chunkier wines than Ventoux, and the finest estate is Domaine de Grangeneuve. Both of the areas were promoted to AC status in 1973. The **Côtes du Vivarais** is situated opposite Tricastin in the Ardèche region. I would give this a miss in favour of the previous two. Finally, there are the **Coteaux de Pierrevert** and the **Côtes du Luberon** where the wines are again made in a Rhône style but lack true impact, and shouldn't feature in your wine diet unless you are there on holiday.

French Country Wines

French Country is a slightly clumsy, catch-all term for any wines not already covered in the classic regions. I have split this into four short sub-sections, featuring my favourite areas and recommended estates. Here we find some of the best bargains on the French wine scene that capture the essential *goût de terroir*.

JURA AND SAVOIE

These two wine regions make classic examples of holiday wines. By that I mean that they taste great when you are skiing or walking in the Alps, but are distinctly dull back home. Situated in southeast France on the border with Switzerland, not far from Geneva, the wines of Jura and Savoie do not travel well. However, if you fall for the peculiar salty, nutty, sherry-like flavour of the Savagnin (not Sauvignon!) grape then there are a few estates to follow. If it is *Vin Jaune* – the yellow wine – you are keen to taste, then Château-Chalon's producer, Henri Maire makes a good example. *Vin de Paille*, a masochist's version of *Vin Jaune*, where the grapes are dried before becoming sherried, is a taste I have never acquired, although some people go into raptures (or is that rigors?). Domaine de Montbourgeau and Château de l'Etoile are the star performers (no pun intended) in the appellation of L'Etoile, where Savagnin again is the weird white grape in charge. Arbois makes Chardonnay and yet more Savagnins (including *Jaune* and *Paille* styles) in a slightly more commercial fashion, and its reds, resembling weak and feeble Côte de Beaune rouges, can be made from Pinot Noir. The other two strange red varieties are Poulsard and Trousseau. Like the detectives in *Tintin*, they are chaotic and rarely get the job done.

Roussette de Savoie can be a nice change from the lean whites usually found in this area. Prieuré Saint-Christophe makes my favourite example. Other whites of Savoie – Crépy, Apremont, Abymes, Chignin and Chignin-Bergeron (the best of the bunch) – are usually fresh, light, insignificant creatures that spend only a few seconds on the palate before disappearing. The reds, using grapes like Pinot Noir, Mondeuse and Gamay, are all light and dry and only really worth it when you are on the piste. Do yourself a favour: book a skiing holiday, drink and be merry, but don't bring any back home.

SOUTHWEST FRANCE

Scattered across a vast area of land in the southwest corner of France are some amazingly diverse and exciting wines. To the east and south of Bordeaux, all the way down to the Pyrenees, there are some superb whites, reds and sweeties worth hunting for, as value for money is in-built into these little-known wines. **Bergerac** makes Bordeaux-style reds and whites using the same grape varieties, and often outclasses many of Bordeaux's cheaper wines. Châteaux de la Jaubertie, Calabre, Moulin des Dames and La Tour des Gendres, made by Luc de Conti, are the leaders here. **Monbazillac** and **Saussignac** are two of the best Sauternes-style sweet wine-producing areas within Bergerac. Here, Domaine de l'Ancienne Cure, Château la Borderie, Tirecul La Gravière, Clos d'Yvigne and Château Richard make great value wines that often replace Sauternes at cunning dinner parties, without even being spotted. **Cahors**, made from the gutsy red grape Malbec (also known as Auxerrois or Cot), used to be known as 'Black Wine' on account of its soupy texture and teeth-staining tannins, although nowadays the wines are often softened with a slice of supple Merlot. Châteaux du Cèdre, Les Laquets, Lagrezette and Clos Triguedina make terrific Cahors – just make sure you have a haunch of beef meaty enough to cope.

Southwest from Cahors towards Spain, we come across some of the most fascinating French Country wines. **Pacherenc du Vic-Bilh**, a white wine made using Gros and Petit Manseng, Arrufiac, Petit Courbu, and other varieties, is a prettier name for what is, to all intents and purposes, Madiran Blanc. It has lovely crushed white fruit aromas with a very dry finish. The sweet version, a *moëlleux* style, can be very exotic; Domaine Berthomieu makes a classic example. The great red wine, **Madiran**, made from the Tannat variety often tempered with a touch of Cabernet Franc, is a chewy monster of a wine. Somewhere between a St-Estèphe and a Gigondas, this wine has not attended finishing school, and will certainly not be charming in public unless it gets a ton of air – decant this brute. The finest versions come from Châteaux Montus, d'Aydie, Boucassé and Domaine Pichard.

The next region we come across is **Juraçon** where Clos Lapeyre, Charles Hours, Clos Guirouilh, de Lahargue, Domaine Cauhapé, Clos Uroulat and Domaine Bellegarde all make stunning dry (*sec*) and sweet (*moëlleux*) wines from the Petit and Gros Manseng grapes. Haunting flavours of pineapple, spice and honey make these wines nearly as sought after as top Viogniers. They are an immensely fashionable aperitif or pudding wine for those in the know. Gros Manseng tends to make the dry wines, whereas Petit Manseng, late-harvested and partially dried on the vine, makes the sweet wines that, when on form, can rival the greatest sweeties in the world.

LANGUEDOC-ROUSSILLON

The vineyards of the Languedoc-Roussillon form an enormous contiguous crescent shape on France's Mediterranean coast. With the bookends of the Pyrenees on the southwest side and the mouth of the River Rhône on the northeast, this collection of vineyards is one of the largest in the world. For most of its two-thousand-year, vine-growing history, this part of France has under-performed shockingly. It took the New World's assault on the global wine market in the late eighties to kick-start it into action. We now have some epic wines filtering out of this huge mass of villages and towns, helped in no small part by New World winemakers themselves, often on work experience tours of the globe. The two main styles of wine found down here are spicy Rhône-style reds that give Châteauneuf-du-Pape a well-earned rest, and sweet and fortified wines for after-dinner enjoyment. Here is a list of the best areas and the wizards behind their success. Remember that these wines are startlingly good value, so look here for everyday drinking favourites.

Corbières can thank the fine wines of Château de Lastours for its reappearance on wine-shop shelves. Along with **Fitou**, these two ACs make chunky Carignan-heavy reds that are designed for short-term gratification. Other good estates in this part of the world are Château Le Palais, Château Etang des Colombes, La Baronne, des Chandelles, Meunier St-Louis, Pech-Latt, Château Vaugélas and Domaine des Gautier. **Minervois** is home to some excellent reds – Borie de Maurel, Le Cazal, Clos Centeilles, Châteaux de Gourgazaud, Lignon, d'Oupia and Fabas make cracking wines that will warm you up on a winter's day. The **Languedoc** is a vast area including a few prime wine villages. Again, Rhône grapes are used for these meaty reds. The star estates in the Languedoc are Gilbert Alquier, de Ciffre and Château des Estanilles in **Faugères**; Camplazens, Château de Capitoul, de l'Hospitalet, de la Negly and Pech-Redon in **La Clape**; Domaine de Coujan, Canet-Valette, Cazal-Viel, des Jougla and Mas Champart in **St-Chinian**; Mas de Daumas Gassac and La Granges des Pères in the **L'Hérault** region; Mas Jullien, Abbaye de Valmagne, d'Aupilhac, Les Aurelles, Mas d'Azelon, Mas de Chimères, Font Caude, Mas Mortiès, Peyre Rose, Puech-Huat, Roc d'Anglade, Château La Sauvagéonne and Mas Champart in the **Coteaux du Languedoc**, and Cazeneuve, Ermitage du Pic St-Loup, de Lascaux, Lascours, Mas Brugière and Domaine de l'Hortus from the famous region of **Pic St-Loup**. Mas des Aveylans, Mourgeus-du-Grès, de Nages, Châteaux Grand-Cassagne, Belle-Coste and de Campuget in the **Costières de Nîmes** are all making stunning wines. The rosés represent good value from this part of the world and they can often out-perform Tavel at a fraction of the price. In **Limoux**, high up in the eastern Pyrenean foothills, you can find superb cool climate Chardonnays and Pinot Noirs. Challenging Burgundy at its own game, and for a fraction of the price, the best estates here are the terrific Domaine Bégude and Domaine de l'Aigle.

The best estates in the **Côtes de Roussillon** appellation are Mas de la Garrigues owned by Marcel Vila in St-Esteve and Château de Jau. **Côtes de Roussillon-Villages** gives us some superb, brooding reds at Clos de Fées and Domaine Gardiés. In **Collioure**, a small appellation just south of the Côtes de Roussillon, some Mourvèdre and Grenache-heavy Southern Rhône blends are made. Domaine de Mas Blanc, de la Casa Blanca, de la Rectoire, Château de Jau and Mas Amiel make stunning reds here, as well as some incredible *Vin Doux Naturel* red wines called **Banyuls** and **Maury**. A good substitute for port (although utilising much lower levels of spirit), these wines are Grenache dominant and can be chilled – and are delicious with chocolate puddings. Other sweet wines from this region are **Muscat de Rivesaltes** (Cazes is a good producer), **Muscat de Lunel** and **Muscat de Frontignan** in that order of preference. These wines are fruity and innocent, and often smell a little too bubble-bathy for my liking. Other superb estates to track down are: Chemin de Bassac, Domaine d'Aupilhac, Domaine Capion and Domaine de Baruel from the **Cévennes**, Domaine des Ravenès from **Coteaux de Murveil**, and Elian de Ros from the **Côtes du Marmandais**.

PROVENCE

Situated on the eastern side of the Rhône delta, running all of the way up the Italian border, this is another great, undiscovered region full of sumptuous wines. It's sad to think that, when there are so many great wines on the doorstep, most of the loaded luvvies who spend their holidays gambling and attending film premières down here probably only drink Bordeaux and Burgundy.

Bandol, made predominately from Mourvèdre, with Grenache and Cinsault included, is the noblest red wine of the region. These wines have spicy, plummy, chocolaty fruit and drink well from five to ten years old. The best estates are Jean-Pierre Gaussen, Lafran-Veryrolles, La Laidière, Pradeaux, Mas de la Bégude, Maubernard, Domaine Tempier (Cuvées La Tourtine, La Migoua, Cuvée Spéciale and Cabassaou are extraordinary), Ray-Jane, Souviou, La Suffrène, Domaine de Pibarnon and Mas de la Rouvière. These estates have all made wines that blow me away. **Bellet** is a tiny appellation behind Nice, where a few estates, like Château de Crémat, and Domaine de la Source make unusual and intriguing wines. Whites are often made from the Rolle grape, rosés from Braquet and the reds from Fuella – weird and wonderful is the order of the day! They are a little expensive, as production is teeny, but it is worth tracking one down, if only to cross it off your 'to do' list.

Palette is a 20ha appellation, of which 15ha are owned by Château Simone. Grenache, Cinsault and Mourvèdre are used in their red (so far so good) but, according to owner René Rougier, so are grapes like Manosquan!, Castet!! and Branforquas!!! These reds age like clockwork, but are a bit on the dear side. His white sticks to well-trodden varieties like Ugni Blanc, Clairette, Grenache Blanc and Muscat, and his rosé is one of the greatest age-worthy versions in France. The pretty fishing village of **Cassis** is our next stop where, for once, the reds take a back seat and the whites, made from Ugni Blanc, Clairette and Bourbelenc, take over. These wines have a very attractive liquorice, herb and spice character under the honeyed fruit. The nicest wines are from Clos Sainte-Madeleine. The **Coteaux d'Aix-en-Provence** is a huge area where one man has captured the palates of the entire wine-loving world. In Les Baux, Eloi Dürrbach, from Domaine de Trévallon, has planted Cabernet Sauvignon and Syrah in the most barren, rocky terrain, and over the last few decades has made stunning red wine. Breaking the AC laws by planting

Cabernet Sauvignon, and presumably upsetting neighbours with his magnificent creations, he has been forced to label his wines *Vin de Table*! I have tasted every wine that this estate has ever made and this is one of very few occasions when I can say wholeheartedly, across the board, that an entire range of wines was incredible. Capturing explosive black-fruit flavours with a Provençal bouquet of rosemary, thyme, lavender and dried herbs, they are not to be missed. Other estates making fine wines from the Aix environs are Hauvette, Château Vignelaure, Château des Gavelles, des Terres Blanches and Mas de Gourgonnier. The famous rosés from this part of France come from the **Côtes de Provence** area of Provence. Carignan is the main red grape with Cinsault, Grenache and Mourvèdre again filling in the gaps. I have never really been taken by Domaine Ott, the most expensive and well known of the wineries in this region, but Domaine de Rimauresq, de la Courtade, Domaine Gavoty, Domaine de St-Baillon and Domaine Richeaume are all worthy adversaries.

GERMANY

The main driving forces behind German wines are world-class skill, buckets of self-belief and true wine passion. You certainly need these elements in a northern European country where winemaking is a serious business and viticulture a constant challenge against (and occasionally with) the elements. But the Germans love a challenge, although, like the Italians, they still have rather a lot of work to do to convince the wine-buying public that they are back on form. The problem was similar to the one in Italy with sub-standard Chianti, when bulk-blended Liebfraumilch, Black Tower and the like flooded the market, forcing prices and expectations spiralling down. These wines were classified as QbAs (*Qualitätswein bestimmter Anbaugebiete* – 'Quality Wine' – see below) but bore no resemblance to any other wines of this quality level and, in fact, were often nowhere near as tasty as many *Tafelweins*. If you have ever tasted one of these wines, and I'm sure you have, judging by the millions of cases still sold every year, then forget it; wipe it from your taste memory banks. There is so much more out there! There is no point even trying to say that great wines have always been made, every year for hundreds of years, in Germany, and that Liebfraumilch was just an awful experiment that blew up in their faces, but I feel I should. So how does it all work and where do we go from here?

THE FACTS

Firstly, what about their classification system – how do they grade their wines? The answer is, by judging the most difficult criteria to come by – natural sugar levels in the grapes at harvest (that makes sense in chilly Germany!?). The more naturally sweet the wine, the finer the grade (for sweet, read ripe). It all seems so excruciatingly difficult, but they are absolutely brilliant at selecting varieties, ripening grapes (Riesling is king here), capturing the perfect balance of fruit and acidity, so that these on-the-surface-delicate white wines can outlive the biggest, butchest Chardonnays by at least a decade.

THE GRADES

In ascending level of importance they are – *Tafelwein* (Table wine), *Landwein* (equivalent of French Vin de Pays), QbA, and QmP (*Qualitätswein mit Prädikat* – 'better quality wine' – which includes *Kabinett*, *Spätlese*, *Auslese*, *Beerenauslese* and *Trockenbeerenauslese*). In addition to this, there are *Trockens* – dry wines, *Halbtrockens* – half-dry or fruitier wines, and *Eisweins* made when the grapes freeze on the vine.

THE GRAPES

The grapes used to make these wines are as follows, in order of importance – Riesling, Müller-Thurgau, Scheurebe, Gewürztraminer, Rülander (Pinot Gris), Sylvaner and a lone red Spätburgunder (Pinot Noir).

THE BEST REGIONS

Mosel is characterised by nose-bleedingly steep, slate slopes running down to the famous river itself. Riesling makes its greatest wines in the Mosel and they are characterised by finesse and elegance. The staggering fact about Mosel Rieslings is that despite looking pretty, racy and refreshing in their youth, they have an ability to age that is extraordinary. Think nothing of uncorking a twenty-year-old wine! The upper reaches of the Mosel are where the **Saar** tributary flows in from the south. Here, where the climate is cooler, Riesling makes tighter, drier styles of wine. The **Ruwer**, another tributary of the Mosel, again grows Riesling with remarkable ageing potential. German Riesling is an essential part of your wine diet, as it is an amazing aperitif, but also manages to cut through a wide variety of dishes. **Rheingau** is regarded as one of the finest regions in the entire German-winemaking scene, producing richer wines with less biting acidity than the Mosel. **Rheinhessen** is Müller-Thurgau, Scheurebe and Sylvaner country; this is where a lot of Liebfraumilch and Blue Nun comes from. **Rheinpfalz** is the warmest district where the meatiest whites come from, made from Riesling, Müller-Thurgau, Rülander and Scheurebe. **Nahe** region makes distinctively perfumed, smooth wines with some weight. **Franken** is where the dumpy bottles that don't fit into bottle banks originate! Here Sylvaner does its weird thing. Reds from the warmer south are fashionable in Germany, but don't really make the grade with the big boys outside the country. The main purpose that Germany fulfils in your cellar is providing world-class Riesling at all price points to lift your mood and cleanse your palate.

THE WINE LABELS

The wine label on a German bottle looks pretty tricky at first glance, but if you split it up into segments it will tell you a number of important things.

1 The region (for instance, Mosel-Saar-Ruwer)

2 The quality level (for instance, QmP plus which QmP level – e.g. Spätlese)

4 The grape variety (for instance, Riesling)

5 The vintage (for instance, 2004)

6 The producer (for instance, Dr Loosen)

7 A Grosslage or collective site area (for instance, Ürziger – from the site of Ürzig)

8 An Einzellage or single-vineyard name (for instance, Würzgarten)

The example here would thus appear in a wine list as: 2004 Ürziger Würzgarten, Riesling Spätlese, Dr Loosen, Mosel-Saar-Ruwer, Germany.

The best producers are: JB Becker, Dr Bürklin-Wolf, JJ Cristoffel, Daniel Vollenweider, Dönnhoff, Egon Müller, Fritz Haag, Heymann-Löwenstein, Koehler-Ruprecht, Künstler, Josef Leitz, Langwerth von Simmern, H & R Lingenfelder, Dr Loosen, Müller-Cattoir, JJ Prüm, Reichsgraf von Kesselstatt, Dr Richter, Reinhold Haart, Robert Weil, Schloss Lieser, Schloss Reinhartshausen, Selbach-Oster, von Schubert-Maximin Grünhaus, St Urbans-Hof, Dr H Thanisch, Weingut Kerpen, Weingut Karthäuserhof and Willi Schaefer.

ITALY

With over a thousand grape varieties, an appalling, meaningless classification system and gallons of poor wine to avoid, Italy ought to be a nightmare chapter destined to be skipped over. But wait, there are hundreds of awesome wines to find; and just because this country makes a quarter of the world's wine production, it doesn't mean we can't sort it out in a trice. I have divided the country into five sections (plus a small section on the islands of Sicily and Sardinia), and then detail the best estates – avoiding the Fiat 126s and concentrating on the Ferrari F430 Spiders.

Map labels: Valle D'Aosta, Lombardy, Trentino-Alto Adige, Piedmont, Friuli-Venezia Giulia, Veneto, oMilan, Venice, Emilia-Romagna, oGenoa, Bologna, Liguria, Marche, Tuscany, Umbria, Abruzzi, Molise, oRome, Lazio, Puglia, Campania, Naples, Sardinia, Basilicata, Cagliari, Calabria, Palermo, Sicily, Syracuse, 200 kilometres

Northwest

Piemonte (or **Piedmont**) is the most important region in this corner of Italy. Southeast of Turin, near Alba, the noble red wine **Barolo** is made from the Nebbiolo grape variety. This tremendously powerful, shudderingly tannic creature must be carefully selected. Poor Barolo (and there is still a surprising amount of it made) is lean, stewed and hollow. Great Barolos last for decades and they pack so much black-cherry, leather and tobacco fruit into the bottle you might think it is a black hole. **Spanna** and **Gattinara** are two other strangely disappointing wines made from Nebbiolo that are rarely spotted outside Italy. **Barbaresco** is made in a similar way to Barolo but is usually less overtly tannic. All wines made from Nebbiolo have an in-built tannic and acidic factor. They should also be very rich in fruit. There is no optimum time to drink these wines – with a carefully chosen menu, they can be enjoyable after only five years of life – but should you get the opportunity to taste an old one, then aim for a twenty-year-old; it would be a nice treat. Just don't expect the tannins to be soft! Also in Piedmont, the red **Barbera** grape is vinified by most estates and can result in plummy, blackcurrant fruit with much lower tannin levels than Barolo. This is a lovely way to be introduced to an estate's wines, because if the Barbera is good, then the Barolo should be even better. **Dolcetto** is another red variety and has a peculiar scent of rubber and blackberries; drunk cool, it makes a grown-up equivalent to *Cru* Beaujolais. The last of the red grapes to watch out for is the red-cherry-scented **Freisa**. Made by a good producer, this grape can be invigorating and rewarding, if initially a little disconcerting.

There are five main white wines in the region. **Arneis**, a rich, flavoured, zesty wine with a unique scent and fine length, is a worthy adversary to a Chablis. **Gavi**, made from the Cortese grape, is a restaurant favourite on account of its fine acidity and honeyed, citrus palate – this makes a welcome change from a Sauvignon Blanc. **Erbaluce di Caluso** is a beautiful wine made from the grape of the same name, the finest example of which comes from Orsolani. Lastly, Moscato is the grape used to make the refreshing sparkler **Moscato d'Asti** and the fizzier **Asti (Spumante)** – a must for summer parties and strawberries. All of these whites should be drunk as young as possible.

The best producers of Piemotese red wines are: Aldo Conterno, Angelo Gaja, Ascheri, Bruno Rocca, Ca' Rossa, Ceretto, Cigliuti, Conterno Fantino, Domenico Clerico, Elio Altare, Fontanafredda, Giacomo Conterno, Giuseppe Mascarello, Luciano Sandrone, Paolo Scavino, Parusso, E Pira, Roberto Voerzio and La Spinetta.
The best producers of Moscato d'Asti and Asti Spumante are: Fontanafredda and La Spinetta.
The best producers of Gavi are: La Giustiniana, Nicola Bergaglio and La Scolca.
The best producers of Roero Arneis are: Bric Cenciurio, Matteo Correggia and Carlo Deltetto.

Lombardy (Lombardia), northeast of Piemonte around Milan, has an interesting red wine called **Franciacorta**, the best example of which comes from Ca' del Bosco. The finest white is a wine called **Lugana**, made from the Trebbiano variety, on the shores of Lake Garda. The best version is the Brolettino *cuvée* made by Ca' dei Frati and owned by the Dal Cero family.

> **The best producers of Lombardy wines are:** Bellavista (Franciacorta), Ca' del Bosco (Franciacorta), Ca' dei Frati (Lugana), Fratelli Muratori (Franciacorta) and Nino Negri (Valtellina).

There are two other areas in northwest Italy, but forget the wines made there – the best thing to do in the **Valle d'Aosta** is ski, and in **Liguria** is sunbathe.

Northeast

There are some amazing wines made in the Tyrolean third of northeast Italy at the foot of the Dolomites. In **Trentino-Alto Adige**, which stretches north–south between Bolzano and Verona, most of the vines are planted on mountainsides, where some of the purest single varietal wines in the world are found. White grapes include Chardonnay, Pinot Grigio, Pinot Bianco, Traminer (Gewürztraminer), Sylvaner, Muscat, Riesling Renano, Sauvignon Blanc and many other indigenous Italian varieties like Nosiola, Goldmuskateller and Rosenmuskateller, which make extraordinary sweet wines. Just take your pick (i.e. the flavour you are after) and follow a good producer. It is the same with the reds – Cabernet Sauvignon, Cabernet Franc, Merlot, Pinot Nero (Noir) and three stunning indigenous varieties – Lagrein, Teroldego and Marzemino – all live here happily. There is no doubt that Trentino-Alto Adige is in a period of enormous expansion, and winemakers are brimming with self-confidence. Most styles drink well young. Watch out for this region, as the wines are starting to filter out into the world and you ought to be first in line.

Around the towns of Padova, Vicenza and Venice, **Veneto** is famous for two wines that have, in the past, had pretty grubby reputations. **Soave** and **Valpolicella** are responsible for upsetting more palates than Liebfraumilch ever has. Soave, at its best, however, is oily, nutty and honeyed, with a long finish, and it is just about the most scrumptious glass of chilled white wine I could hope for on a picnic. These days a handful of committed winemakers have dragged this wine, made from the dull Garganega and Trebbiano varieties, up to speed. Valpolicella is made from Corvina, Rondinella and Molinara, and it ranges from a fresh Beaujolais-style glugger to a very impressive, intensely dark, cherry-imbued beast. There are two unusual styles of Valpolicella made, **Recioto della Valpolicella** and **Amarone della Valpolicella**. The Recioto style has a sweet taste and the Amarone style has a very rich, almost porty (but dry) flavour, resulting from semi-drying the grapes (*passito*) until the water evaporates and the sugar content is raised. The must from these raisins is then fermented until dry for Amarone or left with some residual sugar for Recioto. Soave is sometimes also made in a Recioto style, resulting in a delicious sweet wine.

The Lake Garda's **Bianco di Custoza** (white) and **Bardolino** (red) use exactly the same grape varieties as Soave and Valpolicella, but in both cases are lighter (and less memorable) than our two favourite comeback kids. A small tip – avoid the rosé form of Bardolino called **Chiaretto**; you'll thank me. A very dry sparkling wine is made in Veneto from the Prosecco variety called **Prosecco di Valdobbiadene**. The best producers of this summer fizz are Ruggeri and Bisol. Maculan, based in **Breganze**, makes a sweet wine from semi-dried Vespaiola grapes called Torcolato, a type of Recioto aged in oak barrels. They also makes a botrytised version called Acininobili. All but the top

Valpolicellas and sweet wines drink beautifully young. Amarones can last for up to twenty years.

> **The best Soave producers are:** Ca' Rugate, Gini, Pieropan, Prà and Roberto Anselmi.
>
> **The best Valpolicella producers are:** Allegrini, Ca' del Pipa, Dal Forno, Giuseppe Quintarelli and Masi.
>
> **Miscellaneous estates of excellence are:** (fizz) Ruggeri and Bisol (both Valdobbiadene) and (reds and sweeties) Maculan (Breganze).

On the far north-eastern Italian border in Friuli-Venezia Giulia, white wines are the order of the day. Winemakers, again, favour the single varietal styles, making it easy to select varieties that you like. The Colli (hills) Orientali del Friuli and the Collio Goriziano (shortened to Collio) are the finest vineyard areas. Watch out for Ribolla Gialla (a lemony, floral white variety that makes crisp, mouth-tingling wines), Tocai Friulano (a broad-flavoured, interesting white variety that can be fairly weighty), Malvasia (a variety that makes weird-scented, mineral and honeyed whites) and Picolit (a variety that makes overpriced sweeties). All of the old favourites are planted as well, with the Pinot Grigios, Pinot Biancos and Chardonnays producing the best wines. Some keen estates make wonderful blended whites, endeavouring to jigsaw together the best nuances from a wide range of white grapes. Vintage Tunina from Jermann is the leader in this field, but it is pretty expensive, so find your feet first with a single varietal. A few producers use oak barrels but, in the main, the style of whites from Friuli is one of freshness, youth and up-front fruit flavours. I have rarely been enamoured with the reds from this region, as they tend to taste a little green, lack weight and have intrusive acidity.

> **The best producers are:** Dario Raccaro, Davide Moschioni, Giovanni Puiatti, Girolamo Dorigo, Lis Neris (Alvararo Pecorari), Livio Felluga, Mario Schiopetto, Miani, Ronco del Gnemiz, Roncùs, Tercic, Villa Russiz and Vinnaioli Jermann.

Central East

There are four wine regions in this long, thin stretch of vineyards on Italy's eastern Mediterranean coastline. Situated between the Apennines and the Adriatic coast, in order from north to south, the first one is **Emilia-Romagna**. The infamous stars of this region are **Lambrusco** and the spectacularly overrated white, **Albana di Romagna**. My favourite wine of the area is made from a clone of the Chianti Sangiovese grape, known as **Sangiovese di Romagna**. My pick of producers for this wine is Fattoria Zerbina. The next region is **Marches (Marche)** where **Verdicchio dei Castelli di Jesi** is made. This is Italy's answer to Muscadet and, in the right hands, it can be refreshing and equally as delicious with seafood. The best producers are Coroncino, Brunori, Saladini Pilastri and Umani Ronchi. The finest red wine of the area is **Rosso Conero**, made from the Montepulciano grape variety. Le Terrazze and Umani Ronchi lead the pack, with Umani Ronchi's San Lorenzo being the finest and also best-value version of this wine. They even make a super *cuvée* called Cùmaro that, despite being more expensive and undoubtedly the greatest red of the region, really shows the potential of Marche. **Abruzzi (Abruzzo)** is the next region heading south, where only two truly worthy wine styles are made – **Montepulciano d'Abruzzo** (red) and **Trebbiano d'Abruzzo** (white). Almost all of these wines fall into the ordinary-at-home but fun-on-holiday category, except for Valentini's Trebbiano, which has so much depth and richness it bears no resemblance to any other Trebbiano I have ever tried – no surprise that winemaker Edoardo Valentini is known as the 'Lord of the Vines'. There are a few Montpulciano producers that you could search out whose wines will show you what this grape can do in the right hands – Podere Castorani, Monti, Cornacchia and Valle Reale are the main candidates. **Molise** is the last of the regions in this sweep down the coast, where only one solitary wine is worth hunting down – **Rosso** from Di Majo Norante's Montepulciano grape variety, produced in an area on the coast called Campomarino.

Central West

In Tuscany (Toscana), family estates have been making wine for centuries – Ricasoli started in 1141, and Antinori and Frescobaldi in the 1300s. This historic land is Sangiovese country and home to a large number of Italy's best red wines. There are a few smart whites made in these regions and they tend to be light and fresh styles – with one exception, the decadently sweet Vin Santo, of which more later. Tuscany is the home to an impressive roll call of red wines like **Chianti**, **Brunello di Montalcino**, **Carmignano** and **Vino Nobile di Montepulciano**. Brunello is a Sangiovese clone, as is Prugnolo, the predominant red grape in Vino Nobile, so Sangiovese has very much a controlling interest here. In a good vintage, Sangiovese has a richness and plummy character with fresh herb and tobacco on the nose. Almost always a food wine, Chianti and its Sangiovese partners can live for ten years happily, with the best Vino Nobiles and Brunellos continuing on for a further ten. One last point concerning these reds – the best estates are often very expensive and *riserva* (reserve or special selection) *cuvées* can be very dear. With Chianti, the best estate's *normale* (non-*riserva*) wines will be stunning and, very often, at least as fine as a second-division estate's top-of-the-range wine. With Brunello, watch out for **Rosso di Montalcino**, the earlier-drinking, earlier-released wine that can often be superb. **Vernaccia di San Gimignano**, made from the white Vernaccia grape is the finest of the local white wines. Usually possessing a nuttiness and floral character with trademark Italian zippy acidity, these wines complement seafood and salads, as well as Parmesan and Pecorino. Trebbiano is the most widely planted white grape, making fairly ordinary wines, although Pomino, a blend of Trebbiano, Pinot Bianco and Chardonnay, from Frescobaldi is often well made. **Vin Santo** is the heavenly pudding wine made from drying Trebbiano and Malvasia grapes, crushing and fermenting the sugar-laden raisins, and then ageing the wine in small barrels. The finished glass is a cross between a Fino sherry on the nose and Sauternes on the palate – an expensive slice of heaven.

CLASSIFICATION

It is now time to introduce you to the ugly topic of Italian wine laws. I hinted in the introduction to this chapter that the classification system of Italian wines was a farce; here is why. Trying to copy the success of the French AC system, the Italians introduced a DOC (*Denominazione di Origine Controllata*) equivalent to AC, and DOCG (*Denominazione di Origine Controllatae Garantita*) a further guarantee of the quality of specific 'controlled' elite regions. Zones were mapped out, yield maximums calculated, vinification methods outlined and vine varieties decided upon. DOCs were handed out like flyers, and regulations were not only acting as straitjackets stifling innovation, but were also encouraging sky-high yields, resulting in a dilution in the overall quality of many wines. Regional boundaries were also relaxed, totally missing the point of localised geographical differentiation.

The first five DOCGs to be handed out were Barolo, Barbaresco, Chianti, Brunello di Montalcino and Vino Nobile di Montepulciano. This had a beneficial effect on these regions by reviewing yields and winemaking practices. Then the dodgy decision to award the previously mentioned Albana di Romagna a DOCG (or G) was put down to a political move that did nothing to convince sceptics of the validity of this classification. Fourteen more Gs have been handed out since, mostly going to worthy regions.

Another big problem existed, one that involved some of the best wines in Italy. VdT (*Vino da Tavola*, table wine) was the classification awarded to wines using any grapes outside DOC law. Thus Tignanello, the very first 'Super-Tuscan', fetching astronomical prices for an Italian red wine and upsetting traditionalists, was lumped in with rocket fuel as far as the authorities were concerned. Why? It was made using some Cabernet Sauvignon and small French barriques instead of large Italian botti (barrels). The often-lean Sangiovese was boosted with the fully ripe, blackcurrant-flavoured Sauv grape and created some monumental wines. Ornellaia, Sassicaia, Solaia and countless others followed, advertising the region like never before. So the authorities stepped in again, and a new *Indicazione Geografica Tipica* (IGT) level was created to try to give these extraordinary *Vino da Tavolas* some credibility. Not that they needed it, really, since they already had the kudos. IGT may or may not succeed as a style, but at least it attempts to acknowledge the efforts of thirty years of hard work and passion spent breaking the law.

The best producers of Chianti are: P Antinori, Carobbio, Castello di Brolio, Castello di Fonterutoli, Felsina Berardenga, Le Filigare, Fontodi, Isole e Olena, La Massa, Il Molino di Grace, Poggerino, Querciabella, Selvapiana and Villa Caffagio.

The best producers of Brunello di Montalcino are: Altesino, Argiano, Case Basse, Ciacci Piccolomini d'Aragona, Collosorbo, Corte Pavone, Costanti, Donatella Cinelli Colbini, Fanti San Filippo, Fuligni, La Gerla, Lisini, Mastrojanni, Pietroso, Poggio Antico, Il Poggione, Sesti, Silvio Nardi and Uccelliera.

The best producers of Carmignano are: Ambra and Tenuta di Capezzana.

The best producers of Vino Nobile di Montepulciano are: Dei, Il Macchione, Poliziano and Villa Sant'Anna.

The best producers of Maremma and Morellino are: Costanza Malfatti, Lohsa (Poliziano), Le Pupille and Tenuta di Belguardo & Poggio Bronzone (Mazzei).

The best producers of Vernaccia di San Gimignano are: Montenidoli, Panizzi, Pietraserena and Teruzzi & Puthod.

The best producers of Vin Santo are: Avignonesi, Isole e Olena, Selvapiana and Villa Branca.

The best producers of Super-Tuscans are: Il Borro, Il Bosco (Manzano), Brancaia, Camartina (Querciabella), Campora (Falchini), Il Carbonaione (Poggio Scalette), Casalfero (Barone Ricasoli), Cepparello (Isole e Olena), Cortaccio (Villa Caffagio), Flaccianello della Pieve (Fontodi), Fontalloro (Felsina Berardenga), Ghiaie della Furba (Capezzana), Lupicaia (Tenuta del Terriccio), Masseto (L Antinori), Nambrot (Tenuta di Ghizzano), Ornellaia (Mondavi/L Antinori), Palazzo Altesi (Altesino), Paleo Rosso (Le Macchiole), Le Pergole Torte (Montevertine), Saffredi (Le Pupille), Sammarco (Castello dei Rampolla), Sassicaia (Marchesi Incisa della Rochetta), Siepi (Fonterutoli), Solaia (P Antinori), Solengo (Argiano), Tassinaia (Tenuta del Terriccio) and Tignanello (P Antinori).

After Tuscany's vast range of wines, **Umbria** may seem a bit dull, and you'd be right. **Orvieto** is the lone white of interest and the biggest maker of it is Luigi Bigi. Despite Orvieto being light, dry and rarely inspiring, there is one white wine worth a go. Made on Antinori's estate at Castello della Sala, a fabulous white called Cervaro della Sala, from Chardonnay and the local Grechetto, is by far the most captivating of the region (no surprise it is an IGT!). The lone red wine holding the fort in Umbria is called **Rubesco**, and is made well by Lungarotti. The best version of this wine, a Sangiovese blended with the ancient Tuscan grape Canaiolo, is the Riserva called **Monticchio** that attracted such good press – the local region of **Torgiano** was raised from DOC to DOCG on the back of this wine alone. Other estates of interest are: Arnaldo Caprai, with his terrific and mesmerising Montefalco Sagrantino (a huge red); La Carraia, with their fine Orvieto and red blends; La Fiorita-Lamborghini, with their stunning red blends; Palazzone's Orvietos; and Sportoletti's cracking Merlot.

On south to Rome and **Latium (Lazio)**, where we find the ridiculously named **Est! Est!! Est!!!**, an insipid white wine made from Trebbiano and Malvasia. Another wine that has been ridiculed in the past is **Frascati**. There is no doubt that this variable wine can be dry, lean and tasteless, but new-style Frascati is around the corner. Spearheaded by people like Castel De Paolis, the dull Malvasia and Trebbiano grapes have been introduced to small percentages of Viognier! This has resulted in some of the finest white Italian wines I have ever tasted. One of the top *cuvées*, Vigna Adriana, is nothing short of sensational. Classic Frascati estates that I can recommend are Villa Simone, Fontana Candida's Santa Teresa, Falesco and Pallavincini.

South

There are increasingly more wines in **Apulia (Puglia)**, **Campania**, **Basilicata** and **Calabria**, at the 'boot' end of Italy, that I am happy to recommend. Innovation, investment and international know-how helped transform this outpost into a proper little factory making robust, chunky reds at the bottom end, all the way up to spicy, impressive blockbusters. The baking hot temperatures and lack of rain make light whites virtually impossible to produce (although there are a handful of fantastic Fianos from Campania that taste like the lovechild of Albariño and Viognier). So, meaty reds are the order of the day.

> **The best producers in Puglia are:** Angelo Rocca, Apollonio, Botromagno, Cosimo Taurino, Francesco Candido, Tenuta Rubino and Vallone.
> **The best producers in Campania are:** Colli di Lapio (Fiano experts), Feudi di San Gregorio (Falanghina – another funky white grape worth tracking down), Luigi Maffini, Mastroberardino, Montevetrano and Taburno.
> **The best producers in Basilacata:** D'Angelo, Basilisco and Paternoster.
> **The best producers in Calabria:** Librandi and San Francesco.

The Islands

Sicily, home to the unfashionable fortified wine Marsala, is at a current stage of enormous expansion. Flashy new estates are popping up, using consultant winemakers and making impressive wines. If you want to taste a slice of history, you will find it in the shape of De Bartoli's Bukkaram, a fortified *passito* Moscato, made with grapes from the volcanic island of Pantelleria. It tastes like a wicked, boozy marmalade.

> **The best producers in Sicily and Pantelleria are:** Abbazia Santa Anastasia, Abraxas, De Bartoli, Cusumano, Inycon, Maurigi, Morgante, Planeta, Salvatore Murana and Tasca d'Almerita.

Sardinia's wine trade is also expanding at a rate of knots. Here Rhône varieties are very important. The red Cannonau variety (Grenache) is transformed by Sella & Mosca into a spicy heavy-weight beast. Carignan, known as Carignano, is quite stunning in Santadi's Carignano del Sulcis. They also make Rocca Rubia, a *Riserva* version and a VdT, Terre Brune.

> **The best producers in Sardinia are:** Argiolas, Gallura, Giovanni Cherchi, Santadi and Sella & Mosca.

NEW ZEALAND

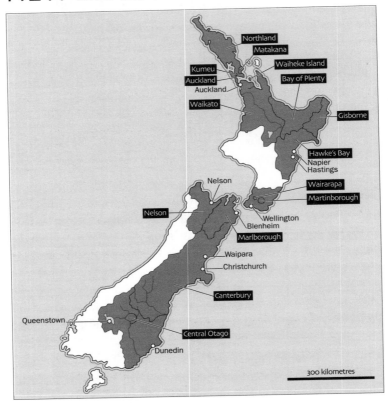

I had never tasted any New Zealand wines before my very first day in the wine trade. In fact, very few New Zealand wines had ever been shipped into England until the mid eighties. However, two wines back then stick in my mind and they still have the same high standards today. Montana and Cloudy Bay Sauvignon Blancs were the wines, and they immediately put New Zealand on the world wine map – forget about the lean Chardonnays and the weedy reds that followed; no one had ever tasted Sauvignon Blanc like it. It was as if Sancerre had been given a makeover, become more sociable and, perhaps, dare I say it, a little flirty. These wines had tropical-fruit flavours like mango and guava, but still stayed gooseberry-like and retained Sauvignon's trademark zippy acidity. Well, a lot has changed since then, particularly with respect to their Chardonnays, other whites and reds! New Zealand winemakers and viticulturalists are regarded in the wine world as some of the greatest geologists, botanists, chemists and technicians in the business. It did not take them long to crack the *terroir* thing. Suddenly Martinborough and Central Otago were Pinot Noir country, Marlborough was ideal for Sauvignon Blanc, and Hawke's Bay, with its gravel seam, was Cabernet and Merlot territory. They seem to have got it all sorted out in only a few years – this is a very new wine country in real terms. Granted prices are creeping up, but the majority of NZ wines are still available for reasonable prices.

I will run through both islands in a vaguely north to south order, noting the main styles in each region and the best wineries therein. Remember that, in traditional New World style, some wineries draw fruit from all over New Zealand and then make a large number of labels from a central winery.

North Island

Matakana, north of Auckland, is a well-trodden tourist route with a handful of small, boutique wineries – Ascension Vineyard and Matakana Estate (great Pinot Gris) are my two picks here. **Auckland** and its environs, just below Matakana and surrounding the city, is home to wineries like Collards, Kumeu River (with its Matés Vineyard, one of my favourite NZ Chardonnays), Matua Valley, Soljans, West Brook, and Villa Maria. This area is still a little too cool for full on reds, but aromatic white varieties and Chardonnay work very well. Syrah/Shiraz (both are used) is also creeping into the vineyards, making cooler, peppery styles of wine. Take a forty-minute ferry ride from downtown Auckland and you arrive at **Waiheke Island**, a stunningly beautiful ex-hippy colony, which is now one of the most chic addresses to holiday in (and grow vines). Top estates here are Cable Bay, Goldwater Estate, Passage Rock and Stonyridge Vineyard. Interestingly, the Cabernet Sauvignons, Merlots and even Malbecs look good here, as do the classy Chardonnays. **Waikato**

and the **Bay of Plenty** have very few wineries, as fruit farming is still the main industry (as it was in most of the north part of the island), but a special mention must go to Mills Reef, an exceptional estate making a wine close to my heart (Elspeth – my daughter's name!). **Gisborne**, on the east coast, is Chardonnay territory and here it picks up a creamy, tropical fruit texture and flavour, with a luscious character that is almost uniquely Gisborne's own. Montana has a large outfit here, and there are loads of smaller producers, but only a few of them export. **Hawke's Bay** is next on the list and this is the place where, in recent years, some of the meatiest Kiwi reds have come from. Gimblett Gravels is the name of a new appellation here, in which Cabernet, Merlot and increasingly Syrah/Shiraz is planted to great effect. Sauvignon Blanc has a fatter, fleshier feel here than the more classic areas like Marlborough, and Chardonnays often lack the richness of Gisborne and come in more chiselled. There are tons of recommended estates here – Alpha Domus, Craggy Range, Esk Valley, Kim Crawford, Ngatawara, Sacred Hill, Sileni, Stonecroft, Te Mata, Trinity Hill, Unison and Vidal make up a fine pack. **Wairarapa**, and its most famous sub-region **Martinborough**, sit at the southern end of the North Island near Wellington. Fantastic Chardonnay, Riesling, Sauvignon and, most importantly, Pinot Noir are made here. Ata Rangi's Pinot Noir is one of New Zealand's best, and Palliser Estate, Dry River and Martinborough Vineyard also make very fine versions. Other wineries of note are Alana Estate, Borthwick Vineyard, Matahiwi, Murdoch James and Solstone.

South Island

Nelson, on the northwest tip of the South Island, is where Neudorf Vineyards makes fabulous Pinot Gris and stunning Chardonnays. It is cooler and wetter here than around the corner in **Marlborough** on the northeastern tip of the South Island; that is where all of the Sauvignon Blanc floods in from! Centred around Blenheim, Marlborough is split into two main areas. The **Wairau Valley** is by far the biggest of the two and all of the famous names are based here. It was originally farmed for fruit, veg and livestock; the first vines (of the modern era) were planted in 1973 by Montana. These days there is only a smattering of non-vine-based farming. The Wairau is a diverse river valley and there are many different microclimates along its length and breadth. The main style here is what I would call 'classic Kiwi Sauvignon', as demonstrated by iconic estates such as Hunter's, Jackson and Cloudy Bay. The other main area is the **Awatere Valley** (pronounced Awa-tree). This is a smaller, cooler region and its Sauvignons tend to be more linear and racy. These wines often taste tighter and more youthful than the neighbouring Wairau styles. Many estates blend the two areas' harvests together in order to build complexity in their wines.

As well as Sauv Blanc, there are a few other grape varieties grown in Marlborough. The main ones are Chardonnay (very good from the top estates), Riesling (usually forward in style and showing promise) and Pinot Noir (just starting to rival Marlborough and Martinborough at the top end). Gewurztraminer and Pinot Gris are both made in fresh, forward, lighter styles (which I adore) and some very good sparklers are produced, too, although they end up looking a little dear by the time they've been exported. Cabernet Sauvignon and Merlot are planted by the brave few, but most sites are a little too cool. There is a new fashion for hillside plantings and some Pinots and other reds look pretty good. I suspect this movement will gather momentum.

There is, not surprisingly, a large roll call of recommended estates: Allan Scott, Astrolabe, Blind River, Cloudy Bay, The Crossings, Dog Point, Forrest Estate, Foxes Island, Framingham, Grove Mill, Hawkesbridge, Highfield, Huia, Hunter's, Isabel Estate, Jackson Estate, Kathy Lynskey, Lawson's Dry Hills, Montana Brancott, Mud House, Saint Clair, Seresin, Spy Valley, Te Whare Ra, TerraVin, Tohu, Vavasour, Wairau River and Wither Hills.

Canterbury and **Waipara**, on the eastern side of the South Island, are cooler and dryer with Pinot Noir and Chardonnay the most planted varieties. Sadly very few of these wines are exported, but of the few, Mountford Estate and Pegasus Bay are my clear favourites.

Just when I thought that every great wine region had already been identified, a brand new one comes along. **Waitaki**, situated north of Dunedin and some 65 km inland on the banks of the great river of the same name, is just such a place. With only 400 or so hectares of vineyard-suitable land, this is only ever going to be a boutique region. Having said that, the examples of Pinot Noir and Pinot Gris that I have tasted (admittedly, only from four- and two-year-old vines respectively) were very impressive indeed. Stay ahead of the pack and hunt down some bottles from wineries such as Craggy Range, Forrest, Lake Hayes, Valli and Waitaki Whitestone, who all source fruit here.

The last main NZ region is in the south of the south island (two hours' drive from Waitaki), and it is one of the very best – **Central Otago**. Home to the world's most southerly grapevines, this is where Pinot Noir, and to a lesser extent Chardonnay, Pinot Gris and Riesling are really setting people's palates alight. There is a handful of cracking wineries and a load of Johnny Come Latelys trying to cash in on this stunning viticultural landscape. Winemaking is often seen as a wonderful lifestyle option for wealthy businessmen as they wind down their careers. This could not be further from the truth. Downscaling into winemaking is as ridiculous as downscaling into helicopter design (I have stolen this quote from a famous Otago personality!). The result is a load of Pinots which imitate the brilliance of the wines made by the following list of overachievers, but never match it. This is one of the most exciting wine regions in the world, not least because I am a Pinot freak, but I must admit that I really don't want to see it dragged down by half-hearted attempts to tackle the world's most beguiling grape variety. In the year 2000 there were roughly fifteen different recognised wine producers in Central Otago. There are now over one hundred – you have been warned!

Central Otago's best producers are: Amisfield, Carrick, Chard Farm, Felton Road, Mt Difficulty, Mount Edward, Mount Michael, Olssens, Peregrine, Pisa Range, Rippon, Rockburn, Sleeping Dogs, Two Paddocks and Valli.

PORTUGAL

Portugal is home to Port and Madeira, two of the most classic and rewarding fortified wines in the world. Less distinguished are some of their rosés, some dry light whites like Vinho Verde and some earthy, tannic, headachy reds. However, like Spain, they are in all-change mode and, as every day goes by, cleaner, fresher whites and funkier, fruit-driven reds are emerging.

Port

Situated in the Douro valley in the north of Portugal, the grapes for Port are grown on some of the most spectacular terraces in the wine world. There are over eighty grape varieties that can go into Port, but usually winemakers select from only about ten or twenty, the best of which are: Touriga Nacional, Tinta Roriz (Spain's Tempranillo), Tinta Barroca, Touriga Francesa and Tinta Cão. There are two distinct styles of Port – oak/cask-aged and bottle-aged. Wood-aged Ports are generally ready to drink on release, as the oak softens the tannins. Bottle-aged Ports spend a short amount of time in barrels and then are bottled without filtration or fining. They need to age for a long period in bottle for the same softening of tannins to occur.

HOW PORT IS MADE

The grapes are harvested and then, instead of being trampled underfoot (yes, it still happens today, although there is mercifully some mechanisation involved, too), they are crushed, macerated and fermented. After only two or three days fermenting, when a sufficiently high level of alcohol is achieved (about 6–8 per cent), about one-fifth of neutral grape spirit, *aguardente* at 77 per cent, is added to the must. This is done to kill the active yeasts and raise the alcohol to about 19 per cent, preserving the remaining sugars in the wine. As the fermentation process is relatively short-lived, the maceration process should be frenzied, extracting as much colour and tannin as possible. Traditionally this is done by treading the grapes, often to music. The soles of your feet are strong enough to break the grapes and squash the skins but not so hard that they split the pips which would release bitter flavours into the wine. The wine is matured in oak barrels and is assessed to determine what quality level of wine has been made. In the second year after the harvest, and only then, is the decision made as to whether a vintage will be declared or not. Samples will be sent to the Port Wine Institute, along with details of quantities of wine made. After the nod has been given, the wine can be bottled for sale – only to be sent away to someone's cellar, banished for a further twenty to fifty years, waiting for the optimum time to pop the cork. Long, protracted, ancient and very, very good! As with a lot of things in life, patience is a prerequisite for pleasure.

STYLES OF PORT

White

Please do not drink this unless you are on holiday (OK, there are a few exceptions – Grahams, Taylors and Quinta do Portal). Try as I might, and that is pretty hard, I cannot see the point to this style, unless it's served with tonic. It is supposedly a nice aperitif, but you'll never get to the food if you have a few too many of these.

Ruby

The fruity, often grippy and most cherry-like of the styles of Port. This wine is aged in bulk and is the youngest released style. It is sometimes drunk chilled as an aperitif – by the French! Or with lemon – by the British in sit coms!

Tawny

Genuine Tawny Port, as opposed to light weak Port, is aged for extended periods in oak barrels, resulting in the deep red Port colour leaching out into the wood and ending up with a 'tawny' hued wine. Tawny Port styles are categorised by age, 10-year-old, 20-year-old, 30-year-old etc., and can be stunning. I prefer the younger ones with more fruit (they are also the cheapest, thank goodness!).

Late Bottled Vintage

Shortened to LBV – this is the best way to enjoy 'vintage' flavours for less money, and you also don't have to wait twenty-five years for the pleasure. They are usually ready to drink on release, as they spend between four and six years in wood, softening the tannins.

Single-Quinta

These wines are usually made in years when a vintage has not been 'declared'. A single quinta is a single estate/vineyard, and connoisseurs who want to enjoy a wine earlier than would be possible for a vintage style, favour this type of Port. Reputable Port houses make S-Q in a vintage mould and then keep them back for bottle ageing, only releasing the wines when they are ready to drink. The best are Warre's Cavadinha, Dow's Bomfim, Graham's Malvedos and Taylor's Vargellas.

Vintage

The big daddy, this style is only made in first-rate vintages when a Port house will 'declare' their intention to do so. Vintage Port is usually made only three or four years in ten. It is the most expensive style and requires extended bottle ageing, as the time spent in oak during the production process is relatively short. Most vintage Ports should be left for a minimum of fifteen years before drinking, but it is not unusual for them to need thirty to fifty years before they start to drink perfectly. They throw a hefty sediment and require decanting.

***

The best big-name houses are: Dow, Fonseca, Graham, Quinta do Noval Nacional, Taylor and Warre.
The best lesser-known overachievers are: Churchill, Niepoort, Quinta do Portal, Quinta do Vesuvio, Quinto do Infantado, Ramos-Pinto and Senhora da Ribeira.

***

Madeira

Made on the volcanic island of the same name, 600 kilometres west of the Moroccan coast, Madeira is an institution among wine drinkers. These wines are the longest lived of all. Think nothing of putting a bottle of Malmsey in your cellar, waiting for 200 years and then tasting it. It will be fine, although you probably won't be. There are only small amounts made. Like Port and Sherry, Madeira rarely seems to be in fashion, but who cares? That leaves all the more for us to enjoy.

WHY MADEIRA WAS MADE

In the late 1600s, trading ships on their way to the Far East would stop at Madeira and pick up casks of local wine. In order to help this wine to get to its destination in one piece, the wine was fortified to make it more stable. The onward journey would involve travelling through the tropics, encountering temperatures as high as 45°C. The cargo was heated up during this time and then cooled down as the ships arrived at their destination. It was only when the Madeira winemakers had an opportunity to taste some wine that was returned unsold, that they realised the flavour was greatly enhanced. They determined that the improvement in flavour had come about, not by the rolling and pitching of the ships, but by the heating and cooling process, so a 'baking' process was introduced during the production.

HOW MADEIRA IS MADE

Cheaper, bulk styles of Madeira are put into the equivalent of a large kettle and heated to high temperatures by means of a coil. The temperature is kept between 40°C and 50°C for three months. Finer styles of Madeira are placed in 600-litre wooden casks in warm rooms. These rooms are heated to between 30°C and 40°C for six months. The very best Madeiras are produced without artificial heating and are stored in casks in the eaves of Madeiran lodges and are naturally heated by the sun. They usually stay like this for twenty years or more before being bottled. These three types of production all use the so-called *estufagem*, or heating, process. Drier styles are fortified before *estufagem*, sweeter styles after. Then the wines enter a *solera* system similar to Sherry (see page 246).

STYLES OF MADEIRA
(EACH STYLE IS A NAME OF A GRAPE VARIETY)

Sercial
Pale, dry, light body and good acidity.

Verdelho
Golden coloured, medium bodied, tangy and medium dry.

Bual
Darker coloured, fuller bodied, smoky and fairly sweet.

Malmsey
Rich, raisiny, full bodied and very sweet.

The best producers are: Blandy's, Cossart Gordon and Henriques & Henriques.

Other Portuguese Wines of Note

Made in the Minho region on the coast north of Porto, **Vinho Verde** should be a searingly dry white wine as it is picked early (Verde = green) to preserve as much acidity as possible. Bring your ladder for harvesting, as the grapes are trained on eight-foot-high trellises. The best producers of Vinho Verde are Palácio da Brejoeira and Quinta do Ameal. There are some seriously good red wines made in the **Douro** alongside Port. My favourite producers are Duas Quintas, Niepoort, Quinta do Crasto, Quinta da Gaivosa, Quinta do Infantado, Quinta do Portal, Quinta de Roriz, Quinta de la Rosa, Quinta do Vale da Raposa and Redoma.

South of Porto in **Beiras**, Caves Aliança is the one outfit I would recommend making hearty reds, while nearby **Bairrada** and **Dão** are widely thought of as two of Portugal's best red wines, made predominantly from Touriga Nacional and Baga respectively. Caves São João and Luis Pato make the best Bairradas, while Alvaro Castro, Conde de Santar, Quinta da Cabriz, Quinta dos Carvalhais and Quinta dos Roques all make meaty Dãos. Further south in **Estremadura**, a weird white wine is produced called **Bucelas** and is in need of major surgery, but other stars are Palha Canas, Quinta da Boavista and Quinta de Pancas, whose plantings of Cabernet Sauvignon soften the local red grapes. In **Colares**, vineyard workers sport baskets on their heads to guard against the three-metre-deep sandy trenches in which the vines are planted from falling in and suffocating them. That's a first. These reds last for ages and the central co-operative makes interesting, if unusual, wine. Inland in **Ribatejo**, Bright Brothers and Quinta da Lagoalva are the top two producers. Further inland again, in **Alentejo**, Cortes de Cima, Quinta de Cabriz, Quinta do Carmo, João Portugal Ramos and Segada are all exporting and doing a cracking job. In **Terras do Sado**, south of Lisbon, João Pires, José-Maria da Fonseca, Pasmados, Periquita and Quinta de Camarate make some terrific reds. **Moscatel de Setúbal**, a fortified Muscat, also pops up with all the charm and poise of a gorilla.

SOUTH AFRICA

No country in the wine world has changed as much over the last decade as South Africa. The South Africans themselves seem a little bemused at the massive interest in their fine produce and are desperately trying to make hay while the sun shines. Famous regions like **Stellenbosch**, **Paarl**, **Wellington**, **Franschhoek** and **Robertson** are being joined by **Malmesbury**, **Elim**, **Walker Bay**, **Elgin** and **Worcester** on wine lists around the world. Wineries are popping up like jack-in-the-boxes and there is a ton of tasting needed just to stay up to date. So, with perfect growing conditions, almost too good in some places, what has the Cape got to offer? Cabernet Sauvignon, Merlot, Shiraz and the indigenous Pinotage in the red camp, and Chenin Blanc (known locally as Steen), Sauvignon Blanc and Chardonnay in the white are all working well. I suspect that Bordeaux blends and classic Syrah/Shiraz styles will be regarded as the way forward for reds, while Chenin, Sauvignon and Chardonnay will all hold their own in the whites. South Africa makes earthy, muscular reds and this suits Syrah more than it does erudite Cabernet, but some very smart 'Cape

Blends' are emerging, where Pinotage is whisked into the mix. Watch this space with regard to these styles – they will provide us with something uniquely South African, as Pinotage isn't planted anywhere else, and I love a good reason to add something to my wine diet. South African Sauvignon Blancs are also very interesting. Situated, not only geographically, between the Loire and Marlborough in New Zealand, the classic Cape style is racy, lean and mildly exotic – somewhere between the two existing classics' own versions. It is also worth pointing out that some of the best dry Chenin Blancs are made in South Africa from very old vines. These can be drunk much younger than their Loire counterparts (thank goodness). The following list grows as each year goes by and, at the very least, South African Syrahs, Cape Blends and Sauvignons should appear on your table from time to time.

My favourite estates are: Avondale, Beaumont, Beyerskloof, Boekenhoutskloof (Porcupine Ridge), Bouchard Finlayson, Brahms, Coleraine, Columella (Sadie Family), De Toren, De Trafford, De Wetshof, Diemersfontein, Dornier (Donatus in the UK), Fairview, Flagstone, Glen Carlou, Graham Beck, Grangehurst, Hamilton Russell, Hartenberg, Iona, Jean Daneel, Jordan, Kanonkop, Ken Forrester, Klein Constantia, Lammershoek, Land's End, Lindhorst, Linton Park, Longridge, Luddite, Meinert, Mischa, Mont Rochelle, Mont du Toit, Morgenhof, La Motte, Nabygelegen, Neil Ellis, Raats, Remhoogte, Rijk's, Rudera, Rupert & Rothschild, Rustenberg (Brampton), Rust en Vrede, Scali, Signal Hill, Simonsig, Southern Right, Spice Route, Springfield, Stark-Condé, Stellenzicht, Thelema, Veenwouden, Vergelegen, Vilafonte, Viljoensdrift, Villiera, Warwick Estate, Waterford (Kevin Arnold) and Wildekrans.

SPAIN

Spain is a huge wine-producing country with, proportionately, relatively few world-class wines. This may seem a little harsh, but I am often very disappointed after big Spanish wine tastings. I must admit, though, they are playing catch-up at a blistering

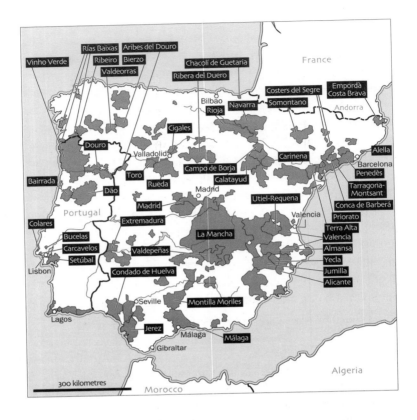

pace, as there is a new wave of stainless steel tanks, clean, fresh whites and under-oaked (as opposed to over-) reds coming through. But this can't happen fast enough. It is welcome news, though, as in the early 1970s, 95 per cent of Spanish wine left Spain in a tanker! While the rest of the world embraced modernisation and deft vinification techniques, Spain just carried on using dirty old barrels. Oxidised whites and stewed reds are thankfully becoming a thing of the past, and indigenous Spanish grape varieties are being allowed to flex their muscles and show off their talents to the rest of the world. OK, some of them are dull – but say 'hello' to Albariño, a stunning white grape destined to feature on connoisseurs' tables around the world. Also, embrace Tempranillo, one of the world's most engaging red varieties in the right hands. Spain is a great-value wine country, and it is worth considering Spanish wines when classic French and Italian bottles are out of reach.

But what prompted this change and woke the industry up? Answer: one man, called Miguel Torres. He had the audacity to enter a Catalonian Cabernet Sauvignon, 1970 Torres Gran Coronas Black Label, in the Cabernet class of the 1979 Gault-Millau 'Wine Olympics' – and walked off with the gold medal, leaving Châteaux Latour, Pichon-Lalande and La Mission Haut-Brion with their not inconsiderable noses out of joint.

Nowadays Miguel is still doing his thing, but there are hundreds of other inspirational figures at the top of the tree, spreading their expertise and goodwill throughout the industry. The one thing that frustrates me more than anything is that, when I visit Spain, the selections on wine lists are simply amazing. We never see this depth and number of outstanding labels exported. Simply put – the Spanish keep all of the great, new, funky, cutting edge stuff for themselves, and, honestly speaking, I can't blame them!

THE GRAPES

Reds include **Garnacha Tinta (Grenache)**, behaving much the same as it does in France, boosting blends wherever it goes, although in Priorato it works phenomenally well on its own. **Tempranillo**, also known as **Ull de Llebre**, **Tinto Fino** and **Cencibel**, is the king of Rioja and Navarra, as well as being Cabernet's partner in the terrific wines of Ribera del Duero. **Cariñena (Carignan)** is planted extensively and used for lower quality reds. **Cabernet Sauvignon** flourishes, lending class and complexity to indigenous varieties, and **Monastrell** is another useful red grape that is generally tucked away in blends. There are a lot of new plantings of **Syrah** going in the ground across Spain, as the climate is spot on and who cares about the local authorities and their Draconian rules?

Whites are less exalted, save for the captivating **Albariño**, the world-famous **Chardonnay**, the world-infamous **Viura**, the fizzy wine twins **Xarel-lo** and **Parellada**, and the underrated **Malvasia**. There is a dribble of other international varieties in Penedès, making mainly aromatic, dry whites.

THE WINE LAWS

The classification is relatively straightforward, but do not expect to see many of the first three examples unless you are on holiday.

Vino de Mesa

A blended table wine from unclassified vineyards.

Vino Comarcal

A regional table wine.

Vino de la Tierra

Equivalent to French *Vin de Pays*.

DO

Denominación de Origen, the equivalent of French *Appellation Contrôlée*.

DOC

Denominación de Origen Calificada, the equivalent of Italy's DOCG – Rioja was Spain's first region to qualify in 1991.

THE STYLES

Joven

A wine that is released young, without any oak ageing.

Crianza

A wine that has been aged for two years before release, of which a minimum of six months or one year is spent in a barrel (depending on the region).

Reserva

A wine that has been aged for three years before release, of which a minimum of one year is spent in a barrel.

Gran Reserva

A wine that has been aged for five years before release, of which a minimum of two years is spent in a barrel.

Rioja and Navarra

Rioja is Spain's most famous red wine. It generally has vanilla-oak and plummy-fruit on the nose, and a deep, mellow, red-cherry palate. It is also generally thought of as being one of the best-value mature red wines available. Rioja outshines Navarra in terms of great wines, although the styles of production are the same. Usually over 70 per cent of a red Rioja is made from Tempranillo, with Garnacha, Graciano and Mazuelo to balance the wine. Viura is the dominant white grape in Rioja Blanco, with Malvasia often making up the numbers. Rioja is split between three areas, the best two being the Rioja Alta and Alavesa, with the Baja area just that bit too hot to produce grapes with fine acidity. **Navarra**, which overlaps the Rioja Baja, tends to make wines with less complexity and longevity. If it is round, tangy, plummy reds with a touch of liquorice and oak on the nose that you want, then you are in the right place. New-wave estates are popping up everywhere in Rioja and a new vogue for super *cuvées* has arrived. These are dark, intense, oak-*barrique*-aged red wines, which don't necessarily conform to the *Reserva/Gran Reserva* mould. They are a little like the super-Tuscans, in that a snazzy bottle and trendy brand name is all you have to go on. In the same way that the Super-Tuscans saved Chianti, I am quietly confident that these wines will catapult Rioja back into our cellars and into our hearts.

Just watch out for the old-fashioned whites, as they are unbelievably oaky (almost medicinal) and not to everyone's taste.

The best producers of Rioja are: Artadi, Barón de Ley, Contino, CVNE, Lopez de Heredia, Marqués de la Concordia, Marqués de Griñon, Marqués de Murrieta, Marqués de Vargas, Muga, Navajas, Remelluri, La Rioja Alta, Roda, Urbina and Viña Salceda.

The best producers of Navarra are: Agramont, Guelbenzu, Julián Chivite, Ochoa, Príncipe de Viana and Vega del Castillo.

Catalonia

The most famous style of wine from this northeastern Spanish region near the city of Barcelona, is **Cava**, Spain's answer to Champagne. Made from rather dull varieties, Xarel-lo, Parellada and Macabéo (local name for Viura), these wines are produced in the traditional method and, if needed, are often boosted with Chardonnay. I have not really come to terms with them, preferring to look to the Loire for cheaper fizz, but some producers make nice enough wines – and, if you dine out in Barcelona, you are guaranteed some good ones to choose from. **Penedès** is the name of the most important region in Catalonia in which Cava is made. It also happens to be Torres's base. The undisputed leader of the pack, the Torres range of wines is stunning – from Esmeralda and Viña Sol, to Spain's best Chardonnay, Milmanda, as well as the entire red portfolio, including the stellar Cabernet, Mas la Plana. The other names to look out for here are Albet I Noya, Can Ràfols dels Caus, Jean Léon, Marquès de Monistrol and Puig i Roca.

Inland and to the southwest of Penedès, is the parched, mountainous region of **Tarragona-Montsant** and **Priorato**. Here, Garnacha and Cariñena are used to fashion thunderous and expensive reds like those from the wines of Celler de Capçanes, Clos Mogador, Clos de L'Obac, Dits Del Terra, L'Ermita and Finca Dofi (Alvaro Palacios), Laurona, Mas d'en Compte, Mas Igneus, Mas Martinet and Scala Dei. A short distance southeast of Priorato is the region of **Terra Alta**, where two noteworthy properties called Bàrbara Forés and Xavier Clu make incredible wines. Further inland, in the region of **Conca de Barberá**, Josep Foraster and the inimitable Miguel Torres hold court. The last of the Catalonian areas worth a shout is up on the Mediterranean border with France, **Empordà-Costa Brava**. Here Mas Estela makes sensational reds.

The northern coast of Spain is home to some of the most weird and wonderful Spanish white wines. **Bizkaiko** and **Getariako Txacolina** in the Basque eastern seaboard is the place to find the beguiling white Txacoli (or Chacolí). Tasting like a mildly effervescent, ultra-dry Muscadet, this seafood wine is at its best from Bodegas Ametzoi and Txomín Etaniz. If we move right the way along to the western Atlantic corner of Spain, in Galicia, we find the region of **Rías Baixas**. This is where the stunning, tropical fruit-scented white grape Albariño does its thing.

> **The best estates are:** Fillaboa, Lagar de Cervera, Lagar de Fornelos, Martín Codax, Pazo de Barrantes, Pazo Señoráns, Valdamor and Valmiñor.

Travelling inland to the east is the vast region of **Castilla y León**. Here in **Bierzo**, Descendientes de J Palacios makes brooding, dark, spicy reds. Further east still, in **Ribera del Duero**, we find the jewel in the crown of Spanish red-wine production – Vega Sicilia's Unico Reserva. This is where the most expensive red wine of Spain is made. Cabernet Sauvignon and Merlot have found their way into the vineyards here and the resulting wines, combined with Tempranillo (known locally as Tinto Fino), are spectacular and incredibly long-lived.

> **The best producers of Ribera del Duero are:** Alión, Cillar de Silos, Condado de Haza, Dominio de Pingus, Pago de Carraovejas, Pesquera, Tarsus, Valduero and Vega Sicilia.

A number of lesser-known regions pop up here, too. In **Valladolid**, Mauro makes the finest wines. In **Rueda**, Agrícola Castellana and Bodegas Dos Victorias make equally good reds and whites (from Tempranillo and Verdejo/Sauvignon Blanc respectively). In the up-and-coming region of **Toro**, Alquiriz (owned by Vega Sicilia) and Viña Bajoz carry the torch. On the Portuguese border, high above the banks of the Douro, is the new region of **Arribes del Duero**. It is here that Durius Alto Duero (owned by the Marqués de Griñon team) is doing some very good work.

In the arid, dead centre of Spain, **Extremadura**, **Castilla-La Mancha** and **Madrid** covers a vast area of bulk-producing vineyards. In **Castilla-La Mancha**, Dominio de Valdepusa makes some fine, earthy reds and in **Valdepeñas** Los Llanos continues to make exceptionally good-value spicy reds, too. Sliding across towards the Med, in **Almansa** Piqueras is my pick and in **Jumilla** Casa de la Ermita is the star. The same can be said for Dominio Los Pinos in **Valencia**.

Heading north, **Calatayud's** best finds come from Marqués de Aragón and San Gregorio, while **Campo de Borja** Bodegas Borsao is the overachiever. The last of these satellite areas is **Somontano** where Blecua (Viñas del Vero) and Enate also make very good wines.

I have tasted one superb wine from **Mallorca** made by Anima Negra, and I have heard there are others, but I will leave them for you to discover when you are on your hols.

Sherry

There is one major Spanish wine style left – Sherry. Sadly, it is a deeply unfashionable drink – but it doesn't deserve to be! Perhaps this time it is the fault of the British, whose taste for cream sherries has taken our eye off the real, true, quality styles made in Jerez de la Frontera, inland of Cádiz in southern Spain. Sherry is a wine made, principally, from the Palomino grape variety. Pedro Ximénez (PX) comes into play to sweeten it, and also makes an intense pudding wine in its own right.

HOW SHERRY IS MADE

The Palomino grapes are harvested and then de-stalked and pressed. The must is acidified with the addition of *yeso* (gypsum) or tartaric acid. Fermentation takes place to total dryness in oak barrels or stainless steel tanks. The bone-dry white wine is then put into casks to mature, leaving an air space at the top. It is now that the magical yeast-strain known as flor may or may not appear in the maturing Sherry casks. Flor, or Saccharomyces beticus, is a filmy scum that forms on top of the wine, feeding off the oxygen in the butt (barrel) and the alcohol in the wine. Butts that don't attract flor are fortified immediately. These casks have now had their fate decided (see below for styles) and are fortified to 18 per cent with a grape spirit called *aguardente*. Flor-infected casks are tasted and monitored to decide upon which style of Sherry the wine will be released as. Once the style has been established, the wines are put into a fractional-blending system called *solera*. This ensures a constant taste for each bodega's brand of Sherry year on year, rather like NV Champagne. A Sherry *solera* is made up of a number of groups of butts known as *criaderas*. Up to one-third of each barrel from the oldest *criadera* is drawn off for each bottling, the space being filled with a wine from the next oldest *criadera*. This 'refreshing' of the butts keeps the flor alive for anything up to ten years. There can be as few as four, or as many as fourteen, *criaderas* in a system. This bottling and topping up process usually occurs two or three times a year.

So why drink Sherry? It is a spectacular aperitif and a stunning after-dinner tipple. Try a Fino instead of a Gin and Tonic or a glass of Champagne before a meal, and an old Oloroso with coffee after. Stick to the top bodegas and avoid cheap cream Sherry at all costs.

> **The best Sherry bodegas are:** Emilio Lustau, Fernando de Castilla, González Byass, Hidalgo, Osborne and Valdespino.

STYLES
Manzanilla is made in Sanlúcar de Barrameda on the coast, and is the lightest and driest of the styles. It tends to have a salty tang from the sea air. Drink as soon as the bottle is opened.

Fino is the most well-known style, and is light, dry, delicate and cleansing. Drink as soon as the bottle is opened.

Amontillado is an aged-Fino style that loses its flor. It is at least eight years old and takes on a deeper, amber colour and a tangy, nutty taste. Keep in the fridge after opening.

Oloroso styles have higher alcohol than Finos, are made from casks that did not attract flor and have raisiny, burnt-toffee flavours with a dry and complex finish. The alcohol levels in these wines can reach 24 per cent as evaporation occurs in older butts. Keep in the fridge after opening.

Palo Cortado is a rare style that sits between Oloroso and Amontillado in taste. Keep in the fridge after opening.

Two miscellaneous wines of note are **Málaga** and **Pedro Ximénez**. These styles are sweet and chocolaty with a nutty, almost liquidised Christmas pudding flavour.

UNITED KINGDOM

In support of its hardworking vineyards, I am writing a short entry for the United Kingdom, rather than including it in the Rest of the World roundup – I know this is biased, but I have a number of vineyards close to where I live! There are 2,500 acres of vines in the UK and everyone ought to taste at least one of their wines, if only to decide it isn't to their taste. With the climate not quite up to Bordeaux standards, it is no surprise that it is hard to get grapes to ripen. However, the Germans manage, and so to Germany the UK winemakers went, in search of early-ripening varieties that could cope with the chilly climes. Huxelrebe, Reichensteiner, Optima, Seyval Blanc, Kerner, Schönburger and, one you may have heard of, Müller-Thurgau, were some of the chosen bunch. Catchy names! With skilful viticulture and vinification, Germanic styles of wine can be made – and even Sancerre wannabes are produced. Some reds are grown in plastic tunnels, but surely the best style of all is the UK's sparkling wine. After all, think of the chalky soils (the white cliffs of Dover) and the Champagne-like climate. The main problem is that equipment is expensive, so co-op style operations are definitely the way forward.

With something like 120 wineries active in England, the least you can do is encourage them by visiting, and tasting their wines. You never know what might happen, the way global warming is going.

UNITED STATES OF AMERICA

California

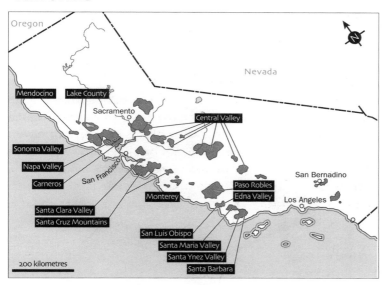

It is perhaps not surprising that there is a touch of Hollywood about Californian winemaking. Big budget 'releases' feature alongside art house, or boutique, creations. Winemakers are as famous and charismatic within the wine industry as film stars are on the silver screen.

THE GRAPES

This is very much Cabernet Sauvignon and Chardonnay land. The Californians were sensible enough to select the two most powerful and universally appealing varieties with which to mount an assault on the world of wine. Merlot, Syrah, Pinot Noir and, of course, the stunning indigenous Zinfandel, as well as various Rhône varieties (grown by Rhône Rangers), play a supporting role for the reds. Sauvignon Blanc, Riesling, some white Rhône varieties and others make up the cast and extras for the whites. But make no mistake, its Cabernet and Chardonnay headlining the show, and they can be blockbusters.

THE FACTS

Extending over nearly 1,000 kilometres of vineyards from north to south, this state produces over 90 per cent of America's quality wine. The styles of wine made are usually rich, pure and varietally correct, with texture and fruit levels corresponding to the climate. Regions within California vary from Germanic chilliness to Saharan heat. Generally the better areas take advantage of moderating ocean breezes and the cooling effect of early morning fogs. The wines are often ready to drink on release, as the tannin levels in reds and the acidity levels in whites are usually in balance from the word go. Some estates, however, make long-lived wines and I have been lucky enough to taste several thirty-year-old reds that were holding up well, but these are rare.

WINE LAWS

In North America, if a wine has a grape variety stated on the label, then it must contain a minimum of 75 per cent of that grape in the bottle. If it states a vintage, then it must contain 95 per cent from said vintage. And if it mentions an AVA ('Approved Viticultural Area'), then 85 per cent must come from that AVA. An AVA is a rudimentary equivalent to the French AC. The AVA system imposes no vinification parameters, yield limits or rules on varieties planted, unlike the French or Italian systems, but, in time, it should enable winemakers to concentrate on soil types and microclimates in order to establish the most suitable varieties to plant in any given AVA boundaries. Since the region as a whole is really only thirty-five years old in serious winemaking terms, it will take some time before these laws can and will be tightened.

THE REGIONS

The **Napa Valley** is surely the best known of the Californian wine regions. It starts, at the cool end, in the San Francisco Bay area and ends up, at the baked end, in Calistoga. Here, Cabernet Sauvignon holds court, producing arguably the greatest reds in all California. Most of the grapes are grown on the valley floor around the towns of Yountville, Rutherford, Oakville and St-Helena, although there is a trend now to head to the hills for improved drainage and aspect – Howell Mountain and Mount Veeder are two of these successful areas. **Carneros** is a region overlapping the southern ends of the Napa Valley and Sonoma County. It is here that some of the best Chardonnay and Pinot Noir are grown, on account of its proximity to the bay and the foggy, cooler temperatures. **Sonoma County** includes the famous sub-regions of the Russian River, Dry Creek, Knights and Alexander Valleys. These are home to wineries like Kistler, Matanzas Creek and Nalle. This is a quieter, less under-the-spotlight region, that is fragmented into particular soil types and microclimates. AVA regions and the notion of *terroir* make more sense here than many other areas of California. The ever-present Cabernet Sauvignon is grown here, but I favour the Zinfandels, Chardonnays and Merlots. Further north are **Mendocino County** and **Lake County**. These two areas are cooler and grow Zinfandel, Sauvignon Blanc and, of course, Cabernet Sauvignon. In Mendocino's chilly Anderson Valley, Chardonnay and Pinot Noir are grown for sparkling wines, with Champagne's very own Roederer Estate making some fine wines.

East of San Francisco, in the first of the Central Coast's regions is the **Livermore Valley**. A small AVA, Livermore is a prime site for Sauvignon Blanc and Semillon. Unfortunately, they are not planted nearly as widely as they should be. To the south, the **Santa Clara Valley**, otherwise known as Silicon Valley, and the **Santa Cruz Mountains** have a small number of useful vineyards – Bonny Doon and Ridge are the big names here, growing Zinfandel and Rhône varieties. **San Benito**, where Calera make Pinot Noir on Mount Harlan, **Chalone**, **Arroyo Seco** and the **Carmel Valley** are other areas dotted around this northern end of the Central Coast. The south Central Coast has some excellent wineries. It is here, in **Santa Barbara**, where two famous AVAs are to be found: the **Santa Maria Valley** and the **Santa Ynez Valley** make awesome Chardonnays and Pinot Noirs, and Rhône varieties respectively. Au Bon Climat and Qupé are based here. **San Luis Obispo County** has two fine AVAs – the baking hot **Paso Robles**, where Zin flourishes, and the cooler **Edna Valley**, home to Chardonnays.

Inland, the vast **Central Valley**, including the **Sacramento** and **San Joaquin Valleys**, is responsible for bulk wines and some lesser labels, and accounts for nearly three-quarters of all wine made in California. RH Phillips and Mondavi's Woodbridge labels are among the better wines made here.

The best Cabernet Sauvignon/Merlot producers are: Araujo, Arietta, Beringer, Bryant Family, Cain, Caymus, Clos LaChance, Corison, Dalle Valle, Diamond Creek, Dominus, Duckhorn, Dunn, Etude, Flora Springs, Forman, Frog's Leap, Gallo Estate, Harlan Estate, Havens, Hess Collection, Joseph Phelps, Justin Vineyards, Lail Vineyards, Matanzas Creek, Moraga, Niebaum Coppola, Newton, Opus One, Pahlmeyer, Paradigm, Paul Hobbs, Peter Michael, Philip Togni, Quintessa, Ridge, Robert Mondavi, St Francis, Shafer, Silver Oak, Spottswoode, Stag's Leap Wine Cellars and Viader.

The best Chardonnay producers are: Arrowood, Au Bon Climat, Beringer, Clos LaChance, David Ramey, Frog's Leap, Gallo Estate, Hanzell, Kistler, Kongsgaard, Landmark, Lymar, Morgan, Paul Hobbs, Peter Michael, Robert Mondavi, Shafer and Sinskey.

The best producers of Sauvignon Blanc are: Beringer, Carmenet, Frog's Leap, Matanzas Creek and Robert Mondavi.

The best producers of Pinot Noir are: Au Bon Climat, Calera, Cinnabar, Etude, Gary Farrell, Hanzell, Kistler, Marimar Torres, J Rochioli, Saintsbury, Sinskey and Talley Vineyards.

The best Rhône Rangers are: Alban, Au Bon Climat, Bonny Doon, Cline, Jade Mountain, Qupé, Sean Thackrey, Tablas Creek, Turley and Wild Hog.

Pacific Northwest

Oregon has long been labelled the perfect place to grow Pinot Noir, on account of its similar climate to Burgundy – but we already know how much Burgundians can be made to suffer at the hands of the weather, so it was always going to be a struggle in Oregon. Since the early 1970s, Pinot freaks have attempted to emulate the wines of the Côte-d'Or. The **Willamette Valley** is the centre of this activity and over the years they have seemed to be nearing the target. These estates tend to be tiny and so production is always limited. They may be hard to track down, but they are definitely worth the trouble. Oh, and they make some nice whites here as well. Chardonnays can be fine with elegance and good acidity and Pinot Gris can be excellent – but, unfortunately, as well as giving you another angle on the tricky Pinot Noir variety, most of the wines are terrifyingly expensive!

The best estates in Oregon are: Adelsheim, Archery Summit, Beaux Frères, Bethel Heights, Cristom, Domaine Drouhin, Duck Pond, Evesham Wood, King Estate, Ponzi and Rex Hill.

Washington State also makes wine – Cabernet Sauvignon, Merlot and Chardonnay are the most successful varieties. I have been mightily impressed with many of the wines from the estates below, in particular the India Wells Vineyard from Ste-Michelle. By the way, you can forget the wines from **Idaho**.

THE REST OF THE WORLD

The remainder of the Old World constitutes another twenty or so countries or regions that make wine. Some are amazing, like **Hungary**'s decadent sweet wine Tokaji – a cross between Sauternes and a top flight Sherry – Disznókö, Oremus and the Royal Tokaji Wine Company are the best producers. **Bulgaria**'s spicy red grapes Mavrud and Gamza are worth tasting for an oft-needed change of flavour, particularly at the cheap end of the spectrum. Serge Hochar's fantastic Château Musar, a blend of Cabernet Sauvignon, Syrah and Cinsault from the Bekaa Valley in the **Lebanon** is definitely worth a try. **Greek** wines are starting to look interesting, particularly the whites using grape varieties like Assyrtiko and Moscophilero. Sweeties from Santorini were the precursors of Italy's famous Vin Santos, so they are also worth a punt. Boutari, Gaia Estate, Gerovassiliou and Tsantali are my favourite Greek estates.

Others not so great include the output from Luxembourg, Swiss reds, Croatia, Cyprus, Corsica, Malta, Tunisia, Morocco (although some Carignans look OK), Turkey, Egypt, Israel, Jordan and Russia. We can only keep on tasting to see if this will all change.

If you think that the Old World gets a rough ride on the rejects, I'm not going to be any more kind to Mexico, Uruguay (a handful of hairy Tannats appear on the market occasionally), Peru, Bolivia, Colombia, Brazil, Paraguay, Bali (although it has the professional outfit, Hatten), Thailand (except the respectable Monsoon Valley wines), China, India (although the Sula Winery is starting to look good) or Japan.

Now I bet you didn't know they all made wine!

Chapter 7

VINTAGES

A vintage is the year in which the grapes are harvested and this alluring word also encompasses the characteristics (weather and, therefore by definition, quality) of that year. Most of the world's vineyards are situated in variable climates. Weather patterns change – frosts, thunderstorms, hail, downpours, cold snaps and droughts can affect the outcome of the harvest. In cooler climates, sunshine hours are the all-important currency for fruit ripeness, and pickers try to shepherd in their crops before any untimely downpours rain on their parade. Some parts of the world don't suffer as badly as others and, in these, the vintage fluctuations are less dramatic and the quality of the wines is therefore more predictable. One thing is certain though, and that is that great winemakers tend to make superb wines in bad vintages as well as in good ones, while mediocre winemakers only fare well when the weather gives it to them on a plate.

Throughout this book I have recommended the world's best Châteaux, Domaines, wineries and estates – these are the people and operations who make something out of nothing. I can safely say that even in notoriously 'difficult' regions like Burgundy, winemakers like Leflaive, Carillon, de Vogüé and Ghislaine Barthod all make stunning wines every year. Granted, in the best years their wines are sublime, but in the 'worst', they still make terrific, world-class bottles. If anything, the bottles just tend to be more forward and are, therefore, able to be drunk earlier than the so-called 'classic' vintages. In Bordeaux, perennial overachievers like Châteaux Latour or Léoville-Barton always keep their end up in desperate vintages, so I feel that, on balance, vintage is very much a secondary consideration to who makes the wine and from where they source their grapes.

Each year, members of the international wine press can be relied upon to trumpet better vintages and slate bad ones, as this is what they are paid to do. Producers will shout 'vintage of the century' at every given opportunity, if they are given half a chance. I don't blame them, as they want to sell their wine. Unfortunately, excessive hype surrounding a cracking vintage only attracts one thing – high prices. As a consumer who is not given to laying down wine for a prolonged period of time, I generally want to find wine to drink in the short to medium term. I find myself willing good (but not necessarily great) vintages for the expensive regions, in the hope that prices will be affordable and wines will drink relatively early. Please don't get me wrong, I love superb vintages as much as the next drinker, but I do not set all of my store in relying on them to find great wines.

Here is a guide to some of the best vintages of the twentieth and twenty-first centuries. You may be able to find somebody's birth year or anniversary year here, and then spoil them with a thoughtful present. Remember that the biggest, richest years last the longest, but try not to gamble with wines that are too ancient, as they may have fallen to bits in the meantime. In these instances, the storage conditions of the wine are as important as the wine itself, and all wines should only be considered within the context of their styles.

France

Red Bordeaux The top wines from the best Châteaux can live happily for thirty or forty years; beyond that cross your fingers and check out the provenance: 1945, 1947, 1949, 1953, 1959, 1961, 1962, 1966, 1970, 1982, 1983, 1985, 1986, 1988, 1989, 1990, 1995, 1996, 1998, 1999, 2000, 2001, 2003, 2004.

Sauternes With the intense sugar levels in this style of wine, they can last for ages: 1945, 1949, 1955, 1959, 1962, 1967, 1970, 1975, 1976, 1983, 1986, 1988, 1989, 1990, 1995, 1996, 1997, 1998, 1999, 2001, 2003.

Alsace Only VT and SGN styles are able to live for more than fifteen years: 1971, 1976, 1983, 1985, 1986, 1988, 1989, 1990, 1993, 1995, 1996, 1997, 1998, 1999, 2000, 2001, 2002, 2003.

Burgundy Try to drink earlier rather than later, as Pinot Noir and Chardonnay only show well up to fifteen years old: 1969, 1971, 1976, 1978, 1983, 1985, 1986, 1988, 1989, 1990, 1992, 1995, 1996, 1997, 1998, 1999, 2000, 2001, 2002, 2003.

Champagne Surprisingly long-lived if kept in good conditions, Champagnes can usually run for much longer than Burgundy, even though they are made from the same grapes. It must be the bubbles! 1964, 1966, 1969, 1970, 1976, 1980, 1985, 1988, 1989, 1990, 1995, 1996, 1997, 1998, 2000.

Loire sweet wines With Chenin Blanc's high acidity, these wines are amazingly age worthy: 1947, 1949, 1959, 1962, 1969, 1976, 1982, 1983, 1985, 1988, 1989, 1990, 1993, 1995, 1996, 1997, 1999, 2000, 2001, 2002, 2003.

Northern Rhône I prefer these Syrahs fairly young, but the big names can age well for twenty or more years: **1978, 1982, 1983, 1985, 1988, 1989, 1990, 1994, 1995, 1996, 1997, 1998, 1999, 2000, 2001, 2003.**

Southern Rhône Likewise with these meaty blends: 1978, 1979, 1983, 1985, 1988, 1989, 1990, 1995, 1998, 1999, 2000, 2001, 2003.

Languedoc/Roussillon With Rhône varieties and plenty of sunshine, these reds can last well: 1985, 1986, 1988, 1989, 1990, 1993, 1994, 1995, 1996, 1998, 1999, 2000, 2001, 2003.

Provence Made from full-bodied grape varieties, Provençal reds last well: **1982, 1985, 1988, 1989, 1990, 1991, 1993, 1995, 1996, 1997, 1998, 1999, 2000, 2001, 2003.**

Italy

Piemonte Nebbiolo's power and tannin levels carry these wines far: 1970, 1971, 1974, 1978, 1982, 1985, 1988, 1989, 1990, 1996, 1997, 1998, 2000, 2001, 2003.

Veneto (Amarone) The structure and power in Amarone means these wines are long-lived: **1970, 1971, 1974, 1976, 1979, 1983, 1985, 1988, 1989, 1990, 1995, 1997, 2000, 2001, 2003.**

Tuscany As with red Rhônes, I prefer to attack these relatively early: 1975, 1977, 1978, 1979, 1982, 1983, 1985, 1988, 1990, 1993, 1995, 1997, 1999, 2001, 2003.

Germany

Rheingau Riesling loves the long haul: 1971, 1975, 1976, 1983, 1988, 1989, 1990, 1992, 1993, 1994, 1995, 1996, 1997, 1999, 2001, 2002, 2003.

Mosel These awesome Rieslings live forever: 1971, 1975, 1976, 1983, 1988, 1989, 1990, 1992, 1993, 1994, 1995, 1996, 1997, 1999, 2001, 2002, 2003, 2004.

Portugal

Port No surprise – the keeper of them all: 1927, 1931, 1935, 1945, 1948, 1955, 1963, 1966, 1970, 1977, 1983, 1985, 1991, 1992, 1994, 1995, 1997, 2000, 2003.

Spain

Rioja I like to drink Riojas when they still have a lot of fruit: 1981, 1982, 1985, 1987, 1990, 1994, 1995, 1996, 1997, 1998, 1999, 2000, 2001, 2003.

Ribera del Duero The top estates take a while to emerge from their tannic shell so are best left for a few years: 1981, 1982, 1983, 1986, 1987, 1990, 1994, 1995, 1996, 1998, 1999, 2001, 2003.

Penedès/Priorat Sturdy reds that need five or more years even to approach drinkability: **1985, 1992, 1993, 1994, 1995, 1996, 1998, 1999, 2000, 2001, 2003.**

South Africa

It is hard to find many older examples of SA wine. My advice is to stick to younger vintages anyway: **1995, 1997, 1998, 1999, 2000, 2001, 2002, 2003.**

USA

California – Napa Valley and Carneros Not achieving the longevity that you might expect, these are good medium-term wines: **1984, 1985, 1986, 1987, 1990, 1991, 1992, 1994, 1995, 1997, 1999, 2001, 2002, 2003.**

Oregon and Washington As for California and South Africa, it is virtually impossible to find old bottles: **1989, 1990, 1992, 1994, 1996, 1998, 1999, 2000, 2001, 2002, 2003.**

Chile and Argentina

It is more important to buy from the best estates, than search for specific vintages.

Australia

Margaret River, WA Cabernets last well from Margaret River: **1991, 1992, 1994, 1995, 1996, 1997, 1999, 2000, 2001, 2002, 2003.**

Barossa Valley, SA Top Shiraz can hang on for twenty or more years easily: **1986, 1988, 1990, 1991, 1992, 1993, 1994, 1996, 1997, 1998, 2001, 2002, 2003, 2004.**

Clare Valley, SA Cabernets and Shirazes are underrated and underpriced from this first-class region. They hold well in the bottle for a decade or more: **1990, 1991, 1992, 1994, 1996, 1997, 1998, 1999, 2001, 2002, 2003, 2004.**

Coonawarra, SA World famous for Cabernet. These wines work well up to fifteen or so years and then only the very best hang on for a few more innings: **1990, 1991, 1993, 1994, 1996, 1998, 1999, 2000, 2001, 2002, 2003.**

Yarra Valley, Vic Pinots don't hold for as long as I'd like, so tread carefully: **1994, 1996, 1997, 1998, 2000, 2001, 2002, 2003.**

Hunter Valley, NSW Shiraz and Semillon both do well here: **1990, 1991, 1992, 1995, 1997, 1998, 1999, 2000, 2002, 2003.**

New Zealand

Hawke's Bay, North Island Almost always drunk young; few reds would last more than ten years: **1990, 1991, 1994, 1998, 1999, 2000, 2001, 2002, 2003.**

Marlborough, South Island Sauvignon Blancs hold for a few years more than you might imagine: **1998, 1999, 2000, 2001, 2002, 2003, 2004, 2005.**

Glossary

VITICULTURAL (GRAPE GROWING) TERMS

Biodynamic Biodynamism is a way of life as much as a holistic guide to sustainable farming. By recognising that the soil itself is alive, and that it is this vitality that supports and affects the quality and health of the vines, the biodynamic farmer pays as much attention to the earth and moon and their cycles, and the health of the soil as he does to the ultra-organic nurturing of the vines. Biodynamic estates, more often than not, make intriguing and, in some instances, very serious wines, so there must be something to it!

Black rot A fungal disease that occurs in wet weather. If the wind doesn't pick up to dry out the bunches after an infection, or you are too slow to counter it, you can lose up to 80 per cent of your crop – disaster.

Botrytis cinerea Usually shortened to botrytis, noble rot or just bot. This is an unwelcome fungus (unless you want to make sweet wines) and swift action must be taken in the vineyard to eradicate it, as it can bring a mouldy tinge and lack of colour to a finished wine. If, however, you are keen to produce a sweetie, botrytis is your best friend. It attacks the bunches and lives off the water within the grapes. The result is a scary, hairy-looking cluster of grapes, but one with very concentrated sugar levels. This means that, after pressing, your grape must is super-sweet and ideally suited to making heady pudding wines. The French term is *pourriture noble*.

Bordeaux mixture A mixture of copper sulphate, lime and water that is very effective in controlling fungal and bacterial diseases on vines. It is permitted in organic viticulture, as it is not made from manmade ingredients.

Budbreak Or 'budburst', is the moment when the first shoots emerge from the buds in spring. Frost at this moment is the main concern, as this can knacker your yields. The clock is ticking – eight months or so to go until harvest.

Budding The process of grafting a single bud to a rootstock.

Bush vine A training system that makes the vine look like a goblet. The vines are free standing, without a trellis and with short trunks, and the grapes grow on short arms resembling a little tree – also called *Gobelet* training in France. Used in low-vigour, hot-climate vineyards.

Canopy management Vine-training techniques that expose the leaves and bunches of grapes to the sun with a view to maximising the ripeness, yield and quality of the fruit

Cépage A French term for a grape variety or varieties in a said wine. When tasting, a question could be 'What is the *cépage*?' The answer could be 'Sauvignon Blanc' for a crisp, white Sancerre, or 'It is a blend of Syrah and Grenache' for a hearty red Languedoc, etc.

Chlorosis A vine disorder caused by iron deficiencies in the soil, which leads to a lack of chlorophyll and results in the leaves losing their green colour and turning yellow.

Clone A specific selection of vine within a grape variety, propagated from a cutting or a bud from a single, successful, mother-vine.

Coulure A French term referring to a natural occurrence that makes flowers or small berries fall off the plant after flowering and results in a diminished crop. It is usually due to adverse climatic conditions (cold and wet weather reducing photosynthesis), disease or lack of minerals in the vine tissue causing the stems to shrivel.

Downy mildew Also known as Peronospera, a fungus affecting vines, particularly in humid summers. Use Bordeaux mixture to treat.

Drip irrigation A watering system that allows drips of water to fall on to the soil beneath the vines from a system of rubber tubing.

Eutypa A fungal disease that rots the wood section of a vine. Often caused by pruning wounds.

Flowering The process prior to fertilisation that leads to fruit set. This usually takes place two to three months after budbreak. Pray for good weather.

Fruit set The process after flowering where the fertilised flower sets to form berries.

Geneva Double Curtain Often shortened to GDC, a training technique that divides the canopy into two hanging 'curtains' thus maximising the sun's effect. Useful on wide-row-spaced vineyards with vigorous soil, resulting in higher quality, larger yields.

Grafting The process of connecting two pieces of plant together to make one vine, usually a specific grape variety on top and a disease-resistant, soil-suitable rootstock below. Essential to avoid the Phylloxera louse living in the soil.

Green harvest A process of reducing the number of bunches per vine, by cutting them off and dropping them on the floor. The objective is to sacrifice some of the grapes each vine has to support, thereby increasing the energy and flavour concentration in the remaining bunches. It might seem wasteful, but the difference in flavour of the resulting wine can be significant.

Grey Rot An infection of the vine, also known as *pourriture grise*. This is the evil big brother of Botrytis cinerea that breaks down the skin of the grape and results in rotten fruit unsuitable for wine.

Guyot A training system named after Jules Guyot. Either single Guyot or double Guyot, referring to the number of laterally trained canes from which the buds burst.

Hectare (ha) Vineyard area measurement equivalent to 10,000 square metres or 2.47 acres (or approximately 1.5 football pitches).

Hectolitre (hl) 100 litres.

Hen and chicken A term for uneven berry sizes on the same bunch, also known as *Millerendage* in French. This is brought about by inclement weather during flowering. It can cause a loss in crop volumes but, conversely, can concentrate the existing flavours within the harvest.

Irrigation The application of water to vines when there is insufficient rainfall – a very clever science that can bring out the best from the vines. Prohibited in certain parts of the world.

Late harvest Vines that are picked later than normal in the quest for extra-ripe grapes with which to make intense dry whites, very full-bodied reds and sweet wines.

Leaf plucking Either done by hand or machine, this process removes leaves from around the fruiting zone (where the bunches hang) thus allowing circulation of air and exposure to direct sunlight. This means rot is less likely to occur and ripening is facilitated. Not recommended in very hot climates, otherwise the bunches can suffer sunburn.

Microclimate The precise climate of a vineyard, or group of vineyards.

Monopole A French term for a vineyard in single ownership – used in Burgundy.

Noble rot See **Botrytis cinerea**.

Oidium Another fungus, this time known as 'Powdery Mildew'. Unlike other fungal diseases this one doesn't need humidity to thrive. It likes shaded canopies and does not like direct sunlight. Spray sulphur, lime and water to control it, or else prune or leaf pluck and open up your canopy.

Phylloxera vastatrix A parasitic louse that feeds on the rootstocks of Vitis vinifera vines. It caused devastating damage to vineyards in the late nineteenth century. The grafting of vinifera vines on to American Vitis lambrusca rootstocks has prevented further damage, as these rootstocks are resistant.

Pruning A combination of shaping the vine, controlling its vegetative growth and concentrating its fruit quality. Achieved by careful lopping off of leaves, wood or grapes by hand-held secateurs or various mechanical devices.

Rootstock The plant forming the below-ground root system of a vine, on to which the fruiting variety (scion) is grafted.

Scion The piece of fruiting vine that is grafted on to the rootstock.

Terroir A French word that rolls all of a particular vineyard's attributes such as microclimate, soil, drainage, altitude, aspect, exposure and slope, into one beguiling term. A complex concept indeed that is celebrated by those who think they have it and rubbished by people who don't understand it. In theory every vineyard 'has' *terroir*. The main issue is whether you can taste it in the wine. Inevitably, the very best wines in the world taste of where they come from, so they, by definition, taste of the *terroir*.

Training The structure along which a vine is encouraged to grow, in order to maximise its quality and quantity of output. Of which Geneva Double Curtain, Lenz Moser, Gobelet, Cordon de Royat, Espalier, Guyot, Lyre, Pergola, Scott Henry, Te Kauwhata two tier and Tendone are but a few.

Tri Usually employed when harvesting botrytised grapes, a tri is one of a series of trips through the vineyard, selecting only bunches that are ready to be picked and leaving the others until they are at their optimum ripeness. Time-consuming and expensive, this technique is usually put into practice for the very finest of sweet wines.

Triage A sorting procedure of the harvested grapes to spot any unripe or out of condition bunches in order to throw them away. This is performed on a bench or conveyor belt, and is essential if you intend to make top-quality wine.

Veraison The moment in the growing season when the small, hard, green berries change into their bigger, softer, yellow- or red-coloured grapes. This is the start of the ripening period.

Vitis lambrusca North American vine species whose rootstocks are Phylloxera resistant.

Vitis vinifera The vine species from which most of the world's wine is made.

Yeast The dusty bloom on grapes is wild yeast and can kick-start fermentation when the grapes are crushed. Some winemakers use this natural process, while others prefer to use cultured yeast.

Yield A word that refers to the amount of grapes or wine that a vineyard produces. As in: a high yield = a big crop, and a low yield = a small and probably concentrated crop, depending on vine density (the number of vines in a said area). 'What is the yield?' 'About 50 hectolitres per hectare.' This is a useful winemaker's calculation of the amount of wine resulting from a standard vineyard area. Yield can be measured in tons per acre. In this case it is a measurement of the weight of the harvested grapes and not the quantity of resulting wine. (On average one ton/acre = 17.5 hl/ha.)

VINIFICATION (WINEMAKING) TERMS

Acid Chemical compounds that give wine freshness and a sharp, clean taste on the back palate (finish). Tartaric and malic are the two most important acids in wine production. Malic acid transforms into lactic acid during malolactic fermentation. Tartaric acid can be added during winemaking if a wine lacks natural acidity. Acids keep wines stable, as they ward off bacteria.

Alcohol The common name for ethanol, measured as a percentage of the volume of the wine. Alcohol is the result of fermentation, when sugar is combined with yeast.

Autolysis A process occurring during bottle-fermented sparkling wine production (i.e. when making Champagne and Traditional Method wines). The flavour of the wine is enhanced due to ageing the wine on its lees (dead yeast cells) for an extended period.

Barrel-fermented A white wine that has been fermented in oak barrels, giving rise to a stronger oaky flavour than those wines just aged in oak barrels.

Barrique Traditionally a 225-litre oak barrel. International term covering just about any 'small' oak barrel.

Bâtonnage French term for 'lees stirring'. This builds depth and richness in a wine by bringing the wine into contact with its solids.

Baumé A scale of measurement of the sugar in grape must.

Bentonite A type of clay used for **Fining**.

Blending Mixing together several different batches of wine (either different grape varieties or different parcels of the same variety) to create a final wine that is, with luck, greater than the sum of its parts. This usually occurs after vinification, just before bottling. The French term is *assemblage*.

Bordeaux blend A universal term meaning a wine consisting of Cabernet Sauvignon, Cabernet Franc and Merlot. Occasionally Petit Verdot can sneak into this equation.

Cap The mass of grape solids that floats on top of red wine during fermentation. The French term is *chapeau*.

Carbon dioxide (CO₂) A gaseous by-product of fermentation that can be deliberately trapped and dissolved into wine, later to be released as bubbles. Also used as a 'blanket' to protect grapes against oxidation.

Carbonic maceration Fermentation of uncrushed grapes in a sealed tank (in a carbon dioxide atmosphere), which results in a vibrant, fruity, forward style of red wine. The French term is *Macération Carbonique*, and it is successfully employed in Beaujolais with the Gamay variety.

Centrifugation A clarification process used to spin out unwanted heavy elements from a wine (yeast cells, for example).

Chaptalisation The addition of sugar or concentrated grape juice to raise the final alcoholic strength of a wine. This is important if your grapes are under-ripe when picked, or lack the required potential alcohol to make the style you are aiming for.

Clarification The removal of suspended solids or lees from grape juice or wine.

Cold stabilisation The extended chilling of a wine to encourage the precipitation of tartrate crystals. These are then removed, thus preventing any crystals forming in the bottled wine.

Cru A confusing French term for a specific vineyard's quality status, as in Burgundy's *1er Cru* and *Grand Crus*, and Alsace's *Grand Crus*. In these cases the individual name of the vineyard would be attached to the *1er* or *Grand Cru* prefix. For example, Meursault 1er Cru Perrières – here the vineyard of Perrières is shown to be the *1er Cru*-rated vineyard from the village of Meursault. (Unless the wine was a blend of several *1er Crus*, in which case it would not list each vineyard involved, rather it would just state *1er Cru*.) The other meaning is 'growth' as in *1er Cru* down to *5ème Cru*, translating as 1st growth, 2nd growth etc. This is the classification of Bordeaux top-ranking Left Bank Châteaux e.g. Château Latour 1er Cru Pauillac.

Crushing The breaking open of the grape skins prior to fermentation.

Cryoextraction Freezing grapes to extract as much sugary juice as possible, leaving the water content behind in the press. Used for sweet wine production, particularly in wet years. A cheat's version of Eiswein.

Cuvaison The total time that a red wine spends in contact with its skins.

Cuve French term for a vat or tank in which fermentation takes place.

Cuvée A catch-all word for an individual barrel, a blend or a style of wine. As in 'Which *cuvée* is this wine?' Answers could be, 'From these one-year-old Allier barrels', 'It is the Cabernet Sauvignon/Merlot blend' or 'It is the regular estate label.'

Débourbage French term for settling out the less desirable solids from must or wine, often involving chilling.

Egrappoir French name for the machine that removes the stems from bunches of grapes. In English we call it a 'de-stemmer', obviously!

Elevage No real translation in English, this word means the 'bringing-up' of a wine in the maturing sense, or the time spent from vinification to bottling (*Elevé en Fût de Chêne* means brought up/aged in an oak barrel).

Fermentation The conversion of sugar to ethanol (alcohol) and carbon dioxide (CO_2) by the addition of yeast.

Filtration The straining of solid particles from a wine.

Fining The clarification and stabilisation of must or wine by the addition of a fining agent, such as bentonite (clay), casein (milk protein), gelatin, isinglass (fish bladders) or egg whites, which coagulate or absorb solids and fall to the bottom of the tank or barrel. The clear wine is then decanted off this sediment. Note that none of the fining agent is left in the wine. Vegans and vegetarians would prefer the use of bentonite rather than some of the others, for obvious reasons.

Fortification The addition of alcohol (usually grape spirit) to a fermenting wine (or after fermentation in the case of sherry), in order to arrest further fermentation by inhibiting the yeast's ability to convert sugar to alcohol. This results in a high level of retained sweetness and higher alcohol levels than normal wine. The result is known as a fortified wine.

Free-run juice The finest-quality grape juice that runs out of the grapes even before the press has been started.

Lees The dregs or sediment that settle at the bottom of a barrel or fermentation tank made up of dead yeast cells, grape-skin fragments, grape seeds and tartrates.

Maceration A period of contact between red grape skins and must or wine – literally a soaking.

Malolactic fermentation The chemical conversion of harsh malic acid to softer lactic acid. Often shortened to 'malo'. This process usually happens after alcoholic fermentation, but can sometimes occur at the same time. White wines that have not been through malo often have punchier acidity. Cooler-climate whites tend to go through malo to soften the overall impact of the acidity on the palate.

Maturation The ageing of a wine. As in 'oak-aged'/'oak-matured'.

Méthode Traditionnelle Along with *Méthode Classique,* Traditional Method is the accepted term for the finest process of sparkling wine production where the second fermentation occurs in the bottle in which the wine is sold. The old term was *Méthode Champenoise.*

Must Unfermented grape juice.

Oak The wood used to make barrels in which wine is fermented and matured. French, American and Eastern European forests are the main source of oak for wine barrels.

Oak programme A winemaker's oak barrel 'formula' designed to result in the best wine possible. Various combinations of: barrel age (new, 1-year-old, 2-year-old etc.); barrel type (*barrique*, *cuve*, *piece*, hogshead, Italian *botti* etc.); origin of oak (American, Slovakian, French – the forests of Limousin, Tronçais, Vosges, Allier, Nevers etc.); cooper (various companies); degree of toasting (low, medium and high); and length of time spent in barrel (from a few months to several years).

Oenology The study of wine and winemaking. Practised by an oenologist (a winemaker). Pronounced 'een-ology'.

Oxidation The chemical reaction of air with crushed grapes, must or wine. More of a danger to whites than reds. Excessive oxidation results in the colour browning and eventually leads to spoilage. Some wines are deliberately oxidised, however, such as Madeira, Tawny Port and Sherry.

Pasteurisation Heating wines to high temperatures to kill off bacteria and yeasts.

pH The level of acidity or alkalinity of a wine expressed as a number. Low pH equals high acidity, 7 is neutral. Wine is generally between 3 and 4.

Pomace The 'cake' of grape skins and pips left over after the wine has been drained off (after fermentation). This is often distilled into brandy. The French term for the pomace itself and the resulting brandy is *Marc*.

Prefermentation maceration The period of time before fermentation when the juice of white grapes is left in contact with the skins, thus enhancing the varietal character of the wine.

Press The grape-squeezing apparatus.

Press wine The strongly coloured and flavoured wine resulting from pressing the pomace of grape skins after fermentation. Used carefully in blending, as it is usually intensely flavoured and often a little coarse, caused by the high 'skin to juice' content.

Pumping over The process of circulating the fermenting red must over the floating cap, in order to release more colour and flavour. The French term is *remontage*.

Punching down French term is *pigéage*. This means pushing the 'cap' down, manually or mechanically, into the fermenting red must to extract more colour and flavour extraction. Also called 'plunging'.

Racking Using gravity to remove clear wine from the sediment in a tank or barrel, by pouring.

Residual sugar The amount of unfermented sugar left in a finished wine, measured in grams per litre. The more 'residual', the more apparent sweetness there is in the wine – although firm acidity can have the effect of disguising the sweetness.

Skin contact The process of extracting more flavour compounds from the skin of a grape into the juice. The same idea as maceration, but this time the term is used for white wines. The French term is *macération pelliculaire*.

Stuck fermentation This is when fermentation stops for some reason or other – time to panic!

Sugar The sugars in a grape ferment to form alcohol. The total sugar content of a grape ('must weight') is a measurement of a grape's ripeness, which in turn can act as a pointer to a harvest date. Sugars are measured in degrees, or 'Baumé', which conveniently translate to potential degrees of alcohol if the wine is fermented out dry. For example, a 12 Baumé would give approximately a 12 (per cent vol.) wine. However, it is not as straightforward with the other methods of measurement: 'Brix' used in America; 'Oechsle' in Germany; and 'KMW' in Austria. They require a calculator and tables to figure out – typical!

Sulphur dioxide (SO_2) Used with care as a preservative in finished wine (it can give rise to an unattractive, pungent odour); an all-purpose disinfectant that kills yeast and bacteria; an antioxidant that prevents oxidation of grapes and wine, thus avoiding colour loss and 'off' flavours.

Tannin The bitter, astringent flavour that is found in grape skins, seed and stalks as well as oak barrels, and softens as red wines age. Often referred to as wine's 'natural preservative', tannins are usually prominent in young, robust red wines. Tannins are undetectable on the nose, but give rise to a drying sensation in the mouth and a harsh feel on the inside of the cheeks.

Tartrates The harmless crystals that are deposited during winemaking and occasionally form in bottles of wines that have not been 'cold stabilised'. In my opinion, the appearance of tartrates in a white wine is a good sign. It means the wine has not been filtered – a process that inevitably causes the wine to lose some of its flavour.

Yeast The 'agent' that transforms the sugar in grape juice into alcohol and CO_2 via the process of fermentation. Yeast is naturally found on grape skins, or can be added by the winemaker in a process called 'inoculation'.

Vin de Liqueur An unusual fortified wine made by the addition of alcohol to grape must before fermentation, resulting in a 17–18 per cent sweet aperitif style of 'wine'. Pineau des Charentes and Floc de Gascogne are two examples, and are made in Cognac and Armagnac respectively.

Vin Doux Naturel A fortified wine made by the addition of alcohol to grape must during the fermentation process. Usually sweet wines and after-dinner drinks, Muscat de Rivesaltes and Muscat de Beaumes-de-Venise are two of the most famous white styles, while Banyuls and Maury are two utterly delicious but lesser-known reds.

Vintage The year in which a grape is harvested.

TASTING TERMS

Acidity A crucial, natural, balancing element that gives a wine freshness, vitality and life.

Aggressive A sensation resulting from an excess of tannin, acidity or both.

Alcoholic A 'hot' feeling on the palate, from high levels of alcohol.

Angular A wine lacking in fruit and depth, without a 'smooth' taste.

Apple A common nose and taste in young white wines. Connected to acidity (malic acid).

Apricot A sure-fire sign of Viognier in a dry wine, or botrytis in a sweet wine.

Aromatic Pungently smelly or strongly scented grapes like Riesling, Gewürztraminer, Muscat and Tokay-Pinot-Gris make aromatic wines.

Asparagus A common tasting note for the nose on a Sauvignon Blanc.

Astringent A dry or sour sensation on the palate, usually from high tannin levels in a red or from high acidity levels in a white. Generally an indication of youth.

Attack The initial burst of flavour in a wine.

Austere Quirky, or maybe a little too young. Wines that seem difficult to appreciate, perhaps 'closed', atypical or funky.

Backward A wine that still tastes young despite its age, leading you to believe that it should be more approachable.

Baked A 'hot' smell or taste, usually from hot-climate wines that give the impression that they were lacking in water in the vineyard. Raisiny.

Balance A wine that is in harmony, with all of its elements complementing each other – the Holy Grail in winemaking and something I look for in every wine I taste.

Banana A red wine's aroma resulting from carbonic maceration.

Big A wine full of flavour.

Biscuity A quality usually associated with the nose and palate of Champagne.

Bite The fresh flavour that acidity brings to a wine.

Bitterness The acid and tannin taste resulting from over-pressing grape skins, pips or stalks.

Black fruit A mix of all black-coloured fruit, and a useful term for the nose and palate if one individual fruit flavour does not particularly stand out.

Blackcurrant The classic Cabernet Sauvignon aroma and taste.

Blind tasting A tasting where the identity of the wine is unknown.

Blowsy A low acidity wine that appears too fruity and out of balance.

Body The weight of a wine on the palate (light, medium and full).

Bottle shock A recently shipped (or recently bottled) wine that appears to be jet-lagged and needs to settle down and gather its thoughts.

Bottle stink An initial unpleasant pong when opening a bottle of wine that disappears with a little contact with air.

Bouquet The smell, aroma or nose of a wine.

Brettanomyces (Brett) A curious yeast that gives rise to a peculiar 'mousey' smell on a wine. Not unpleasant in small amounts, just a little unusual – unless, of course, you are particularly sensitive to it. Not really a true wine fault, as such, just an idiosyncrasy, which in these days of cleaner and cleaner wines is not tolerated as much as it was in the past.

Briary A term used to indicate a mixed-berry-fruit flavour, coupled with spicy notes.

Bright The appearance of a clean, clear wine.

Brilliant Apart from the obvious explanation, this word is also used to describe the clear colour of a wine.

Buttery A classic Chardonnay tasting note on the nose and palate.

Caramel A burnt-toffee flavour found on old Sherries and Madeira.

Cassis French for 'blackcurrant' – a Cabernet Sauvignon tasting note.

Cat's pee Not being a 'cat-man' I cannot vouch for this term, but it is a popular description for the nose on Sauvignon Blanc.

Cedarwood The nose on an oak-aged Cabernet Sauvignon or Merlot, particularly found in fine clarets.

Chaptalised Describing a slightly disjointed character in the wine, due to the addition of sugar to fermenting must in order to raise the alcoholic strength of a wine.

Cheesy Not an uncommon nose on expensive Chablis. However, cheesiness is usually a sign of poor hygiene in a winery!

Cherry Black or red, a useful aroma to spot on Burgundies, Beaujolais, Nebbiolos, Zinfandels, Riojas and many other red wines. The ultimate cherry-tasting note is the chocolate and cherry combination of Blackforest Gâteau – found on some Californian Zinfandels.

Chewy This refers to the palate of a richly textured, often high-alcohol wine. The flavour is so dense you can almost 'chew' it.

Chocolate Dark chocolate can be found on many big red wines, perhaps in the combination of aroma and texture.

Cigar-box Another classic red Bordeaux term for the aroma of oak and fruit combined.

Classic Overused in my tasting notes, denoting a wine that tastes exactly as it should from previous experience.

Classy A distinguished taste. Usually referring to a complex, balanced flavour – more often than not from an expensive bottle.

Clean A pure, unencumbered smell or taste. Usually referring to white wines.

Closed A wine that is somewhat subdued, not giving much away in the way of aroma or flavour. Usually needing more time to age or more air in a decanter.

Cloudy A bad sign. A wine that has not been stabilised and is exhibiting suspended yeast, bacteria or micro-organisms. Or the result of sediment in a red wine being shaken up unwittingly.

Cloying Mouth-coating, usually referring to a sweet wine and often a sign of a wine lacking in balancing acidity.

Clumsy A simple, if slightly out of balance, wine, lacking in elegance.

Coffee A self-explanatory, red-wine descriptive term often found on New World Cabernet Sauvignons and Merlots.

Commercial Not a derogatory expression, but rather an indicator of a crowd-pleaser – and what could be better than that?

Complex The sign of a fine wine, having a multi-layered flavour. A wine that reveals different aromas and flavours every time you taste it. The main aim for every winemaker is to produce complex, balanced wines.

Confected Seemingly a 'chemistry-set wine' that is 'made' in the winery rather than 'grown' in the vineyard. A wine reminiscent of confectionery.

Cooked A feeling that the fermentation was too hot and the wine ended up being 'stewed', leading to high alcohol and lacking in balance.

Corked (-y) A faulty wine spoiled by a mouldy cork – which happens far too often, in my opinion. (Does not refer to bits of broken cork in the wine.)

Crisp A white wine with refreshing levels of acidity.

Depth The concentration or richness of flavour.

Developed A term to indicate maturity: under-developed – too young; well-developed – ready to drink; over-developed – too old.

Dirty Unpleasant, unclean winemaking.

Dried-out A wine lacking in fruit flavours.

Drinking Ready to drink or at its peak.

Dull Uninspiring wine that lacks character or interest.

Dumb A wine with no aroma (nose) at all.

Dusty A palate sensation usually associated with highish tannin levels, almost as if there was a dusty coating to the wine.

Earthy Another dimension to the aroma and palate, coming from the soil. A welcome element in the complexity of a wine.

Eggy Urgh! A bad sign indicating high levels of sulphur in a wine.

Elegant An even, lingering flavour that is pleasing and refined, and not too overblown.

Eucalyptus Found on the nose, this distinctive smell often pops up on New World Cabernet Sauvignons.

Explosive A massive, unexpected nose or flavour!

Extract The 'guts' of a wine, making up its body.

Farmyardy An accurate, if surprising, aroma on red Burgundy.

Fat A 'big' rich wine lacking in definition, full-bodied and a little too heavy.

Fine There are two meanings to this. 'Fine Wine' is a catch-all term for expensive and possibly rare wine. 'Fine' on its own, implies a degree of 'class' and 'complexity'.

Finesse Often used in the same breath as 'elegance', this is another word used to describe a complex, if slightly lighter-bodied, wine. Nearly always mentioned in the context of expensive Champagne.

Finish The end flavour left on the palate (aftertaste), measured in terms of length (of time).

Flabby A wine lacking in balancing acidity, one stage worse than blowsy.

Flat A muted nose and palate on a wine. Not quite as uninspiring as 'dull', but not far off!

Flinty A gunflint or smoky scent picked up on Loire Sauvignon Blancs, associated with the French word *fumer*, to smoke (as in Pouilly-Fumé).

Flowery A bunch of flowers aroma (floral), evoking a fragrant summer meadow.

Forward A wine that can be drunk earlier (in its lifetime) than expected.

Fresh A wine with perky acidity and a lively flavour.

Fruity A reassuring, ripe-grape nose and palate.

Funky Not always complimentary, this term can mean that a wine is a touch faulty but not enough to detract from the overall impression of the wine. If we were talking about furniture, the term might be 'distressed'.

Gamey As the word implies, a scent or taste of game that is meaty, fairly strong and a little rotten – in the nicest sense of the word. Only found on red wine (usually older bottles). Another Burgundy trait, although often associated with any of the Rhône grape varieties.

Generous As in any polite word meaning 'in abundance'. Top-heavy, ample, copious, voluptuous, overflowing etc. Phew!

Glugger A jokey word for a simple, undemanding, easy-to-drink wine that would please everybody's palate. Perfect for a party.

Glycerine The oily feel in a wine that makes it taste more textured on the palate.

Gooseberry The benchmark Sauvignon Blanc nose.

Grapey The actual smell and taste of grapes, only really applicable to wines made from the Muscat variety.

Grassy The 'green' smell, often reminiscent of cut grass and cricket pitches, found on Sauvignon Blanc and Cabernet Franc in particular.

Green An unripe smell and taste often found on thin Merlots and Cabernet Francs, associated with an unripe crop resulting from overproduction or a bad vintage. Green wines tend to have 'raw' acidity on the finish. Green can be used as a positive description for Sauvignon Blancs, referring to its attractive herbal aroma. Interestingly, Cabernet Sauvignon and Sauvignon Blanc both possess flavour compounds that result in herbaceous notes – these are called methoxypyrazines.

Grip The firm feeling on the back-palate brought about by dominant acidity or tannin. Essential in very ripe wines.

Hard Almost always followed by 'tannins', i.e. too young to drink.

Harsh Another acidity and tannin adjective, suggesting a high degree of one or the other, or both.

Heady A dizzy-making feel to a wine. Not for quantity reasons, just alcohol levels.

Heavy Used to explain the weight of a wine on the palate.

Herbaceous Not to be confused with 'green', this word conveys the scent of greenhouses, or garden centres. Often a pleasant extra dimension to a wine.

Herbal As the word suggests, any scent or flavour reminiscent of fresh or dried herbs.

Hollow A wine that has 'attack' and a 'finish' but a gap in between. A disappointing dip in the concentration on the palate – a doughnut.

Honeyed A common tasting note for sweet wines, particularly Sauternes and Loire sweeties. Sometimes used for dry whites to imply a degree of texture and richness.

Horizontal tasting A wine tasting consisting of a number of different bottles from the same year (vintage).

Horsey A bit like 'farmyardy' and 'leathery', although more specific. I'm sure you can imagine the smell. Not a bad term, particularly when connected to red Burgundies.

Hot Wines with high alcohol.

Insipid Watery wines lacking in structure and character.

Jammy Self-explanatory, smells akin to the fruit preserve, often as a result of hot climates.

Lanolin An oiliness found in some heavy white wines.

Leafy See 'Herbaceous'.

Leathery Another superb descriptive word that conjures up new shoes, motorcycle gear, tack rooms and all manner of leather goods. Leather is found on Syrah, Grenache and many of the Bordeaux reds. Similar to the 'cigar-box' and 'tobacco' feel.

Legs The patterns made by wine sliding down the inside of a wineglass as a result of its viscosity. Also known as 'tears'. Not a sign of quality, as such, but of alcohol level.

Lemon Usually found on youthful white wines with a citrusy freshness.

Length The time that the wine's flavour lingers on the palate – the 'finish'.

Light Used to explain the weight of a wine on the palate.

Liquorice Can be picked up on many red and white wines, offering an unexpected and often enjoyable flavour, thus adding an element of complexity.

Lively A reference to the keen acidity in a young wine.

Long The most desirable degree of length.

Luscious A ripeness and smoothness found in equal measure.

Lychees Found on the distinctive nose of a Gewürztraminer.

Maderised The sweet pungent aroma of over-mature or oxidised wines, often accompanied by a browning colour – not good. At its most typical, and enjoyable, in the wines of Madeira.

Malic acid The aroma of unripe green apples, suggesting that a wine has not completed its malolactic fermentation.

Meaty Always with reference to a huge red wine – you may need a knife and fork!

Mellow A character trait brought on by age, this usually means soft and smooth with a harmonious palate.

Metallic Sometimes found on the palate of inexpensive wine, arising from sloppy winemaking. Not very pleasant.

Minty A New World Cabernet Sauvignon hallmark.

Mocha Somewhere near a coffee aroma usually found on New World Shiraz or Bordeaux Blends.

Mouth-feel A superb self-explanatory term referring to the sensation of a wine on the palate.

Mulberry Another berry flavour often associated with Sangiovese and Merlot.

Musty A stale aroma or taste, caused by a hygiene problem somewhere along the line. Usually disappears with aeration. If it doesn't, bin the bottle!

Nose The aroma, bouquet or smell of a wine.

Nutty Usually a nose-detected quality resulting from oak ageing, somewhat akin to dry-roasted nuts. Smart Chardonnay often has this aroma.

Oaky The smell and taste of oak barrels. Should not be too intrusive.

Organoleptic A fancy word for 'testing by using one's senses' or 'sensory assessment' with regard to wine (and food).

Out of balance Self explanatory (see **Balance**). I shorten it to OOB in my tasting notes.

Out of condition Faulty. I shorten this one to OOC in my tasting notes.

Oxidised A wine spoiled by oxidation. Browning in colour and stale on the nose and palate.

Palate The flavour of a wine and also a word for your mouth.

Peaches A Viognier pointer. Found on loads of aromatic white wines.

Pepper Absolutely guaranteed on the noses of Northern Rhône red wines made from Syrah. Also found on Syrah blends from the Southern Rhône and Provence. Evident on Syrahs from further afield, too – Shiraz from California, Australia and so on. Can also be found on top quality Cru Beaujolais.

Perfumed Highly scented or fragrant nose.

Petrol Older Rieslings tend to have this unusual, pungent scent.

Plummy A rich, ripe red wine, particularly Merlot or Pinot Noir, can have a nose and flavour reminiscent of plums.

Poor Not nice.

Price Point Game A guessing game played when tasters are trying to assess whether a wine is good value or not. Quite simply, have a guess at the price. If you guess too low then you would obviously not want to pay more for the wine so, in your opinion, the bottle was not worth the money. If you guess too high, then you must think that the wine is good value and you may want to buy a bottle for yourself. This thought process is used whenever a wine buyer selects a wine.

Pungent Strongly scented.

Quaffing Drinking with purpose. This is what you would do with a case of gluggers!

Raspberry A lighter red wine aroma associated with Pinot Noir and Gamay.

Red fruit A collection of red-skinned fruit, like strawberries, raspberries, cranberries, redcurrants etc. A red-wine tasting note when no specific red fruit descriptor jumps out at you.

Reductive A word associated with a 'skunky' smell on a wine. This smell is of sulphur compounds, such as hydrogen sulphide, that should subside with aeration. So decant the wine and wave it around!

Residual sugar The remaining sugar in a wine that accounts for its degree of sweetness.

Rich A word used to describe texture and smoothness in a medium to full-bodied wine.

Ripe The taste of a wine that has reached its physical peak of development at harvest.

Robust A firmly structured wine. Always used for red wines, never whites.

Rose Either rose-petal or rose-water can be found on the nose of some aromatic varieties like Gewürztraminer. Occasionally red wines can have a rose nose, too.

Round This refers to a wine's body, meaning that a wine is balanced and complete. (Nothing to do with 'flabby' or 'fat'.)

Rubber A sulphurous nose if too strong, but can actually be an attribute of some cheaper New World reds or Italian Dolcettos.

Salty Most often found on sherry, particularly Manzanilla. Also can be picked up on some top flight Muscadets.

Sediment The solids found at the bottom of some old red wines.

Sharp A term used for acidity beyond that in a balanced wine.

Short A disappointing 'length'.

Shows As in 'exhibits'. This wine 'shows' mint on the nose means you can smell mint on this wine. Or, this wine is 'showing' well means this wine is 'drinking' nicely.

Silky Very smooth on the palate.

Sinewy A lack of juicy fruit character, exposing the acidity and tannin elements of a red.

Smoky In reds, smokiness can be found on a range of wines, particularly Syrah, Nebbiolo, Mourvèdre and Grenache. In whites, it is only really used for Pouilly-Fumé (see **Flinty**). Flinty is a much better term for Pouilly.

Spicy Regularly making it into my tasting notes, spicy means just that. Often countering a fruity flavour, a herbal spiciness on whites and a dried-spice character on reds is commonplace and welcome.

Spittoon The correct term for the bucket that you spit into during wine tastings.

Spritz A gentle prickle of fizz on the palate. Found on young white wines.

Stalky One stage beyond that of 'green', this word is used for a particular type of harsh tannins, resulting from the inclusion of too many grape stems in the fermentation.

Steely A lean, acidic 'crispness' in a white wine that can be refreshing i f balanced with sufficient fruit flavours.

Strawberry The benchmark Burgundy fruit nose and flavour, it is also unmissable on Rioja.

Structure The physical framework on which a wine's flavours are hung.

Subtle Subdued flavours that are in balance, but require some concentration to track down.

Sulphur Similar to the smell of a 'struck-match', sulphur can be detectable on the nose but should disappear when the wine comes into contact with air.

Supple A lush, round style of wine with no obvious, hard acidity or tannin.

Tangy A pleasant feeling of acidity on the palate of white wines.

Tannic The natural 'preservative' for red wines, found in grape skins, that lends a 'dry', 'harsh' flavour to a wine in its youth, but softens with age. There are many expressions for tannic wines including cheek-sucking, teeth-furring and mouth-puckering.

Tart A 'raw' feeling of acidity on the palate of white wines.

Toasty The nose associated with oak-aged wines, on account of the insides of the barrels being charred or toasted during their production.

Tobacco See **Cigar-box**.

Truffles A really beautiful mushroomy aroma found on some red wines, usually red Rhônes and Nebbiolos from Piemonte – both, curiously, where actual truffles are found.

Unctuous Intense, oily character usually associated with sweet wines.

Up-front The immediately appealing characteristics on a wine. An up-front nose or palate means that they are instantly on display and are recognisable.

Vanilla An aroma resulting from oak-ageing, particularly in American oak.

Varietal A wine that displays textbook grape variety characteristics. For example, 'gooseberries and asparagus on the nose, with keen acidity and fresh citrusy fruit on the palate' depicts a 'varietal' (typical) Sauvignon Blanc.

Vegetal A word that groups together various vegetable smells and tastes, mostly with reference to red wines. Not always a derogatory term.

Velvety The smoothest and most luxurious of textures on the palate. Merlot and other sensuous red varieties can attain this character if they are of the finest quality.

Vertical tasting A wine tasting consisting of a number of different vintages of the same wine.

Violets Purely a nose note, violets can be found on a number of red grapes, for example, Sangiovese, Pinot Noir and Cabernet Franc.

Volatile Acidity (VA) Acetic acid that, in certain concentrations (above 1.5g/l), gives an off-putting vinegary smell. This is usually brought about as a result of shoddy winemaking.

Woody Over-oaked – when the nose or palate stops tasting like well-integrated oak and start tasting like tree!

Yeasty The fresh-baked-bread nose found on Champagne and other white wines, mainly with Chardonnay.

Zesty A citrus taste associated with acidity and also with some white grape varieties like Sauvignon Blanc and Sémillon.

Zippy A term used to describe refreshing levels of acidity. 'Perky' and 'zingy'.

NB – I have not included 'cheeky', 'train-brakes', 'impudent', 'wet park benches', 'bashful' or 'precocious', as these terms reveal more about the taster than the wine!

A Few French Tasting Terms That Could Come in Useful

Agressif High acidity, harsh.

Agrume Citrus.

Arome Aroma or nose.

Bouchonné Corked.

Brut Dry.

Charpente Literally carpentry – this refers to wines with good structure and smart oak.

Clairet Light red colour, deeper than rosé.

Crémant Literally creaming – slightly sparkling or frothing.

Dégustation Tasting, as in wine tasting.

Demi-Sec Literally half-dry – therefore medium-dry.

Doux Sweet.

Equilibré Balanced.

Fruité Fruity.

Goût de terroir A French term meaning the distinct 'taste of the soil' found in wines typical of specific regions or villages.

Moelleux Sweet with reference to pudding wines, although sometimes this means rich, smooth and ripe but not overly sweet.

Mousse The fizz on the surface of a glass of sparkling wine or Champagne.

Pétillant Gently sparkling.

Piquant A refreshing level of acidity.

Robe The colour of a wine.

Sec Dry.

Souple Supple, balanced, harmonious.

Tendu Tight – as in acidic.

Vif A lively, youthful flavour.

Vin de Garde A French term for a wine that is worth laying down, as opposed to drinking young.

GENERAL WINE TERMS

Abboccato An Italian term for 'medium-sweet'.

Abocado A Spanish term for 'medium-sweet'.

Amabile An Italian term for 'sweet'.

Amarone An Italian term for wines made from dried grapes, such as Amarone della Valpolicella.

Ampelography The study of vine species and varieties.

AOC *Appellation d'Origine Contrôlée*. Often shortened to AC. A control system that protects and polices regionally specific wines in France.

Aperitif A drink used to get the taste buds humming before a meal. See **Kir**.

Auslese A German style of wine, meaning 'selected harvest'. The grapes will be harvested later and so riper than normal, often giving rise to sweet wines.

AVA American Viticultural Area. A somewhat confused attempt at a meaningful AC system – see above.

Azienda Agricola The Italian equivalent of 'Domaine' – where the grapes are grown and made into wine on the estate.

Bacchus The Roman God of Wine – what a job!

Bereich A German term for a wine district containing Grosslagen areas.

Beerenauslese A German term for a sweet style of wine made from individually selected overripe berries, one notch up from Auslese.

Blanc de Blancs A French term for a white wine made using white grapes only. On a bottle of Champagne it would signify a wine made solely from Chardonnay.

Blanc de Noirs A French term for a white wine made using red grapes only by removing the skins from the must before any colour leaches out.

Bianco Italian word for 'white' usually followed by 'di' then a place name.

Blanco The Spanish word for 'white'.

Bodega The Spanish word for a winery.

Butt A barrel used for the production of Sherry, usually made from American oak and with a capacity of approximately 600 litres.

Capsule The covering protecting the cork on a bottle of wine. Nowadays made from all manner of weird and wonderful materials. They used to be made from lead.

Casa Vinicola The Italian equivalent of a French *négociant*.

Case The traditional trading unit of a dozen bottles of wine.

Claret An old-fashioned English term for any red wine from Bordeaux.

Climat A Burgundian term for an individually named vineyard site.
See **Lieu-dit**.

Clos A French term for a walled vineyard.

Co-operative A winery owned by a number of different members who
pool their resources, combine their harvests, and save considerable
money on buying winemaking equipment, as they all share the one site.

Coteaux A French term for a collection of hills.

Côte A French term for a slope or hillside.

Crianza A Spanish term for a wine that has been aged for two
years before release, of which a minimum of one year is spent
in a barrel.

Cru Bourgeois A Médoc classification for wines one step below that
of Cru Classé.

Cru Classé Literally a 'classed growth', this French term refers to a
classification system covering the finest left bank Bordeaux Châteaux.

Decanting The process of pouring a wine out of its bottle into a
decanter or jug, for the purpose of removing its sediment or letting
it breathe.

Digestif A smart word for an after-dinner drink. Whether it be
Cognac, Armagnac, Calvados, Eau de Vie, Whisky or any of the other
huge range of nose and swirl drinks, I feel that it is a fine curtain-call
to finish off any good dinner.

Dionysus The Greek God of Wine – another enviable position, though, on current form, I would prefer to be in Rome rather than Athens for cellar-selection.

DO *Denominación de Origen*, the Spanish version of *Appellation Contrôlée*.

DOC *Denominazione di Origine Controllata*, *Denominación de Origen Calificada* and *Denominação de Origem Controlada* – respectively the Italian, Spanish and Portuguese version of *Appellation Contrôlée*.

DOCG Add *e Garantita* to the Italian DOC term and this is the classification for the supposedly finest Italian wines.

Domaine A French word for a winery that owns its own vineyards and makes its own wine.

Double-decanting Pouring a wine into a decanter then back into its original bottle, after having washed out any sediment. This means that you can enjoy the wine without the worry of the sediment ruining the last few glasses, and also still see what wine you are drinking.

Eau de Vie A spirit made from distilled fruit. Some people keep their bottles in the freezer, like vodka, so that when it is poured it is as cold as possible. This is not the best way to appreciate these 'digestifs'. The bottles should be kept in a normal fridge, and the *glasses* kept in the freezer. The aroma will explode on the nose when the liquid hits the freezing glass and will taste superb.

Einzellage A German term for a named single vineyard site, like a *lieu-dit* in French.

Eiswein A German name for wine made only in vintages where the grapes freeze on the vine. They tend to be affected with 'noble rot' and, when frozen, the water content is captured in such a way that the juice emerging from the winepress is so concentrated in sugar that they result in tooth-achingly sweet wines and cost a bomb. This style of wine is made also in Austria and Canada. See **Cryoextraction**.

En-Primeur Any wines that are offered for sale before they have been bottled, similar to buying a 'future'. In theory, the buyer gets the opportunity to reserve a wine at a 'low' opening price with a view to speculating on the quality of the wine and its eventual worth. This is one way to invest in wine, attempting to realise a profit as the wine matures and nears its period of drinking. Duty, shipping costs and taxes are due when the wine is released from the winery.

Fût de chêne A French term meaning oak barrels.

Generoso A Spanish or Portuguese term for a wine that is fortified.

Gran Reserva A Spanish term for a wine that has been aged for five years before release, of which a minimum of two years is spent in a barrel.

Grosslage A German term for a collection of vineyard sites.

Halbtrocken A German term meaning 'half-dry', one up from Trocken (with a little more residual sugar).

Hectolitre 100 litres.

Icewine See **Eiswein**.

IGT *Indicazione Geografica Tipica*, the Italian equivalent of French *Vin de Pays*, except it can be used for some 'Super'-style Italian wines instead of *Vino da Tavola*.

ISO International Organisation for Standardisation.

Jeunes vignes A French term for 'young vines'.

Kabinett A German term for the first grade of QmP wines, usually light and dry.

Kir A refreshing aperitif made by adding dry white wine to a few drops of

Crème de Cassis in the bottom of a wineglass. Firstly, check with the drinker how strong they would like it. Crème de Cassis is very potent and only a dribble is needed to give the wine flavour and colour. Use the best Crème de Cassis you can afford, as this is the predominant flavour. Use a very neutral white wine – nothing oaked and nothing off-dry. Usually a French table wine is best for the job, traditionally Aligoté would be used.

Landwein The German equivalent of French *Vin de Pays*.

Lieu-dit A French term for a specific named vineyard site. This name might appear on the wine's label, thus raising it to a higher quality level than a straight *village* wine.

Millésime French term for 'vintage'.

Mousseaux French term for 'sparkling'.

Négociant A French wine producer who buys in grapes or wine for vinification, bottling, labelling and selling. The opposite of a Domaine.

New World This term refers to winemaking countries outside Europe and the Mediterranean. Most of them are, in fact, not that 'new' in establishing vineyards – South Africa 1659, California 1782, Australia 1788 and Chile in the middle of the 16th century – but in terms of having commercial wineries which export wine around the world, most are relatively 'new'.

Old World European and Mediterranean-bordering winemaking countries.

Organic A wine made from grapes grown without the use of manmade chemical herbicides, pesticides or fertiliser.

OWC Original wooden case.

Passito An Italian term for a wine made from dried grapes.

Puttonyos The level of sweetness of Hungarian Tokaji (1–6).

QbA A German term, *Qualitätswein bestimmter Anbaugebiete*, meaning 'quality wine'. Don't believe it, this term is on bottles of Liebfraumilch! These wines are usually boosted with added sugar.

QmP A German term, *Qualitätswein mit Prädikat*, meaning 'better quality wine'. This is the one to look for, as no sugar is added. This term covers all levels of ripeness from *Kabinett* to *Trockenbeerenauslese*.

Recioto An Italian term for a strong sweet wine made from dried grapes.

Récolte A French term for 'harvest'.

Reserva A Spanish term for a wine that has been aged for three years before release, of which a minimum of one year is spent in a barrel.

Rosso Italian word for 'red', usually followed by 'di' then a place name.

Screwcap The closure of choice for any self-respecting winemaker who wants their product to make it to the consumer in exactly the condition they put it into the bottle. Screwcaps suffer from a slight image problem, but the most forward-thinking wineries in the world use them so the wine will be in perfect nick. Stelvin is a brand name for a type of screwcap.

Sélection des Grains Nobles The ultimate in sweet wines from Alsace or the Loire. Literally meaning 'a careful selection of noble-rot-affected grapes'.

Single varietal A wine made from a single grape variety.

Spätlese A German style of wine that is late-harvested but not always sweet. Usually less sweet than Auslese, these wines can be fermented out dry to result in a higher alcohol more 'foody' wine. See **Trocken**.

Sur lie French for 'on its lees', with reference to higher quality Muscadet and other white wines that are made in contact with their lees.

TCA The full name is '2,4,6-trichloroanisole', the unpleasant, musty-smelling compound that reveals a cork-tainted wine.

Tenuta Italian word for an estate, or collection of vineyards including a winery.

Throw As in 'to throw a sediment'. A quaint expression for a wine that has developed sediment.

Tinto Spanish and Portuguese word for 'red'.

Trocken A German term for 'dry'

Trockenbeerenauslese A German mouthful in all senses of the word. A mega-sweet, mega-expensive style of wine made in tiny quantities from noble-rot-affected grapes. Even the winepress is miniature. Usually shortened to 'TBA' to save five minutes' effort.

Unfiltered Just that, a wine that is not filtered. More likely to throw a sediment and may, in time, require decanting. French term is *non filtré*.

Ullage The space between the top of the wine and the bottom of the cork in a bottle of wine.

VDQS French for *Vin Délimité de Qualité Supérieure*, this is the breeding ground for wannabe AC regions, higher than *Vin de Pays*.

Vendange French for 'harvest'.

Vendange Tardive French for 'late picked or late harvested'. Used for sweet wines.

Vendemmia Italian term for 'vintage'.

Vieilles vignes French term for 'old vines'. This should signify a superior wine with a more concentrated flavour.

Vigna The Italian word for a 'vineyard'.

Vigneron A French vineyard worker.

Vin de Pays French classification for 'country wine', an intermediate category for French wines falling between *Vin de Table* and AC. The term *Vin de Pays* is always followed by 'de...' indicating where the region is (e.g. Vin de Pays de l'Ardèche).

Vin de Table French classification for 'table wine', the basic level of French wine. In Germany the term is *Tafelwein*, in Italy *Vino da Tavola*, in Spain *Vino de Mesa* and in Portugal *Vinho de Mesa*.

Viña The Spanish word for a 'vineyard'.

Vino Comarcal A regional Spanish table wine.

Vino de la Tierra The Spanish equivalent to French *Vin de Pays*.

Vino de Mesa A blended Spanish table wine from unclassified vineyards.

Maipo 141
Malaga 248
Malbec 16, 112
malic acid 48, 267-268
Mallorca 246
Malmesbury 238
Malmsey 237
Malvasia 221, 223, 241
Manjimup 124-125
Manseng, Gros and
Petit 31, 115
Manzanilla 247
Maranges 183
Marches (Marche) 222
Maremma 225
Margaret River 123-124,
125, 260
Margaux 149-150
Marlborough 95, 230-231, 261
Marqués de Aragón 246
Marsala 227
Marsannay-la-Côte 171
Marsanne 31-32, 117
Martinborough 230
Mas Estela 244
Mas la Plana 4, 244
Masseto 6
Matakana 229
Matanzas Creek 251
Mataro 16-17, 112
Matés Vineyard 229
Maule 141
Mauro 245
Maury 10, 112, 211
Mavrud 16
Mazis-Chambertin 171
MC (maceration
carbonique) 59-60
McLaren Vale 126, 129
McWilliams 135, 138
Médoc 148-149, 153
Melon de Bourgogne 32,
115-116
Mendocino County 251
Mendoza 121
Menetou-Salon 198, 199
Mercurey 184
Merlot 5-6, 113
méthode Champenoise 61
Meursault 180
micro-wineries 157
Mildara Bass 135
Mills Reef 230
Milmanda 244
Minervois 210
Miranda 138
mise en bouteille 71
Molise 222

Monastrell see
Mourvèdre
Monbazillac 33, 208
Monsoon Valley 254
Montagny 184
Montana 230, 231
Montée de Tonnerre 168
Montefalco Sagrantino
226
Montepulciano
d'Abruzzo 222
Monthélie 179
Monti 222
Monticchio 226
Montilla 33
Montlouis 197, 198
Montmains 168
Morellino 225
Morey-St-Denis 172
Mornington Peninsula
132
Moscatel de Setubal 26,
238
Moscato Bianco 26
Moscato d'Asti 116, 218
Moscato di Pantelleria
26
Mosel 214-215, 259
Moulis 150
Mount Barker 124
Mount Benson 130
Mountford Estate 231
Mourvèdre 16-17, 112
Mudgee 137
Müller-Thurgau 32-33,
248
Murray Darling 135-136
Murrumbidgee
Irrigation Area (MIA)
138
Muscadelle 33, 116
Muscadet 32, 53, 115-116, 195
Muscat 25-26, 111
Muscat Blanc à Petits
Grains 25-26
Muscat d'Alsace 25
Muscat de Beaumes-de-Venise 25, 64, 206
Muscat de Frontignan
25, 211
Muscat de Lunel 211
Muscat de Rivesaltes
26, 64, 116, 211
Muscat of Alexandria 26
Muscat Ottonel 26
Musigny 172-173
Muskadel see
Muscat
must 52-53

Nagambie Lakes 134
Nahe 215
Nalle 251
Nantes 195
Napa Valley 251, 260
Navarra 243
Nebbiolo 12, 113
négociants 74, 166-167
Nelson 230
Neudorf Vineyards 230
New South Wales 136-138
New Zealand 40, 228-232, 261
Nicolas Potel 167, 175
Noble One 138
noble varieties 2
nose 84-86, 94-96
Nuits-Saint-Georges 7,
174-175

oak aged wines 55
oak barrels 49-51
Port 233, 234
red wine 58-59
sherry 246
white wine 23, 53,
169, 199
oak flavours 88-89
Oloroso 247
Ontario 139
Orange 137-138
order, drinking wine
103-104
Oregon 253, 260
Orlando 138
Ornellaia 224
Orvieto 226
oxidation 46, 54, 94,
272

Paarl 9, 238
Pacherenc du Vic-Bilh
209
Pacific Northwest 253-254
Pacific Rim dishes 115,
117
Padthaway 130
palate, the 89-90
Palazzone 226
Palette 212
Palo Cortado 247
Palomino 33, 116
Pantelleria 227
Parellada 31
Paso Robles 252
passerillé 63
pasteurisation 47
Pauillac 151-152

Paul & Henri
Jacquesson 183
Pedro Ximénez 33, 116,
248
Pegasus Bay 226
Pemberton 125
Penedès 244, 260
Penfolds 127
Penfolds Grange 9
Pernand-Vergelesses
176
Perpignan 10
Perricoota 138
Perth Hills/Swan Valley
123
Pessac-Léognan 154
Peter Lehmann 127
Petit-Chablis 168
Petit Verdot 17
Phylloxera vastatrix
41-42, 147
Pic St-Loup 211
Picolit 221
Piemonte (Piedmont)
217-218, 258
Pierro 124, 125
Pinot Blanc/Pinot
Bianco 26-27, 116
Pinot Gris/Pinot Grigio
27-28, 113
Pinot Meunier 17-18
Pinot Noir 7-8, 113
Pinotage 18, 111
Piqueras 246
pomace 57
Pomerol 6, 158-159
Pomino 223
Pommard 178
Pompe à Bicyclette 62
Porongurup 124
Port 68, 233-235, 259
Portugal 145, 233-238,
259
Pouilly 185
Pouilly-Fuissé 185
Pouilly-Fumé 198,
decanting 101-103
serving temperature
101
sparkling 64
winemaking 51, 53,
56-60

Qualitätswein bestimmter
Anbaugebiete (QbAs)
214
Qualitätswein mit
Prädikat (QmP) 214
Quarts de Chaume 196,
197